Microsoft 365 Business for Admins

by Jennifer Reed

for
dummies®
A Wiley Brand

Microsoft 365 Business for Admins For Dummies®

Published by: **John Wiley & Sons, Inc.**, 111 River Street, Hoboken, NJ 07030-5774, www.wiley.com

Copyright © 2019 by John Wiley & Sons, Inc., Hoboken, New Jersey

Published simultaneously in Canada

For general information on our other products and services, please contact our Customer Care Department within the U.S. at 877-762-2974, outside the U.S. at 317-572-3993, or fax 317-572-4002. For technical support, please visit https://hub.wiley.com/community/support/dummies.

Wiley publishes in a variety of print and electronic formats and by print-on-demand. Some material included with standard print versions of this book may not be included in e-books or in print-on-demand. If this book refers to media such as a CD or DVD that is not included in the version you purchased, you may download this material at http://booksupport.wiley.com. For more information about Wiley products, visit www.wiley.com.

Library of Congress Control Number: 2018968493

ISBN 978-1-119-53913-1 (pbk); ISBN 978-1-119-53917-9 (ebk); ISBN 978-1-119-53922-3 (ebk)

Manufactured in the United States of America

C10007668_011619

Contents at a Glance

Table of Contents

Introduction

To be productive and successful in today's modern computing world, where instant sharing and immediate feedback are the new standards, organizations and teams need to respond to new information with agility and speed. The way we work today is more iterative and collaborative than ever before. This reality is driving the need for small- and medium-size businesses to figure out ways to improve workplace productivity.

Small businesses must also deal with the omnipresence of mobile devices — owned by the company or the employee — in the workplace. And just because your employees are at work doesn't mean that they don't use their mobile devices for personal purposes. If you have a habit of checking Facebook, Twitter, or Instagram at least 14 times a day, you know what I mean.

Against this backdrop, small businesses must also contend with today's threat landscape. With a limited budget and a highly competitive job market for security professionals, it's not unusual for some business owners to find it easier to just bury their heads in the sand and hope they don't get hacked. I think we can agree that this is not a good idea.

For a market that accounts for 66 percent of net new jobs in the United States and powers the economy with their labor force and capital expenditures, small businesses are long overdue for an enterprise-class solution that doesn't break the bank.

If you're running a small business or managing the IT infrastructure for a small business, your wait is over. Microsoft 365 Business is here. It's the coming together of three key cloud services from Microsoft: Office 365, Enterprise Mobility + Security, and Windows 10 Business. It's not your parent's solution, either. It has artificial intelligence, machine learning, and advanced features that used to be out of reach for small business. And the best part about Microsoft 365 Business? Even dummies can use it.

About This Book

The intent of *Microsoft 365 For Admins For Dummies* is to provide SMBs an understanding of the capabilities of Microsoft 365 Business: an integrated solution with built-in security and collaboration features to enable today's modern workplace.

For business owners, this book will provide peace of mind knowing that their workforce can manage their work productively and securely across devices. For IT teams, this book is a timely source of information about the features and functionalities as well as guidance on implementing the solution. For end users, this book serves as a guide for making the most out of the company's investment in the technology.

Microsoft 365 For Admins For Dummies serves as a rich resource for all the components included in Microsoft 365 Business and the purpose they serve. I call out the dependencies across the components to ensure that the reader is aware of issues that may arise when implementing or using the solution.

I include insights and real-life scenarios based on my experiences as a consultant and solution architect with over 10 years' experience in the industry. It is written in the *Dummies* format, which breaks down a highly technical subject matter into easily understood concepts.

If you're planning to implement Microsoft 365 Business or to upgrade to Microsoft 365 Business, you've picked up the right book to help demystify the complexities of the bundled solution and set you up for a successful deployment of the solution.

Foolish Assumptions

This book is written for the benefit of the novice or intermediate IT admin who wants to implement and manage a cloud solution for a small business organization. I assume some basic knowledge of the tasks and responsibilities of an IT team. In addition, a senior-level IT professional might glean some nuggets on the end user experience as well as insights into driving technology adoption.

Icons Used in This Book

The familiar *For Dummies* icons are used in this book to spotlight notable topics through visual cues. The following icons are used in this book.

TIP

The Tip icon is your cue for shortcuts or guidance to doing things more quickly or easily.

REMEMBER

The Remember icon marks information that's especially important to know and provides insights into the nuances of Microsoft 365 Business, an evolving cloud solution.

TECHNICAL STUFF

The Technical Stuff icon marks information of a highly technical nature that you will inevitably encounter as an IT admin. I have, however, used layman's language as much as possible.

WARNING

The Warning icon tells you to watch out! It marks important information that may save you from the pitfalls of implementing a new cloud technology..

Beyond the Book

As a software-as-a-service offering, Microsoft 365 Business is updated and improved on a regular basis. Here are some links to stay up to speed on the goings-on of Microsoft 365 Business:

>> **Cheat Sheet:** Visit www.dummies.com/cheatsheet/microsoft365business for a cheat sheet to help you take advantage of the features and functionalities of Microsoft Business 365.

>> **Author's Amazon Page:** Read about the latest features of the service from my Amazon.com author's page at www.amazon.com/author/jennreed.

Where to Go from Here

Novice IT admins will find it helpful to read the pages of this book in order because some instructions in later chapters point back to configuration instructions in earlier chapters. But if you want to jump right into a chapter that interests you most, go right ahead! I've pointed out the location for prerequisite information where needed to provide you with additional context.

1

Transforming the Small Business

Understand how a multi-generational workplace is influencing the way we work.

Take advantage of cloud technologies to shift from a traditional to a modern IT environment

Get an overview of the Microsoft 365 solution, the services it includes, and the licensing model for the solution.

Grow your business by using built-in business applications in Microsoft 365 Business.

Chapter 1

Understanding the New World of Work

Today's computing environment has leveled the playing field for small businesses. The availability of fast Internet connections has afforded entrepreneurs access to technologies typically only used by big corporations with huge IT budgets. As major cloud service providers compete for market share, a top priority is answering the technology needs of small and medium size businesses (SMB). Sophisticated productivity and security solutions that used to be reserved for large enterprises with huge IT budgets are now available as cloud services at prices within the reach of even a mom-and-pop store.

Against this backdrop, you can see how it's an exciting time to start a new or manage an existing small business. The days of using free email services full of ads that do nothing to promote a company's brand are far behind us. For the cost of a cup of coffee, you can pay for a full month's subscription to the same email solution that Fortune 500 companies are using.

If yours is a startup business, you're in luck. Without the baggage from the olden days of running an IT infrastructure, you can immediately launch a born-in-the-cloud startup with funding and support from major cloud services providers. Microsoft for Startups (https://startups.microsoft.com/en-us/program-details/), for example, provides product, technical, and go-to-market benefits to start-up entrepreneurs to help accelerate their growth.

Now that cloud computing and the use of personal mobile device in the workplace are becoming mainstream, small businesses have even greater opportunities to compete with the big guys — on a global scale. These opportunities, however, require a change in how you work and how you run a business. And with these changes come challenges.

This chapter lays the foundation for small businesses to start their journey into the new world of work. It covers current productivity and security trends and provides guidance and best practices for taking advantage of the cloud to grow a small business without falling prey to security challenges in today's threat landscape.

Creating a Productive Workplace

Baby boomers (1946–1964), Gen X (1965–1979), Gen Y (Millennials, 1980–1994), and now Gen Z (Centennials, 1995–2012) are the four cultural generations now converging in the workplace. If you think simply having a cookie-cutter approach for driving productivity in the workplace is all that's needed, think again.

Consider this. Baby boomers grew up during a time of prosperity and see work as a 9-to-5 career until retirement. Gen Xers, on the other hand, have the highest level of education in the US, saw the fall of the Berlin Wall and the tragedy of Tiananmen Square, and see work as a contract — just a job. Millennials grew up with a computer and the initial stages of Internet at home. They do best in a flexible work arrangement and will account for 50 percent of the workforce by 2020. Centennials are the multitasking fiends, super-connected kids who can troubleshoot a baby boomer's cell phone while building a website and Snapchatting with a friend.

With such a diverse workforce and different work styles, businesses need to figure out a way to provide a flexible and productive work environment while ensuring data privacy and security. The best way to address this challenge is to embrace cloud technologies and adopt a business strategy to run a secure and productive enterprise.

Realizing the value of Microsoft 365 Business

Bring your own device (BYOD), touchdown stations, outcome-driven versus process-driven goals, flexible work arrangements, and data security and governance are just a few of the catchphrases you hear at work today. As businesses shift from the old-school approach to a modern workplace, they do not need to spend a lot of money and procure several solutions from different vendors.

Microsoft 365 Business is a complete, intelligent, and secure solution delivered through the cloud that empowers employees to be productive with tools built for teamwork but designed to fit individual work styles. With one subscription, an employee gets a comprehensive productivity, security, and device management toolkit that doesn't require expensive consultants and highly trained systems engineers to implement.

Figure 1-1 provides a high-level comparison between several stand-alone solutions versus the bundled Microsoft 365 Business solution. Clearly, SMBs can benefit from the cost-effective, simplified, and integrated solution Microsoft 365 Business offers.

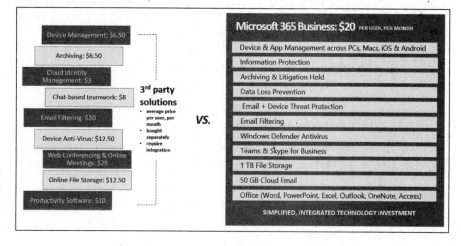

FIGURE 1-1:
Stand-alone solutions versus Microsoft 365 Business.

Promoting teamwork in a diverse workforce

We all work differently and have our own preferred method for communication and collaboration. In a team with representation from all four cultural generations, you could end up with someone who prefers phone calls, another who prefers email, someone else who thinks anything other than instant messaging is lame, and yet another team member who mainly communicates with emojis and office memes.

Lucky for you, Microsoft 365 Business has a way to bring all these people together with a universal toolkit for collaboration: Office 365.

Office 365 comes with four key workloads, or services:

>> **Exchange Online** powers email, calendar, tasks, journaling, and more. It has built-in intelligence to protect users from phishing, spoofing, and so on.

>> **SharePoint Online** provides online storage with built-in capabilities for real-time co-authoring and data protection. OneDrive for Business is part of this workload.

>> **Microsoft Teams** (soon to replace Skype for Business) serves as a digital collaboration hub for online meetings, web conferencing, instant messaging, and more.

>> **Office ProPlus** includes the familiar Office desktop applications: Word, PowerPoint, Excel, Outlook, OneNote, and Access.

In addition to these key workloads, Office 365 includes productivity and security tools that integrate seamlessly across the entire suite of services. Following is a partial list of services included in Office 365:

>> **Delve and Yammer** help you identify people in your organization with certain expertise.

>> **Office 365 Groups** automatically gives team members a shared mailbox, file folder, and notebook.

>> **StaffHub** is a retail store's solution for managing shift schedules for workers or associates, allowing them to share files, swap schedules, and connect to company resources.

>> **Stream** is your YouTube at work. You can upload and view videos, create channels for your team, and even watch videos with transcripts and closed captions.

WARNING

Putting together a complete list of services is challenging because Office 365 is a software-as-a-service (SaaS) offering and Microsoft is constantly rolling out new features. Stay on top of notifications you receive from Microsoft regarding updates to the service. In that way, you will know about new features and will be prepared for functionalities scheduled for retirement or deprecation.

If you're wondering how you could possible use all these services, consider the scenario on Figure 1-2. On any given day, an employee in a modern workplace can work smarter by using at least four capabilities in Office 365.

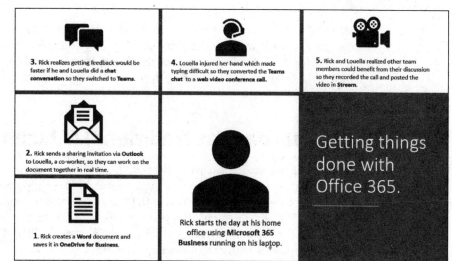

FIGURE 1-2: How modern workers collaborate in Office 365.

Keeping Business Technology Current

Running a small business is no small feat. Some people have the mistaken belief that start-up entrepreneurs live glamourous lives. I'll never forget a comment from a former colleague when she learned I had started my own IT consulting firm. She exclaimed, "That's awesome! You must sleep in a lot."

I almost choked trying not to burst out laughing at the suggestion that someone running an IT consulting company would routinely enjoy leisurely sleep-in mornings. Anyone who's ever tried to launch a business knows that sleep is a luxury and never a priority. A small-business owner typically wears many hats. In the first few months of starting my business, for example, I was the salesperson, technical support department, CEO, CFO, marketing department, consultant, and IT director. Wearing all those hats, I never slept late and often didn't sleep at all.

It shouldn't come as a surprise, then, that small businesses tend to deprioritize the work required to keep their technology current. I've met several clients who are still running Windows XP even though support for the operating system ended in 2014. Although the security implications of such an environment are astounding, some businesses just can't find time to update their current systems.

Keeping up with technological changes is disruptive, time-consuming, and expensive. It seems like every time you update your technology, within a few weeks the update is obsolete and the update process must be repeated.

Microsoft 365 Business attempts to address such challenges. The solution is designed to make it easier for SMBs to keep their technology current, minimize the risk for cyberattacks, and reduce the cost of running a modern IT infrastructure so the business owner and employees can focus on the strategic work required to grow the business.

Looking back at traditional IT businesses

Running a small business used to mean working 9 a.m. to 5 p.m., Monday through Friday, with everyone showing up at the same office. Employees were given a company-owned device configured with legacy applications accessible only while at the office. The devices for sales team members may have been configured with a network connection, such as virtual private network (VPN), to allow them to access company resources while out on the field.

A day in the life of an IT admin supporting an SMB typically meant manually configuring devices, providing technical support to users, and reacting to technical updates in the industry. For those running Windows operating system, Patch Tuesdays meant long nights testing, deploying, and resolving issues related to the security patches Microsoft released on the second or fourth Tuesday of each month.

If an SMB didn't have an in-house IT team, scarce dollars were spent on a managed service provider who was usually a lone wolf who may or may not have been available when service was needed.

Running a business today is no longer the same as it was ten or even five years ago. Most SMBs, however, still use the tools, processes, and mindset of a traditional IT environment. Clearly, these SMBs are at a disadvantage when competing with businesses that have adopted a modern IT environment.

Running a modern IT environment

With cloud technologies becoming mainstream, mobile devices turning into a necessity more than a luxury, artificial intelligence pervading our daily lives, and the amount of digital data exploding in the last few years, businesses must transform to stay relevant.

The concept of digital transformation is simply a matter of taking advantage of current technologies to rethink and rework the products and services a business delivers to its customers. Such changes, in turn, alter the processes and strategies by which a business is run.

In many ways, SMBs are better positioned than large enterprises to adopt digital transformation. With fewer hoops to go through in the decision-making process, SMBs have the agility to adopt new and emerging technologies, especially if the cost is budget-friendly.

Most SMB clients I've met were at the forefront in adopting a bring your own device (BYOD) policy. The BYOD model was partly driven by the owners' desire to cut the cost of company-supplied devices. From the employees' perspective, especially the younger generation, being able to use their own mobile devices for work might be a deciding factor in accepting a job offer or not.

Safeguarding Business Data

When you run a business, you deal with data. When you sell to customers, you collect data. When you buy something for your business, you're giving away data. With the possession of data comes great responsibilities. A business is required to follow laws and regulations governing data.

The large amount of data in our connected world has paved the way for big data. *Big data* is simply a huge volume of data that can't be stored or processed in the traditional way. Imagine processing the data from the millions of tweets a day or analyzing the patterns and behaviors of YouTube viewers watching billions of videos every day. That amount of data could provide insights and competitive advantage.

Data is the new business currency. Data is so valuable that hackers want to steal your company data. Do you have a plan in place to safeguard your business data?

Security is everyone's business

Small businesses typically don't have a risk management executive tasked with maintaining the company's information security program. This may not be a bad thing because some employees in big companies have the mistaken belief that data security is the responsibility of the company's information security officer. The reality is that security is everyone's business. When you're a small business and don't have a designated security officer, it's easier to instill a culture of security as everyone's responsibility.

For example, even though an employee might own his smartphone, company emails received on his phone are not free game for social media posting. Or if an employee is trying to fast-track a customer transaction, she shouldn't send a customer's social security number and other personal information through email.

Although technology enable us to accomplish more things faster, it has also increased our exposure to security risks. You can mitigate these risks in many ways, but the best first step is to ensure that everyone in the organization makes a commitment to take security seriously. The shared understanding of that responsibility can then be complemented by the security features in Microsoft 365 Business, such as the ones in the Security & Compliance Center, shown in Figure 1-3.

FIGURE 1-3:
Microsoft 365
Security &
Compliance
Center.

Taking a layered approach to security

Implementing security best practices in the workplace doesn't mean just enforcing strong, complex passwords. If you rely on complex passwords, users will simply write them down on a sticky note and tack them on their monitors. Shocker.

Microsoft 365 Business takes a layered approach to security to complement your company's security policies. First, your devices are centrally managed with enterprise-level security features of Windows 10 Business. Features such as Windows Hello for Business and Credential Guard replace passwords with biometrics and facial recognition. Malware can be eliminated with Secure Boot, Device Guard, and Windows Defender. In addition, sensitive data can be automatically encrypted with Windows Information Protection.

You get protection from hidden threats in email and attachments in emails or embedded in Office files by using the built-in security features in Office 365 Advanced Threat Protection.

TIP

It may seem as though I am venturing out of Microsoft 365 Business territory when I start writing about Microsoft Azure. However, both technologies are provided by Microsoft, so they work well together. For example, you can prevent data leaks by ensuring that sensitive information such as social security numbers and credit card information aren't shared outside your company by using Azure Information Protection. You can also manually or automatically encrypt an email or a file with this service and even control who has access to the information by applying restrictions such as do not copy or do not forward.

These security features are just the beginning in terms of what you can do to safeguard your data in Microsoft 365 Business. Microsoft has already done the heavy lifting by figuring out 80 percent of the common security configurations that apply to small businesses. Your IT admin can customize the other 20 percent to fit your specific company requirements.

Chapter **2**

Getting to Know Microsoft 365 Business

f I had wanted a drone 12 years ago, I would have had to come up with $100,000. Lucky for me, the cost of drones declined so much and so rapidly that I finally got one as a birthday present from my husband and son last year. The cost of the drone? $100. Watching our puppy run in circles in our backyard chasing the drone overhead? Priceless.

Drones are just one of the key technologies that has seen a drastic drop in prices in a short time span. According to a white paper published by the Word Economic Forum, 3D printing used to cost an average of $40K in 2007. Seven years later, that price dropped to $100. In 1984, the average cost for solar power per kilowatt hour was $30. In 2014, that cost went down to 16 cents.

The astounding drop in prices for these and other advanced technologies under-scores just how rapidly our world is changing. Moreover, affordable smart devices have made us increasingly connected. With an estimated 1 trillion devices connected to the Internet by 2030 and the mainstreaming of science-fiction-like technologies such as artificial intelligence, businesses of all sizes will have no choice but to adapt to the changing digital landscape to succeed or simply survive.

At home and in the workplace, we are already seeing humans and machines working together to drive efficiency. For example, my Echo Dot (a hands-free, voice-controlled device from Amazon) and I get along well — especially in the morning while I get ready to go to work — when it tells me the top news, the weather, and the traffic on my commute route, and even attempts a lame joke. The Echo Dot does all that from a simple "Alexa, start my day" voice command.

These technological advancements dictate that even a small business needs to have a technology strategy just like its big brother, the enterprise. SMBs need to reevaluate legacy systems that require a lot of maintenance, out-of-support platforms rife with security holes, and fragmented productivity solutions that started out free but ended up costing a lot of money to integrate.

This chapter outlines the value proposition of Microsoft 365 Business and how the solution can help define the technology strategy of an SMB (small- to medium-sized business). I provide guidance for integrating a few of the recent technological innovations into the workplace. I also clarify the use case between the Business and Enterprise editions of Microsoft 365 to enable small-business decision makers to make the right purchasing choice.

Understanding the Microsoft 365 Plans

Although a small business and a large enterprise operate differently, common trends in the workplace affect any organization's capability to achieve its goals.

The influx of Millennials drives the demand for flexible work arrangements, workspaces that lend themselves to easy interactions, and the use of personal mobile devices. Today's employees demand an open flow of information and quick access to company data anywhere and anytime so they can get things done. In addition, we see a prolific cottage industry of bad actors and almost daily news about security breaches.

These trends are the impetus for Microsoft 365. Delivered through the cloud, Microsoft 365 simplifies the complicated tasks IT admins would have to perform to run a modern IT environment.

Microsoft 365 is available in two types of plans for businesses: Business (300 or fewer users), and Enterprise (more than 300 users).

Although the focus of this book is on the Business plan, it's helpful to understand the feature sets in the Business and Enterprise plans to inform procurement decisions, especially because an organization might have a mix of both types of plans.

Breaking down the Enterprise plan

The Microsoft 365 Enterprise plan provides organizations with more than 300 users increased levels of security and compliance management. The plan includes business intelligence and analytics tools not found in the Business plan.

Three key workloads work together seamlessly in Microsoft 365:

>> **Office 365:** A software-as-a-service (SaaS) solution designed to drive productivity and enhance collaboration

>> **Enterprise Mobility + Security:** An identity-driven cloud solution for security, data privacy, and mobile device and app management

>> **Windows 10 Enterprise:** The operating system for Windows devices with built-in security and simplified platform management

Microsoft 365 Enterprise comes in E3, E5, and F1 plans. The E3 plan has robust features to meet the needs of most users. The E5 plan has additional advanced features such as business intelligence and analytics tools. The F1 plan is targeted for first-line workers, who typically do not sit in front of their computers all day and may not even have their own dedicated devices. In a retail store, these users might be sales associates dealing with customers all day.

WARNING

Pricing for Microsoft 365 Enterprise plans varies from one Microsoft reseller to another based on discounts and added services. Cloud611 (a company I founded and a Cloud Solutions Provider partner for Microsoft), for example, offers the E3 plan at $35 per user per month, the E5 at $62 per user per month, and the F1 at $12 per user per month. Published prices from the Microsoft website apply when you purchase directly from Microsoft.

Deciding whether the Business plan is right for you

The Business plan is designed to meet the needs of SMBs with 300 or fewer users. It bundles the collaboration tools in Office 365 Business Premium, security features and device management capabilities, and simplified deployment and servicing of Windows 10 Business.

This plan is ideal for small businesses that have little or no IT staff and do not want to manage an on-premises IT environment. Prices vary from one reseller to another. At Cloud611 (www.cloud611.com), Microsoft 365 Business licenses are available at $20 per user per month. You can also sign up for a 30-day free trial of the plan subject to promotional availability.

If you're wondering how simple it would be to deploy Microsoft 365 Business for an organization, consider this: My 20-year-old son has no prior IT experience but was able to deploy the solution for a customer with 20 users over a weekend. The same customer's 16-year-old son is now training to be the IT admin for the organization. These two young and tech-savvy Centennials are, in fact, the inspiration for this book.

The fastest way to find out whether Microsoft 365 Business is right for you is to use the decision tree in Figure 2-1. If your situation has some nuances outside the chart, reach out to a Microsoft Cloud Solution Program (CSP) partner such as Cloud611 (info@cloud611.com) for additional guidance.

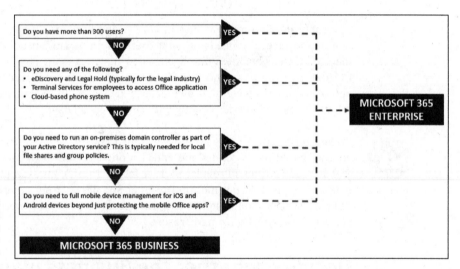

FIGURE 2-1:
Microsoft 365
decision tree:
Business or
Enterprise plan?

If you make the decision to go with the Business plan and realize you need some but not all of the advanced features in the Enterprise plan, you can purchase add-on services on top of the Business plan. Figure 2-2 give you a quick comparison between the standard and advanced services available in Microsoft 365 Business, Enterprise E3, and Enterprise E5.

		Microsoft 365 Business	Microsoft 365 Enterprise E3	Microsoft 365 Enterprise E5
Standard services	Pricing from Cloud611 (https://cloud611.com)	$20	$35	$62
	Maximum number of users	300	unlimited	unlimited
	Install Office on up to 5 PCs/Macs + 5 tablets + 5 smartphones per user	Business	ProPlus	ProPlus
	Exchange, OneDrive, SharePoint, Skype, Microsoft Teams	●	●	●
	Business Apps – Outlook Customer Manager, Bookings, MileIQ[1] Business center[1], Listings[1], Connections[1], Invoicing[1]	●		
	Legal compliance & archiving needs for email – archiving, eDiscovery, mailbox hold		●	●
	Information protection – message encryption, rights management, data loss prevention		●	●
	Advanced Threat Protection, Office 365 Cloud App Security, Threat Intelligence, Advanced Compliance	Add-on	Add-on	●
	End User and Organizational Analytics (MyAnalytics), PowerBi Pro	Add-on	Add-on	●
	Audio Conferencing	Add-on	Add-on	●
Advanced services	Phone System, Calling Plan[3]		Add-on	●
	Windows: Windows 10 Business (Windows Information Protection, Windows Defender, Store, Cortana Mgmt Controls, Auto-Install Office apps, Upgrade rights to Windows 10 Pro for 7/8.1 Pro licenses)	●		
	Windows: Windows AutoPilot	●	●	●
	EMS: Microsoft Intune, Azure Active Directory Premium P1	●[2]	●	●
	Windows: Microsoft Desktop Optimization Package, VDA		●	●
	Windows: Windows Information Protection, Windows Hello, Credential Guard, Device Guard, App Locker		●	●
	EMS: Microsoft Advanced Threat Analytics, Azure Information Protection P1		●	●
	Windows: Windows Defender Advanced Threat Protection			●
	EMS: Azure Active Directory Premium P2, Microsoft Cloud App Security, Azure Information Protection P2			●

[1] Available in US, UK, Canada
[2] Only selected features: App protection for Office mobile apps, MDM for Windows 10 PCs, Selective wipe of company data, AAD Auto-Enroll
[3] Phone System Required

FIGURE 2-2:
Microsoft 365 plan comparison.

Exploring Admin Center

Microsoft 365 Business is like a matryoshka doll, those nested Russian dolls of decreasing size. Each of the workloads in Microsoft 365 Business contains more services. Unlike the Russian dolls, however, these services do not decrease in size — they expand and extend the capabilities of Microsoft 365 Business.

The Microsoft 365 Admin Center is the IT admin's management portal for the workloads included in the service. It's also the landing page for other types of specialist admins who need to administer some aspect of the service.

Getting to know the Admin Center home page

If you were one of the early adopters of Office 365, you would typically navigate to https://portal.office365.com to administer your Office 365 tenant. Since March of 2018, you may have noticed that your URL is redirected to https://admin.microsoft.com and the top bar displays Microsoft Admin Center instead of Office 365 Admin Center.

If you're new to Microsoft 365, don't worry — you didn't miss anything. In fact, you're in luck because you've skipped the pains that previous IT admins had to deal with in the old Admin Center.

To log in to Microsoft 365 Admin Center, you must be an administrator. Bear in mind that Microsoft 365 has various types of admins based on a person's role in the organization. You might be a global admin, who has access to everything, or you might be a security admin, who has access to only Security Admin Center.

Figure 2-3 shows the current home page experience for Admin Center. The left pane displays the menu navigation. By default, the menus are collapsed, but when you click the arrow to the right of a menu, it will expand to display the submenus.

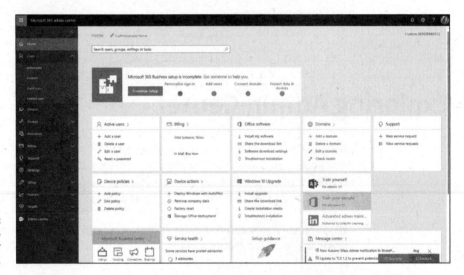

FIGURE 2-3:
Microsoft 365
Admin Center
home page.

WARNING

In this chapter, I am using the classic or current experience of Admin Center. Be aware, however, that updates to Microsoft 365 Admin Center are in progress. Depending on your update release settings and when you're reading this book, you might see the Try the Preview toggle switch to enable the new experience. I go into more details about the new experience in Part 6.

To the right of the menu are several elements. The Search box at the top is a quick way to jump directly to an item or a task. For example, you can type the name of a user in the Search box and then click the name of the user to perform tasks such as resetting the password or updating the license for the user.

When you first set up Microsoft 365 Business, the Setup wizard shown below the Search box in Figure 2-3 appears. After the setup is complete, the wizard will go away.

TIP

The most common tasks for administering Microsoft 365 Business are displayed as cards in the Admin Center home page. Although you can access these tasks also on the menu, using the cards is faster.

Discovering admin centers

Remember the discussion about workloads in Microsoft 365? Well, each of those workloads has its own admin center, which you can access by expanding the — surprise! — Admin Centers menu in the left navigation pane, as shown in Figure 2-4. This image was taken with the classic, or current, experience (as opposed to the new experience, which is in preview as of December 2018).

FIGURE 2-4:
Expanded view of Admin Center in the classic experience.

As you peek inside each admin center, you'll find a universe of additional services you can configure and customize. Do not fret, though. Microsoft 365 Business is already configured for the most common SMB scenarios, so you need to customize only some features based on the need of your business. For example:

» **Exchange Admin Center:** Enables an IT admin to configure additional policies and rules. In the Advanced Threats section, for example, you can turn on advanced threat protection for SharePoint, OneDrive, and Microsoft Teams to prevent users from opening and downloaded malicious files in those locations.

- **Teams and Skype for Business Admin Center:** Provides a consolidated dashboard for managing communications and web conferencing services. You can set up meetings and messaging policies and enable external and guest access so people outside your organization can, for example, join teams. It even has cards with help articles to help you administer teams.

- **SharePoint Admin Center:** Displays the activities across SharePoint Online. You can manage sites, restore deleted sites, and even migrate data from on-premises SharePoint sites.

- **Security & Compliance Center:** Displays the security management, compliance configurations, reporting, tracking, and even your organization's secure score! (A *secure score* is like your credit score but instead reveals your current risk profile so you can know what, if anything, you need to do to improve your security posture.)

REMEMBER

With cloud technologies, services are never in their final state. By nature, cloud services are designed to be ever-changing to keep up or respond to the current computing environment. The same is true for Microsoft 365. In this chapter, I refer to admin centers in the current experience. When the new experience is fully rolled out sometime late 2019, these admin centers will be referred to as *specialist workspaces.*

Growing Your Business with the Bookings App

Hair highlights, pet grooming, photo shoots, and tax advice all have one thing in common: appointments. When your small business provides services to customers, having the capability to automate the appointment setting process and allow customers to self-serve is a major stress relief.

The Bookings app in Microsoft 365 Business allows business owners to reduce the time spent setting up appointments by allowing customers to do it themselves from the web. After an appointment is set, you can send auto-reminders to minimize no-shows.

Administering Bookings licenses

The Bookings app is enabled by default for the entire organization in Microsoft 365 Business, as shown in Figure 2-5.

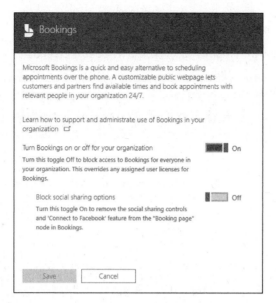

If you want to disable the Bookings app for a user, do the following:

1. **Navigate to** `https://admin.microsoft.com`

2. **Click the Users menu on the left navigation and select the Active Users submenu.**

3. **Select a user from the list, and then click Edit on the Product Licenses row.**

4. **Toggle the switch next to Microsoft Bookings to Off, and then click Save.**

5. **Click Close, and then click Close again.**

   You return to the Active users screen.

Installing the Bookings app

To install Bookings, do the following:

1. **While logged in to the Microsoft 365 Admin Center, click the app launcher icon (shown in the margin).**

   The icon appears at the top left of the screen.

2. **In the list of apps, click Bookings.**

   If the Bookings app icon is not displayed, click the All Apps link below the icons.

3. **On the Bookings page, click the Get It Now button.**

4. **In the window that pops up, click Add a Booking Calendar.**

5. **In the Welcome to Setup window, enter your business name and business type and then click Continue.**

   The system will take a few minutes to set up Bookings. When it's finished, the Bookings page will display a new user interface with a wizard for configuring Bookings.

To configure Bookings, simply follow the Setup wizard, starting with the first card on the left (Set Your Business Hours). After you finish the tasks for each of the cards, click the Home icon in the left pane to get back to the Bookings home page.

2

Implementing Microsoft 365

Get your organization ready for enhanced collaboration with security in mind.

Move email systems to Exchange Online and migrate data to SharePoint Online and OneDrive for Business

Deploy Windows 10 Business for better control and management of your company devices.

Secure your IT environment with built-in security features and protect data with encryption.

Chapter **3**

Preparing for Implementation

When it comes to successfully implementing a new technology like Microsoft 365 Business, there is no substitute for planning and preparation. Whether the user base is 10 or 10,000, without thoughtful planning, you will be setting yourself up for a lot of grief and, most likely, failure in your deployment.

One of the lessons I've learned from having been involved in numerous technical projects is that when end users participate in the implementation, the chances for a successful deployment are higher. When end users feel that they are part of the journey, they feel invested, which paves the way for better adoption of the technology. Your investment in Microsoft 365 Business is only as good as the end users adopting it. So why not make the most out of your technology dollars by rallying end users to champion its use?

Involving end users in your journey to a modern IT environment starts with clearly communicating the plan. You don't need to have everyone approve the plan, but if you can get as many end users as possible excited about the benefits of the initiative early on, you'll save yourself a lot of pain down the road.

Obviously, you can't communicate what you don't know, so this chapter provides a high-level overview of a Microsoft 365 Business implementation so you can at least have a framework when describing your implementation and communication plan.

Setting the Stage for the Rollout

In Chapter 2, I cover the different workloads included in Microsoft 365 Business: Office 365, security and device management, and Windows 10 Business. Those workloads, however, are not the full story. Other Microsoft cloud services such as Azure Active Directory underpin those key workloads. These services are found in Microsoft Azure, a cloud-computing platform that offers an array of compute, storage, and networking services that organizations can use to run their business.

To successfully deploy and manage Microsoft 365, you need to know about multiple management portals and admin centers: Microsoft 365 Admin Center, Microsoft Azure portal, Azure Active Directory management portal, and more. If deploying Microsoft 365 Business in your organization is starting to feel daunting at this point, don't worry. You will get your confidence back as you read this chapter.

Introducing Microsoft Azure

To recap, Microsoft 365 Business is a software-as-a-service (SaaS) offering. This means that the software is delivered via the Internet and paid for typically with a subscription-licensing model.

A lot of work in the backend is required to make a SaaS offering work. In fact, an army of tech demigods works day in and day out to ensure that services are running, connectivity is working, data is protected, and users are supported. This backend is like a planet of its own, with huge data centers managed by system engineers with expertise in various fields, offices around the world where teams of programmers and developers are coding features and functionalities, and boardrooms where leaders orchestrate how all these efforts come together so SaaS can be made available to customers like you and me.

The compute, storage, and networking power of this planet is called Microsoft Azure (Azure for short) and is defined by Microsoft as follows:

> "Azure is an open and flexible cloud platform that enables you to quickly build, deploy, and manage applications across a global network of Microsoft-managed datacenters. You can build applications using any language, tool, or framework. And you can integrate your public cloud applications with your existing IT environment."

For mere mortals like us, this definition simply means that when you use Microsoft 365 Business, you're using a single version of a software program hosted in Azure that is then replicated across multiple instances globally so that each organization can run the software in its own isolated environment called a *tenant*. So the next time you hear someone say, "I have a Microsoft 365 tenant," it simply means they are subscribed to Microsoft 365 services and paying a monthly fee while Microsoft takes care of the complicated and mind-numbing work of server and software management, including patching and updating.

Getting to know Azure Active Directory

Users with an Azure tenant use a shared infrastructure, which contributes to the lower cost of the service compared to the cost of running your own servers in your own data center (on-premises, or on-prem for short).

Don't get heartburn because I said that Azure uses a shared infrastructure. A shared infrastructure doesn't mean that data between tenants is open and accessible to everyone using Azure. Controls are in place to isolate one tenant from another to prevent data leakage and to prevent the actions of one tenant affecting another.

Azure Active Directory, or Azure AD, is one of those controls. This technology ensures that each tenant has a boundary to protect a customer's content from being leaked or accessed, as shown in Figure 3-1.

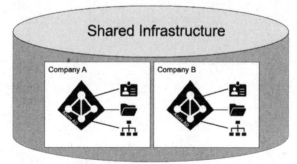

FIGURE 3-1:
Azure AD tenant
isolation.

So what exactly does Azure AD do? Azure AD is a cloud-based directory service that manages the identities of the users in SaaS applications such as Microsoft 365 Business. It stores tenant objects such as the entries that are made when users log in to the services. IT admins can enable self-service password reset with Azure AD to free up the IT team from doing this time-consuming task. The service is also useful when configuring single sign-on (SSO) so users don't have to enter their username and password every time they log in to a company-sanctioned application. With Azure AD, you can configure the sign-in pages for your Microsoft 365 environment with your own branding to make the end user feel at home. These are just a few examples of what Azure AD can do.

REMEMBER

When you purchase licenses for certain Microsoft cloud services such as Microsoft 365 Business, an Azure AD tenant is automatically created to manage the identities of the users accessing the services. In fact, when you first provision a Microsoft 365 tenant, the first user created in Azure AD is the global admin for the tenant.

The Azure AD management portal provides quick access to information and tasks in your environment (see Figure 3-2). To access the portal directly, log in to `https://portal.azure.com` with your global administrator account and then click the Azure Active Directory menu navigation on the left. Alternatively, you can access the Azure AD management portal from the list of admin centers in Microsoft 365 Admin Center.

FIGURE 3-2:
Azure AD management portal.

Building the implementation road map

Implementing Microsoft 365 without a road map is an invitation to technical issue nightmares, bad experiences for end users that can turn a hardworking IT admin into pariah, and flushing scarce dollars down the drain.

I'm going to go ahead and burst your bubble if all the slick marketing materials your may have read online gave you dreamy expectations of how easy it is to implement Microsoft 365 Business. Yes, the deployment steps are straightforward and 80 percent of the typical tasks usually performed by highly skilled system engineers are already configured. Deployment, however, is just part of the picture. Before you deploy, you must prepare and plan. And after deployment, maintenance work and routine tasks are required to continue to enhance the new IT environment. Throughout the transition to the cloud, you must continue to communicate, communicate, and communicate. Add to all those activities the need to train end users, and that, dear IT admin, is the reason why you need an implementation road map.

To give you an end-to-end view of what a typical Microsoft 365 Business implementation looks like, check out Figure 3-3. Note that the intent of the road map is to provide high-level guidance, not a prescriptive approach or a comprehensive plan.

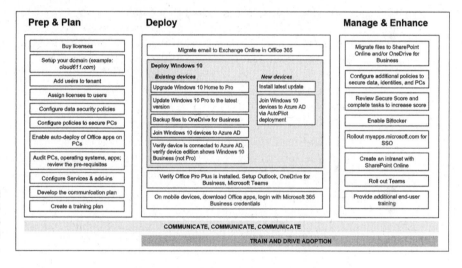

FIGURE 3-3: Microsoft 365 business implementation road map.

Because each organization is different, no hard-and-fast rules exist for the order in which you should deploy the workloads in Microsoft 365. In my experience, however, those who migrated their email system into Exchange Online in Office 365 first were the ones with the fewest deployment challenges, largely because email is most organization's bread and butter. Nailing that aspect of the implementation first lays the groundwork for the rest of the deployment, especially because a user's email address is also the login credentials for the rest of the workloads in Microsoft 365.

Taking Care of Prerequisites

Part of the preparation and planning exercise for implementing Microsoft 365 Business is to ensure that prerequisites are met and identified issues are addressed. If you skip this step, you're bound to run into trouble during the deployment, resulting in a lot of wasted time and effort. I want you to be successful, so in the following sections I've captured the documented prerequisites from Microsoft as well as some of the nuances I have discovered when I implemented Microsoft 365 Business for my customers.

Getting ready for Windows 10 Business

In case you're wondering, Windows 10 Business is not an edition of Windows 10 you can buy anywhere. When you join a device in your environment to Azure AD using your Microsoft 365 license, the Windows 10 Pro edition becomes Windows 10 Business edition. The code of the software doesn't get changed in the process. It's just that now the device is enrolled to the mobile device management (MDM) services, allowing policies to be pushed to that device.

To get your existing devices ready for Windows 10 Business, take note of the following.

>> Audit the Windows operating systems running in your environment. This step is important because the management and security capabilities of Microsoft 365 require Windows 10 Pro, version 1703 (also called the Creators Update) or later.

>> If you have Windows 10 Home, you first need to upgrade the operating system to Windows 10 Pro. Currently, no free upgrade from Home to Pro is available.

>> If you have Windows 7 Professional, Windows 8 Pro, or Windows 8.1 Pro, you can upgrade these devices to the Windows 10 Pro Creators Update version for free. You can upgrade in three ways by using the link www.microsoft.com/en-us/software-download/windows10:

- From the device you want to upgrade, navigate to the link and follow the instructions to perform the upgrade.

- Email the link to end users and have them perform the upgrade.

- Navigate to the link and create an installation media such as a USB flash drive and use the same media to install the upgrade on the devices.

>> Remove your devices from any mobile device management (MDM) solution they are enrolled in, if applicable.

Flying on autopilot with Windows AutoPilot

If you want to get fancy and automate the deployment of Windows 10, consider Windows AutoPilot, which uses a collection of technologies to automate the steps to join a device to Azure AD.

Original equipment manufacturers (OEMs) who are participating in the Windows 10 AutoPilot program have devices with company IT policies preconfigured that can be shipped directly to end users. When the end user receives the new device, he or she completes a few guided steps to join the devices to the organization's Azure AD. An IT admin does not need to first unbox the new device, wipe all the programs installed on it, and then load the Windows 10 image.

How this magic happens lies in prep work in the Microsoft 365 Business Admin Center. In the backend, the IT admin preloads the device's hardware information to inform the system that the company owns that device. Then, when an end user turns on the device and enters the appropriate credentials, the system will recognize the device and automate the step for joining Azure AD. I cover the step-by-step instructions for Windows 10 AutoPilot deployment in Chapter 5.

The prerequisites for deploying with Windows AutoPilot follow:

>> The device must be registered as a company-owned device.

>> The company branding must be configured. I cover this topic in the following section.

>> Some organizations have group policies that prevent users from accessing certain sites. For Windows AutoPilot to work, a device must be able to access the following URLs:

- `https://go.microsoft.com`
- `https://login.microsoftonline.com`
- `https://login.live.com`
- `https://account.live.com`
- `https://signup.live.com`
- `https://licensing.mp.microsoft.com`
- `https://licensing.md.mp.microsoft.com`
- `ctldl.windowsupdate.com`
- `download.windowsupdate.com`

>> Devices must be preinstalled with Windows 10 Pro, Enterprise, or Education, version 1703 or later.

>> Devices must be able to connect to the Internet.

>> The user must have a Microsoft 365 Business license.

Branding sign-in pages

Even though Microsoft 365 Business is a SaaS solution with standard configuration already set up, you can still have your own look and feel to the service. Azure AD allows you to customize the branding of your sign-in pages so that end users will be presented with an interface bearing the company logo and background image after they enter their credentials on the sign-in page. For an example of a sign-in page, go to www.office.com.

Company branding for sign-in pages is a requirement for deploying Windows 10 with Windows AutoPilot. Here are some of the prerequisites before you customize company branding:

>> **Banner logo:** Displayed on the sign-in and Access panel pages. The logo must be in JPG or PNG format and no more than 36 pixels high and 245 pixels wide.

>> **Sign-in page image:** Shown as the background of the sign-in page on desktops and laptops but not on narrow mobile devices. The image must be JPG or PNG format, less than 300KB, and 1920 pixels wide and 1080 pixels high.

>> **Square logo image:** Displayed when Windows AutoPilot runs on a device. Subsequently, the image is displayed on the password entry pages for Windows 10. The image must be JPG or PNG (preferred) format, less than 10KB, and 240 x 240 pixels.

After you have these three elements handy, you can customize your company branding in Azure AD as follows.

1. Navigate to http://portal.azure.com and log in with your Microsoft 365 credentials.

2. From the left menu, select Azure Active Directory.

3. From the left pane, select Company Branding.

4. From the top left of the main panel, or *blade,* click Configure, as shown in Figure 3-4.

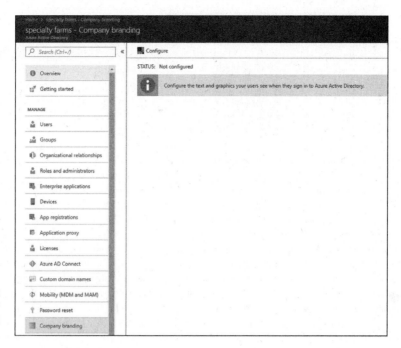

FIGURE 3-4:
Company
branding
Configure button.

5. **Upload the images for the Sign-in page background, banner logo, and square logos. You can leave the other boxes blank or enter custom information.**

   For more information on what to enter in the other boxes, hover your cursor over the information icon (*i*) to display the tooltips.

6. **From the top of the blade, click Save.**

   A notification window pops up to let you know that the system is saving your changes.

7. **After the changes are saved, click the close icon (X) to close the blade, as shown in Figure 3-5.**

It may take up to an hour for your customization to appear, so don't be alarmed if you try signing in and you don't see your company branding. After the changes are in effect, the login experience for end users will look like Figure 3-6.

FIGURE 3-5:
Save and close
icons on the
Configure
Company
Branding blade.

FIGURE 3-6:
A branded sign-in
experience.

» **Exploring the options for migrating files to SharePoint Online**

» **Setting up your organization's digital collaboration hub**

Chapter **4**

Migrating to Office 365

The IT professional of yesterday is fast transitioning into today's and tomorrow's cloud professional. Cloud pros do not deal with cumbersome legacy technologies and applications that work only on-premises. They take advantage of cloud-ready technologies and keep in mind the question: What technology will my company use in five years?

If you're an IT admin looking to implement Microsoft 365 Business, congratulations! You have taken a major step toward becoming a cloud pro. You have left the pack of dinosaurs and are now with the "It crowd" (pun intended) of cloud technologists who are in demand and have an exciting career ahead.

Microsoft 365 Business is nothing without Office 365. The chat-based workspace, email, calendar, voice and video meetings, real-time co-authoring, intranets, and even workplace social networking all happen in Office 365. In fact, the mass adoption of Office 365 drove the need to bundle other Microsoft cloud services into a single offering in Microsoft 365 Business to simplify not just the licensing but also the management of the services.

True to the theory of *Diffusions of Innovations* by Everett M. Rogers (Free Press), Office 365 adopting is at its peak (Figure 4-1) and is expected to double its growth each year, as shown in Figure 4-1.

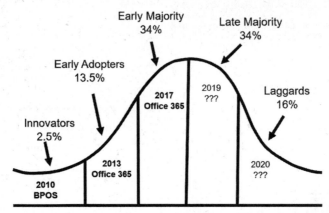

FIGURE 4-1:
Overlay of Technology Adoption bell curve and Office 365 adoption.

Everett M. Rogers, *Diffusions of Innovations*

I was one of those who adopted the technology back in 2010 when it was called the Business Productivity Online Services (BPOS) suite. Since then, I have kept up with the innovations in the service and shared my knowledge through a book I co-authored, *Office 365 For Dummies,* and of course, this book. My adoption of cloud technologies has opened many doors for me in the IT industry, which is unusual because my bachelor's degree is in business administration, not computer science. If you question the career advantage of being a cloud pro career-wise, I hope my story helps remove any doubt.

In this chapter, you get insights into the effort required to migrate email systems into Exchange Online in Office 365. The intent is to provide general guidance for migrating email rather than step-by-step instructions to do a migration, because each organization's email environment is unique. You learn how to take advantage of the online storage capabilities of SharePoint Online and get hands-on instruction for enabling your end users to self-serve.

Moving Your Email System to Exchange Online

Being an innovator or an early adopter has advantages. The tribal knowledge of how the technology has evolved can be helpful when troubleshooting issues. And with your feedback, you get to contribute to the incremental improvements of the technology.

Inversely, being the first to try out a new technology has its share of disadvantages. For example, email migration in the very early stages of Office 365 was complicated and often required consultants and highly trained systems engineers to accomplish. SMBs were at a disadvantage especially if they had emails hosted on-premises and didn't have thousands of dollars budgeted for a migration project. Migration best practices were sparse because systems engineers themselves were still trying to figure out the quirks of the system.

TIP

Today, you can find many online videos and articles describing how to migrate email to Exchange Online in Office 365. Search for "Exchange migration docs. microsoft.com" to find articles from Microsoft's repository. You will also find a robust library of resources for migrating email in different scenarios in Microsoft 365 Admin Center, as described in this section.

Basic email migration overview

If your small business is still using an email system that doesn't have a custom domain name, you're missing out on the opportunity to reinforce your brand and build trust. Worse, your competition could register a domain name you should have and divert potential business away from you.

I tell my clients that the first step in migrating email to Exchange Online — if they don't have an existing mail server — is to register their domain name. Several domain registrars, including Microsoft, offer discounted rates for domain name registration.

TIP

If you already have a domain registered with a registrar, you should have the capability to add records to your domain name system (DNS). This feature is important when setting up your domain in Office 365 because you will be asked to manually add the records or have Office 365 add them automatically. To understand the pros and cons of both approaches, visit `https://support. office.com/en-us/article/domains-faq-1272bad0-4bd4-4796-8005- 67d6fb3afc5a#bkmk_howdoesoffice365managemydnsrecords`.

A WORD ABOUT CHOOSING A DOMAIN REGISTRAR

When choosing a domain registrar, make sure to go with a company that allows you to add all the required DNS records: MX, CNAME, SRV, and TXT. If any one of these records is not supported, it will affect the usability of the service. For example, if TXT records are not supported, hackers could use your domain to send spam or malicious emails.

For small businesses running their own mail servers or that have their emails hosted by a third-party provider, the general process for migrating email for all users at the same time is four-fold:

1. Create a Microsoft 365 tenant by buying or trying out Microsoft 365 Business licenses. This step automatically creates an Azure AD tenant where users will be hosted in the cloud.

2. Add users to Azure AD from Microsoft 365 Business Admin Center manually. For organizations with on-premises Exchange servers, users are synchronized from the on-premises directory to Azure AD by using a tool called Azure AD Connect.

3. Replicate email data from the current email system to Exchange Online in Office 365. During the replication, users can continue to send and receive email with the current email system.

4. Flip the switch (also called *cutover*) so emails start flowing through Exchange Online instead of through the old email system.

TECHNICAL STUFF

The ideal scenario for a small business is to use the new cloud-based system exclusively to reduce the IT infrastructure footprint. If you're currently running Exchange servers on-premises, relying solely on Azure AD requires a change in the way you think about managing your identities and resources. There are tenured Exchange server systems engineers with decades of experience who will undoubtedly disagree with me and will insist that on-premises Exchange servers should not be retired, essentially shackling a business to the costly chain of managing on-premises infrastructure forever. This debate has come up often in my team of solution architects, and it's interesting to see the arguments on both sides. At the end of the day, this book is about transforming and modernizing how you run a business, so I stay firm in my belief that, especially for small businesses, it's time to shed the old ways and embrace a paradigm shift in how you manage your IT environment.

Capitalizing on the Office 365 Mail Migration Advisor

Outlining a step-by-step process for email migration is challenging because each email environment is different. In fact, the detailed activities for each of the four migration steps outlined in the preceding section can drastically vary from one organization to another.

There is, however, good news. The Setup Guidance card in Microsoft 365 Admin Center, shown in Figure 4-2, is your gateway to a successful email migration.

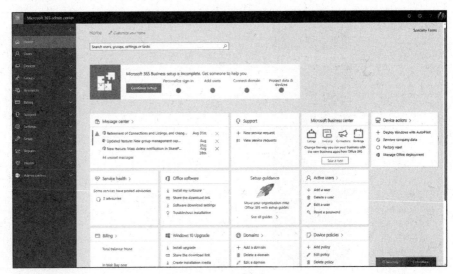

FIGURE 4-2:
Setup Guidance card in Microsoft 365 Admin Center.

Click the See All Guides link on the card, and the Setup Guidance page appears. From there, click the Office 365 mail Migration Advisor (see Figure 4-3) to get started on your mailbox migration journey.

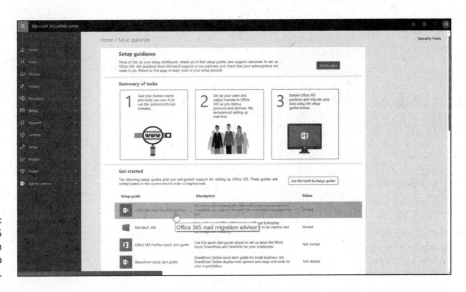

FIGURE 4-3:
The Office 365 Mail Migration Advisor setup guide.

The Mail Migration Advisor is a wizard that takes you step-by-step through the email migration process. It's built to accommodate different scenarios, so you know you're not being given a cookie-cutter approach to migration. For example, when you get to the What's Your Mail System? section, most common email scenarios are already accounted for, as shown in Figure 4-4.

FIGURE 4-4:
Email systems options in the Mail Migration Advisor wizard.

You don't have to complete all the steps in one sitting. You can save your work and go back to it later. After you've added a mail system, however, the left pane will display the rest of the steps to complete the migration, so you can track your progress, as shown in Figure 4-5.

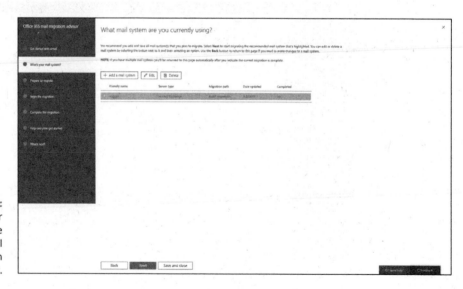

FIGURE 4-5:
Tracking your progress in the Office 365 mail migration advisor.

Migrating Files to SharePoint Online

Your subscription to a Microsoft 365 Business license includes 1TB of cloud storage in OneDrive for Business per licensed user. In addition, your organization gets 1TB of storage in SharePoint Online plus 10GB per licensed user.

Let's say for example you have 10 users, each with a Microsoft 365 Business license. Here's what your free cloud storage would look like:

> 10 users x 1TB per user in OneDrive for Business = 10TB
>
> 1TB in SharePoint Online
>
> 10 users x 10GB per user in SharePoint Online = 100GB (0.1TB)
>
> Total cloud storage: 11.1TB

If you're wondering how much data you can store in 1TB of storage, consider the infographic from http://itelementaryschool.com/wp-content/uploads/2015/10/Terabyte.png. In it, the author claims you'd have 60 piles of typed paper stacked as tall as the Eiffel Tower to consume 1TB of data.

With that much storage, you might wonder why SMBs are still using file shares and third-party SaaS applications such as Dropbox. For a majority of small businesses, the challenge is moving their existing data to SharePoint Online or OneDrive for Business.

Traditionally, migrating data to SharePoint Online required complicated tools requiring senior engineers. If a business did not have a budget for such tools or expertise, an IT admin would have to spend an enormous amount of time manually moving files and dealing with sync issues.

The good news is that Office 365 is designed to break traditions. What was challenging a few years ago is now a simple, free, self-service tool. With a few clicks, an IT admin can now confidently migrate files to document libraries in SharePoint Online or OneDrive for Business.

Do-it-yourself with the SharePoint Migration Tool

The SharePoint Migration Tool is a handy application taking the guesswork out of moving files to Office 365 from either your hard drive, third-party SaaS storage provider, or on-premises SharePoint environment. You basically just need to download the tool and, with a few clicks, the tool will do its magic while you, depending on the size of data you are moving, grab a cup of coffee or turn on Netflix to watch your favorite show while you wait for the tool to finish its job.

Here's how it works.

1. **Download the tool at** `http://aka.ms/spmt`.

2. **Double-click the downloaded file to run the tool and then click the Sign In button, shown in Figure 4-6.**

   The Where Is Your Data? screen appears.

FIGURE 4-6:
SharePoint
Migration Tool
sign-in screen.

3. **Select the source of your data (for this exercise, choose the File Share option):**

  - *If you're moving files from an on-premises SharePoint environment, choose SharePoint on-premises.*

  - *If you want to move files from your hard drive or file shares, choose File Share. If you want to move files from Dropbox, make sure the Dropbox app is running on your desktop and select the File Share option.*

  - *If you have multiple sources of data, choose JSON or CSV File for bulk migration. Note that you'll need some programming skills to create a JSON file.*

4. **In the Select a Source and Destination screen, click the Choose Folder button.**

5. **In the Browse for Folder window, choose the folder you want to migrate and then click OK.**

  The Select a Source and Destination screen reappears.

6. **Click the Next button.**

  A new box appears in the same screen so you can paste the URL for SharePoint Online or OneDrive for Document.

7. **In the Enter a URL box, enter or paste the URL of the destination library. In the Choose a Document Library drop-down menu, choose the appropriate document library. Then click the Add button.**

8. **On the next screen, review the entries for the Source and Destination, and then click the Migrate button to start the migration process.**

  The tool displays the migration status. If you need to change the Source or Destination entry, you must restart the process.

9. **When the migration is complete, click the Close button.**

The tool captures logs from the migration job, which you can view after the migration. Seeing the logs can be helpful for troubleshooting.

If you must close or accidentally close the tool before the migration job is complete, you can resume the job from any computer, provided that the job has run for at least 5 minutes.

TIP

Another cool feature of the tool is its capability to perform future incremental migrations. If someone in your team didn't get the memo and continues to save files to your file share, you can run the tool again and move just the new or updated files from the source location. To take advantage of this feature, click Yes when the tool asks if you want to keep the migration settings for future incremental runs after the migration is finished.

Syncing files with the OneDrive client

Another way to migrate files to SharePoint Online or OneDrive for Business is through the OneDrive sync client. After the sync client is running, you can simply drag files from the source location to the appropriate library in either OneDrive for Business or SharePoint Online.

If Windows 10 has been deployed with the Microsoft 365 Business license, the OneDrive for Business sync client is automatically set up for the account using the device. As such, OneDrive for Business folders will be available in File Explorer.

If you're migrating files to a SharePoint Online document library by using the OneDrive sync client, you first need to sync the SharePoint document library to your desktop. You do this by navigating to the SharePoint Online document library, and then clicking the Sync icon on the command bar, as shown in Figure 4-7. The sync client will prompt you through the rest of the steps, which are straightforward.

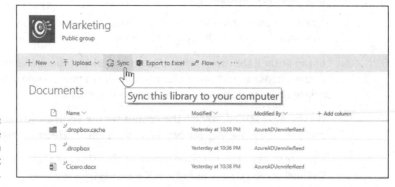

FIGURE 4-7:
Sync icon on the command bar in SharePoint Online.

Customizing the Microsoft Teams Tool

Microsoft Teams is the core collaboration tool in Microsoft 365 Business. With chat, voice, and video communication capabilities, Microsoft Teams answers the needs of team members working and collaborating today. The service has built-in productivity apps like the Office Apps and integrates with other services such as SharePoint, Planner, and Outlook.

As a digital collaboration hub, Microsoft Teams enables users to customize their workspace to fit the unique needs of the team. Third-party SaaS applications — even bots! — can be added to the service. People outside the organization can also be added to Microsoft Teams, extending collaboration outside the walls of the organization. Because Microsoft Teams is part of Office 365, security and compliance is standard in the service.

The out-of-the-box configuration for Microsoft Teams is usually sufficient for most small businesses. However, if your organization has specific policies, you can customize the settings from Microsoft Teams & Skype for Business Admin Center, which you can access as follows:

>> Navigate to Microsoft 365 Admin Center ⇨ Admin Centers ⇨ Teams & Skype

>> Navigate directly to https://admin.teams.microsoft.com/.

Like other admin centers in Microsoft 365 Business, the Dashboard page for Microsoft Teams Admin Center contains cards. Although Figure 4-8 displays only four cards, expect this page will have more cards in the future to streamline the work for IT admins.

In the left pane, note the sections where you can customize settings. Under Org-Wide Settings, for example, you can turn external access on or off. You can also enable Microsoft Teams users to communicate with users who are using the consumer Skype platform, as shown in Figure 4-9.

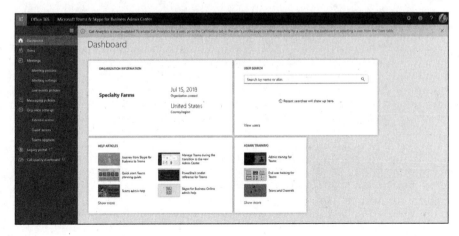

FIGURE 4-8:
Microsoft Teams & Skype for Business Admin Center.

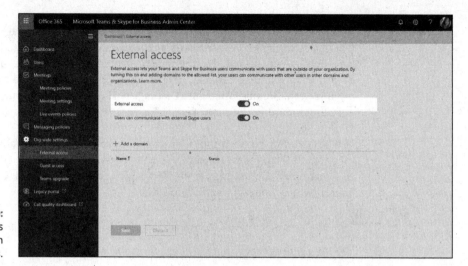

FIGURE 4-9:
External access
settings in
Microsoft Teams.

Microsoft recently implemented a Microsoft Call Quality Dashboard (as if we don't have enough dashboards already) so you can view reports about call quality, voice quality, and more. To check out the new dashboard, click Call Quality Dashboard in the left pane. This dashboard is new, so expect more features and improvements to be added soon.

Chapter 5

Deploying Windows 10

The day of reckoning is nearing for all businesses still running Windows 7. In less than a year, on January 14, 2020 to be exact, extended support for the Windows 7 operating system will end. Security updates will no longer be available for this version of the operating system when extended support ends. Considering today's cyberthreat landscape, you do not want to be running a business without security updates.

If you think you're safe because you're running Windows 8.1, think again. Mainstream support for Windows 8.1 ended on January 9, 2018. Although security updates are still available through the end of extended support on January 10, 2023, non-security updates will no longer be available. Requests for product design changes and features enhancement are no longer accepted and no-charge support programs are discontinued when mainstream support ended.

But wait—there is good news. Your Microsoft 365 Business license makes you eligible for a free upgrade to Windows 10 Pro! In Chapter 3, you learn that to prepare for a Windows 10 rollout, the first step is to upgrade Windows 7 or 8.1 devices to Windows 10 Pro Creators Update following the instructions here: www.microsoft.com/en-us/software-download/windows10.

After all the devices are updated, the stage is set for an IT admin to perform the Windows 10 deployment wizardry by using the Microsoft 365 deployment advisor and other tools.

If new laptops or desktops pre-installed with Windows 10 Pro from Lenovo, Dell, HP, or Microsoft are being deployed, consider unlocking Master Wizard level for the IT admin. End users will witness magic when they first turn on their device and realize that with a few clicks their device will be fully managed and protected with the technologies in Microsoft 365 Business.

This chapter is all about empowering an IT admin to deploy Windows 10 with the confidence of a wizard. You begin with an overview of the benefits of the operating system that Microsoft considers to be the most secure. Read about what Windows as a service means, and then get down in the weeds and step through two approaches for deployment. You then elevate your wizard level by automating the installation of Office ProPlus on devices during the Windows 10 deployment process.

Making the Case for Windows 10

A notable story in *Steve Jobs* by Walter Isaacson (Simon & Schuster) is when Jobs complained about the how long it took to boot up a Macintosh computer. When an engineer started to explain and give excuses, Jobs cut him off and asked if he'd shave 10 seconds from the boot time if it meant saving a person's life, to which the engineer replied, "probably." Jobs then proceeded to calculate that if 5 million people could save 10 seconds per day booting up their Macintosh computers, that added up to 300 million hours or so per year, the equivalent of at least 100 lifetimes saved per year. Apparently, the engineers came back a few weeks later to report that they'd managed to boot the computer not just 10 seconds faster, but 28 seconds.

So why am I talking about Macs in a book about a Microsoft technology? Well, for one, I have memories of cooking a fried rice dish while waiting for my Windows XP machine to boot way back when. With my Windows 10 device today, it takes no more than 20 seconds to boot my Surface Book 2.

Beyond just boot times, however, Windows 10 saves IT admins tons of hours in deployment and servicing. An IT director for a Fortune 500 company has said that the Windows-as-a-service model has reduced their deployment time by 75 percent. If you consider that time saving against 500 million plus devices running Windows 10 today, you'll see how much potential lifetimes we'd save per year simply by deploying Windows 10.

Getting cloud-ready with Windows 10

The future is here. Managing devices and identities no longer requires deep technical expertise and expensive infrastructure that takes a long time to build and deploy. Today, all you need are an Internet connection and a subscription to Microsoft 365 Business to have access to Azure AD and Windows 10 for a cloud-based identity and device management.

Windows 10 has built-in intelligent security. It's intelligent because it uses machine learning and artificial intelligence to combat sophisticated threats from bad actors. Updates are released on shorter cycles at regular intervals to ensure that security holes are plugged and risks are proactively managed.

Cloud-based provisioning in Windows 10 means an IT admin never needs to touch a device to manage it. Management can be in the form of wiping data if the device is lost or stolen, resetting the device to original settings so it can be reissued to another user, or pushing scheduled updates to the operating system. An IT admin can even remotely install the Office suite (Word, PowerPoint, Excel, Outlook, and so on) on a managed device.

The smart people at Microsoft have come up with a simple graphic that encapsulates the difference between traditional IT and modern IT, as shown in Figure 5-1. This is the future of how IT is delivered, and that future is now. Are you in or are you out?

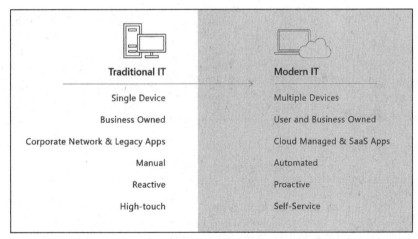

Traditional IT	Modern IT
Single Device	Multiple Devices
Business Owned	User and Business Owned
Corporate Network & Legacy Apps	Cloud Managed & SaaS Apps
Manual	Automated
Reactive	Proactive
High-touch	Self-Service

FIGURE 5-1: Traditional IT versus modern IT.

Microsoft Ignite 2017 Presentation

Windows as a service (WaaS) at a glance

Windows as a service (WaaS) is a concept that simplifies how the Windows operating system is managed and maintained. It is designed to be iterative, with additional features and improvements rolled out more quickly than in the past.

WaaS has two types of updates:

>> **Features updates:** Released twice annually, usually in the fall and the spring. This release cycle aligns with the feature releases for Office ProPlus (Word, PowerPoint, Excel, Outlook, OneNote, and so on).

>> **Quality updates:** Released monthly with fixes for bugs and other security updates. They contain cumulative updates, so if you have a PC that hasn't been turned on for three months, it will still get up to the latest version of Windows 10 when the update is applied.

By delivering these updates more often and in smaller packages, the chances of running into huge incompatibility issues with the operating system and your apps are lower.

The updates are rolled out in four stages, as shown in Figure 5-2. With both monthly and semi-annual updates, you can imagine the teams of engineers, project managers, testers, and more orchestrating the overlapping releases on any given day. Or night for that matter. I know. I've been there.

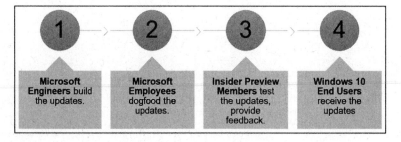

FIGURE 5-2: WaaS timelines.

>> **Microsoft engineers:** Updates are developed by Microsoft engineers in an iterative process.

>> **Microsoft employees:** *Builds* (something tangible coming out of a software code) are periodically released to thousands of Microsoft employees who participate in the *dogfood* (slang for an organization using its own product) program.

>> **Microsoft Insider Preview members:** After the engineers are satisfied with the build after taking feedback from the dogfooders, the update is released to the millions of people who have signed up for the Insider Preview program. During this stage, Microsoft is collecting feedback and feeding it into the development process.

>> **Windows 10 users:** When feature updates are final based on the feedback from the Insider Preview members, the build is released to organizations that have users licensed for Windows 10. Depending on how the servicing is configured, the update may be rolled out to end users in stages or all at once.

When it comes to deploying Windows 10, one size does not fit all. Each organization has its own unique needs. Even small businesses in the same industry with the same number of users will reveal subtle differences in how they use the technology.

In the next sections, I cover two approaches for deployment that would typically meet the needs of SMBs. Note that the steps outlined may require customization based on the business requirements.

Completing the Setup Wizard before Deployment

Before you begin deploying Windows 10, you must first complete the tasks in the Setup wizard from Microsoft 365 Admin Center, as shown in Figure 5-3. If you have completed the email migration as described in Chapter 4, most likely you have already added a domain and therefore the first step (Personalize Sign-In) will not appear.

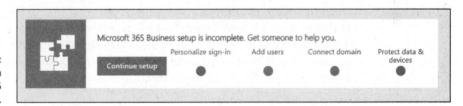

FIGURE 5-3:
Setup wizard in Microsoft 365 Admin Center.

As you continue through the wizard, you can just click Next if no action is required. For example, in the Add Users step, you can click Next if all users have been added or if you prefer to add them later.

After the Add Users step, the next screen asks you whether you want to migrate email messages, as shown in Figure 5-4. If you choose Migrate Email Messages, you will be taken out of the Setup wizard and directed to the Migration wizard. Don't worry; you can go back to the Setup wizard later to finish the tasks.

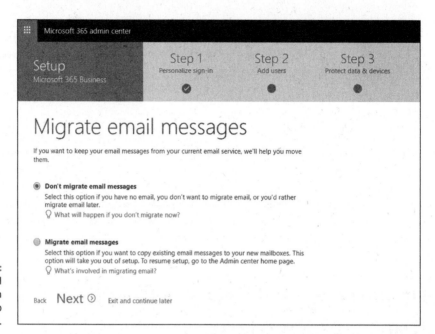

FIGURE 5-4:
Migrate Email
Messages screen
from the Setup
wizard.

The Migration wizard guides you through the process of migrating email from various sources, as shown in Figure 5-5. Note that you need to complete additional steps outside of the wizard to finish the email migration.

When you have completed the email migration, run the Setup wizard again and it will pick up where you left off.

The next task is to configure the settings for protecting work files on mobile devices under the Protect Data & Devices step. Figure 5-6 displays toggle switches to turn various settings on or off. By default, Protect Work Files when Devices Are Lost or Stolen is turned on. Delete Work Files from Inactive Device After is set to 90 days but you can change that setting.

Each toggle switch has quite a few policies automatically configured in the backend. In the past, configuring those policies would have required a systems engineer with deep technical expertise.

When you're satisfied with your settings in the Protect Work Files on Mobile Devices screen, click Next to move to the next task: Set Windows 10 Device Configuration.

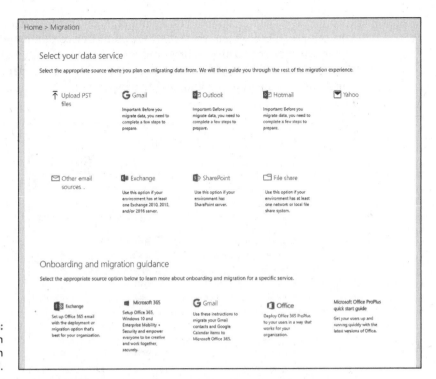

FIGURE 5-5:
Email sources in the Migration wizard.

FIGURE 5-6:
Protect work files on mobile devices from the Setup wizard.

Like the preceding screen, the Set Windows 10 Device Configuration screen has toggle switches for turning policies on or off, as shown in Figure 5-7. Note that these policies will be applied to all users whose devices are managed when they join Azure AD as part of the Windows 10 deployment.

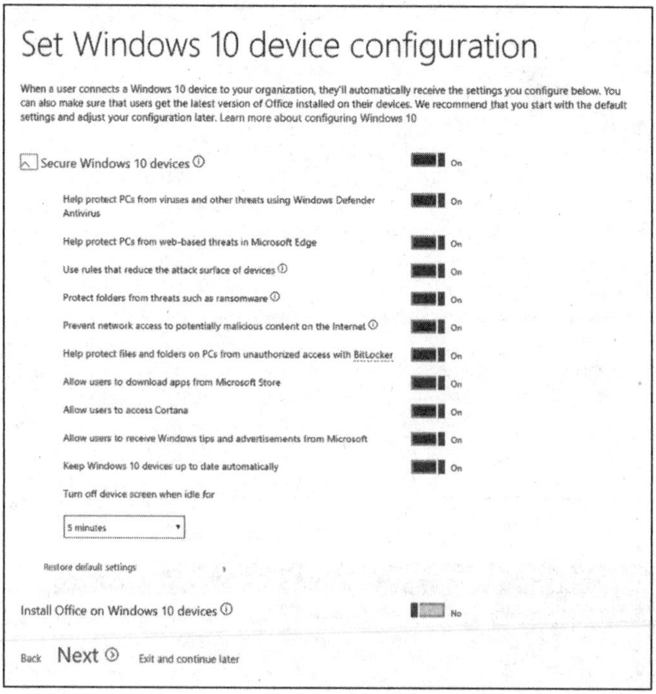

FIGURE 5-7:
Set Windows 10
device
configuration.

On the same screen, you can automate the installation of Office ProPlus by toggling the switch to On for Install Office on Windows 10 Devices. When you're satisfied with the settings, click Next to complete the Setup wizard tasks. You're now ready to deploy Windows 10.

Manually Deploying Windows 10 Business

For existing devices that have already been upgraded to Windows 10 Pro Creators Update (refer to Chapter 3), follow these steps to deploy Windows 10 Business:

1. **On the bottom left of your screen, click the Windows Start icon (Windows logo).**

2. **Click the Settings icon (gear).**

3. **In Settings, select Accounts.**

The Your Info page appears.

4. **In the left pane, select Access Work or School, as shown in Figure 5-8, and then click Connect.**

The Set Up a Work or School Account window appears.

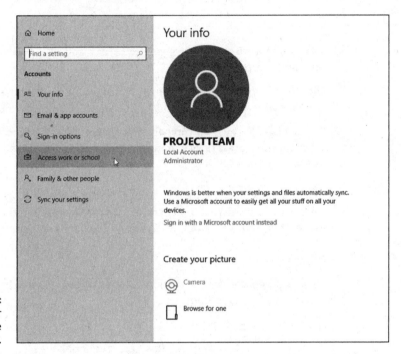

WARNING

5. **Select Join This Device to Azure Active Directory.**

Do not enter your email address in the box in the window!

The Let's Get You Signed In window appears.

6. **Enter your email address for Microsoft 365 Business, and then click Next.**

7. **Enter your password, and then click Sign In.**

The Make Sure This Is Your Organization window pops up, as shown in Figure 5-9.

8. **Click Join.**

The You're All Set! page appears.

9. **Click Done.**

The Access Work or School page reappears.

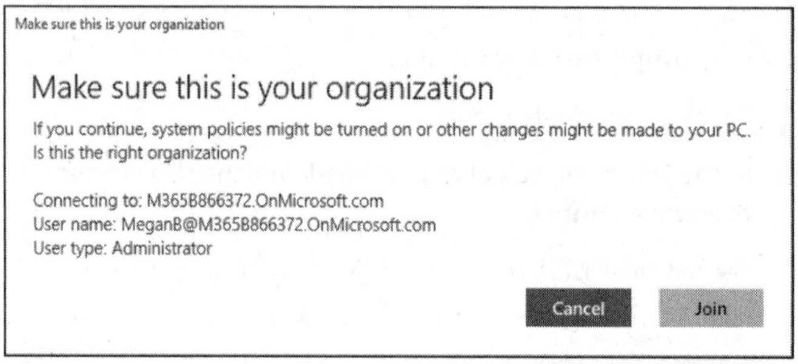

Make sure this is your organization

If you continue, system policies might be turned on or other changes might be made to your PC. Is this the right organization?

Connecting to: M365B866372.OnMicrosoft.com
User name: MeganB@M365B866372.OnMicrosoft.com
User type: Administrator

Cancel   Join

FIGURE 5-9:
Make Sure
This Is Your
Organization
pop-up window.

10. **Select Connected to [*your company name*] to display the Info and Disconnect button.**

11. **Click the Info button to get the sync status and verify that the device is synching with Azure AD.**

12. **On the Managed by [*your company name*] page, click the Sync button to make sure the latest device management policies are applied to the device.**

Now that you've deployed Windows 10 to the device, the next step is to log in to the device with your Microsoft 365 credentials and start using the device with all the features that come with your Microsoft 365 Business subscription. Here's how.

1. **Click the Windows Start icon.**

2. **Right-click the icon for the current account logged into the device, and then select Switch account.**

   The Windows 10 login page appears.

3. **Log in with your Microsoft 365 Business credentials.**

4. **If you see the "Another user is signed in" notification, click Yes.**

5. **Verify that Windows 10 Pro has been upgraded to Windows 10 Business by clicking the Windows Start icon and then selecting System.**

6. **In the left pane, click About.**

7. **Under Windows Specifications, make sure that the edition is Windows 10 Business, as shown in Figure 5-10.**

   Congratulations! You've just deployed Windows 10 manually!

TIP

If you follow the preceding steps — including additional steps Microsoft might require from updates — and the edition does not display *Windows 10 Business*, restart your computer. If the issue persists, submit a ticket to Microsoft (if licensing directly with Microsoft) or through your licensing provider's support channel.

FIGURE 5-10:
Windows 10 Pro upgraded to Windows 10 Business.

Windows specifications

Edition	Windows 10 Business
Version	1803
Installed on	8/3/2018
OS build	17134.228

Change product key or upgrade your edition of Windows

Read the Microsoft Services Agreement that applies to our services

Read the Microsoft Software License Terms

Deploying with Windows AutoPilot

To deploy Windows 10 by using Windows AutoPilot, Azure AD first must know that the company owns the device. This means that the device will need to be registered in Microsoft 365 Admin Center with the device's hardware ID. After the device is registered, it is ready for Windows AutoPilot deployment. I cover the steps for registering the device in this section.

Capturing the device ID

If you want to repurpose a computer or laptop for Windows AutoPilot, you must first extract the device ID of the device by using PowerShell, a utility tool installed on any Windows 10 device.

In this exercise, you will be doing some geeky stuff, but don't worry. No prior coding experience is required. The only skill required is the ability to read and type.

Capturing the device ID involves three steps:

1. Get the script that will extract the information from the device.

2. Save the script in a shared folder or a USB flash drive for later access.

3. Run the script on the device from which you want to extract the device ID.

Step 1: Get the PowerShell script

I'm all for not reinventing the wheel, so I recommend using a PowerShell script that's already been shared and tested in the geek community. Here's how to get the script that seasoned professionals use:

1. **From a device already running Windows 10, click the Windows Start icon and then type** PowerShell.

2. **Right-click Windows PowerShell and choose Run as Administrator, as shown in Figure 5-11.**

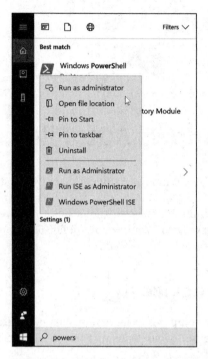

3. **Copy and run the following commands, which are the Get-WindowsAutoPilot script:**

```
Set-ExecutionPolicy Unrestricted
Save-Script -Name Get-WindowsAutoPilotInfo -Path
Install-Script -Name Get-WindowsAutoPilotInfo
```

4. **Accept the change by typing Y in the Execution Policy Change section, as shown in Figure 5-12, and then press Enter.**

The PowerShell window displays an error in red.

5. **In the PATH Environment Variable Change section, type Y and press Enter.**

6. **In the Nuget Provider Is Required to Continue section, type Y and press Enter.**

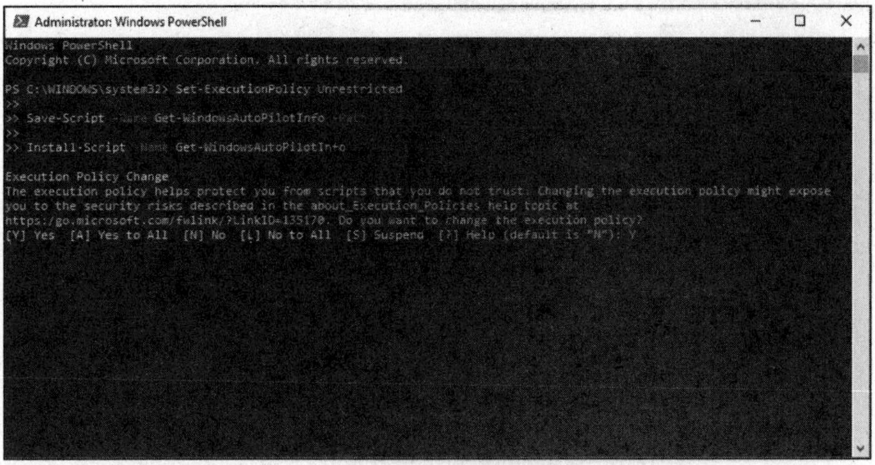

FIGURE 5-12:
Running
the Get-
WindowsAutoPilot
script.

7. **Under Untrusted Repository, enter Y and then press Enter.**

   After the command has run successfully, the last line in PowerShell will be

   ```
   PS C:\WINDOWS\system32>/
   ```

8. **Close the PowerShell window by clicking the X in the upper-right corner.**

Step 2: Save the script

After you complete the preceding steps, you can add PowerShell in your IT admin's toolkit — and be able to honestly add to your resume your experience using the tool. That's just the beginning. Next, let's save the script so you can it to capture the device ID.

1. **Open File Explorer by clicking the folder icon on the taskbar, and then navigate to**

   ```
   C:\Program Files\WindowsPowerShell\Scripts
   ```

2. **Verify that the Get-WindowsAutoPilotInfo.ps1 file is there, as shown in Figure 5-13.**

FIGURE 5-13:
PowerShell script
successfully
fetched.

3. **Copy the file to both a shared location such as OneDrive for Business or a document library in SharePoint and to a USB flash drive.**

   You will need to access that script from the device for which you want to capture the device ID.

Step 3: Run the script

Now that the script is readily accessible, let's capture the device ID. You will step through two scenarios in this process:

» Scenario 1: Capture the device ID from a device that is already in use.

» Scenario 2: Capture the device ID from a new device that has not been turned on yet and has not gone through the Out-of-the-Box Experience, or OOBE.

To capture the device ID from an existing device:

1. **From the device, navigate to where the PowerShell script is stored. Copy the file to the C drive, placing it in the root folder for easy navigation in PowerShell.**

2. **Open Notepad and type the following:**

   ```
   .\Get-WindowsAutoPilotInfo.ps1
      -ComputerName {ComputerName} -OutputFile .\MyDeviceID.csv
   ```

   Make sure to replace *{ComputerName}* (including the braces) with the name of your computer. Don't close Notepad. You will need it in Step 5.

TIP

   So you and your computer have been buddies for a while, but now you realize that you don't know your computer's official name! Fortunately, your computer won't take offense. Just click the Windows Start button, click Settings, and then select System. In the left pane, click About to find the device name under the Device Specifications group.

3. **Run PowerShell as an administrator per the instructions in the preceding section ("Step 2: Save the script").**

   PowerShell will default to the following path:

   ```
   PS C:\Windows\systems32>
   ```

4. **Point PowerShell to the folder where the script is saved from Step 1 by entering the following command:**

   ```
   cd\
   ```

PowerShell displays the following path (see Figure 5-14):

```
PS C:\>
```

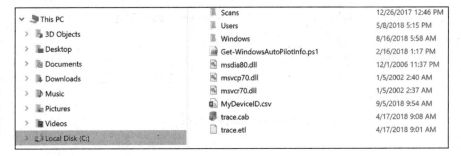

FIGURE 5-14:
PowerShell script
ran to capture
device ID.

5. **Copy the code you wrote in Notepad in Step 2 and paste it after the ›
character in the resulting PowerShell path (PS C:\›) in Step 4. Then press
Enter.**

PowerShell runs the script in the background. When it's finished, it reverts to
the C:\> path (refer to Figure 5-14).

6. **In File Explorer, navigate to Local Disk (C:). You will find the file with the
device ID called MyDeviceID.csv, as shown in Figure 5-15.**

FIGURE 5-15:
Device ID
captured and
stored in the
C drive.

The .csv file will contain information about the device in the following order:

Column 1: Device serial number

Column 2: Windows product ID

Column 3: Hardware hash

With the device information in hand, you're ready to register the device in the
Microsoft 365 Admin Center for Windows 10 AutoPilot deployment.

Registering the device for AutoPilot deployment

In this step, you upload the .csv file with the device information to Microsoft 365 Admin Center, and then create and assign an AutoPilot profile to the device. Here's how:

1. **In Microsoft 365 Admin Center, find the Device Actions card, and then select Deploy Windows with Autopilot, as shown in Figure 5-16.**

The Prepare for Windows page appears.

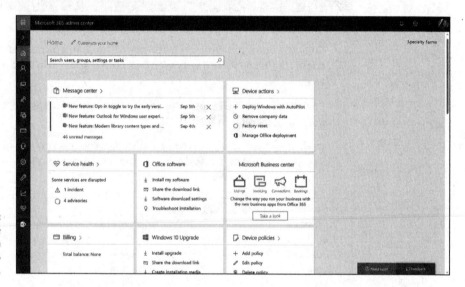

FIGURE 5-16: Device action card in Microsoft 365 Admin Center.

2. **Click the Start Guide button.**

The Upload .csv File with List of Devices page appears.

3. **Click the Browse button to locate the .csv file you created in the preceding section.**

4. **Navigate to the C drive on the device, select the MyDeviceID.csv file, and then click the Open button.**

The Upload .csv File with List of Devices page appears.

5. **Click Next.**

The Assign Profile page appears.

6. **Create a new deployment profile by entering a name in the Name Your New Profile box, as shown in Figure 5-17, and then click Next.**

   The You Are Done! screen appears.

7. **Click X (close).**

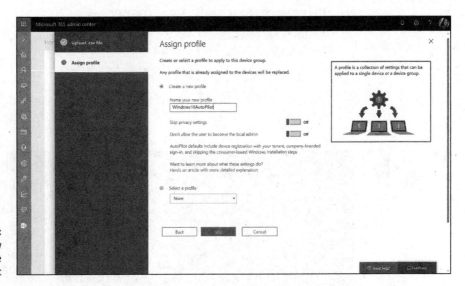

FIGURE 5-17: Creating a new profile for the AutoPilot

It will take a few minutes for the device to show up on the list of devices registered for AutoPilot. When it does, the end user will be taken through the simplified out-of-the-box experience (OOBE) for joining the device to Azure AD when he or she turns on the machine.

Stepping through the OOBE

Because Microsoft, HP, Dell, and Lenovo are part of the Windows AutoPilot program, these manufacturers can load the required device ID for your organization in preparation for an AutoPilot deployment. If you purchase new devices from these companies, ask them about loading the device IDs for you. If you prefer to have a Microsoft Partner help you with device purchases and working with manufacturers, contact info@cloud611.com.

After the devices are registered for AutoPilot, the end-user's experience for joining the device to Azure AD for management is greatly simplified.

For the IT admin, the AutoPilot process eliminates the need to even touch the device. So, if you have employees out in the field and one of them loses his device while out on a trip, that employee can basically go to a computer store, purchase a laptop, have the IT admin register the laptop for AutoPilot, turn the device on, enter the credentials, and — voila! — the laptop is now protected and managed.

The following sequence provides a glimpse into the end user experience when users first turn on a new device that has been registered for AutoPilot:

1. The end user selects a language and region.

2. The end user validates the keyboard layout and confirms whether a second keyboard layout needs to be added.

3. The end user connects to the network.

4. The end user enters his or her Microsoft 365 Business credentials, as shown in Figure 5-18.

FIGURE 5-18:
The end user
enters credentials
to join the device
to Azure AD.

5. The system finishes the setup (about 5 to 10 minutes) and then displays the default Windows 10 desktop.

   If the IT admin has configured the deployment to also install Office ProPlus, the applications will automatically start to install after a few minutes.

If you followed along with these steps and successfully deployed Windows AutoPilot for your company, congratulations! That was no small feat in the past, requiring deep technical expertise or the hiring of consultants and systems engineers.

If you ran into issues, help is available. If you purchased licenses directly from Microsoft, you can call Microsoft support. If you prefer to have a Microsoft Partner guide you through the deployment process and resolve issues, I would be happy to assist. Please send an inquiry to info@cloud611.com.

Chapter **6**

Configuring Security Features

John Chambers, former Cisco CEO, said that there are only two types of companies: those that have been hacked, and those who don't know they have been hacked. Considering that Cisco is the worldwide leader in IT, networking, and security solutions, notable personalities in the industry (including James Comey) have echoed the same sentiment for a good reason.

Sadly, that statement is today's reality and the new normal for anyone running a business of any size. On any given day, we face the risk of being attacked by malicious threat actors whose intent is to cause business disruption or harvest valuable company data to be resold on the dark web. Companies that have vulnerable servers and devices from lax (or the lack of) patch management and outdated practices are usually the entry points for hackers.

And if that weren't enough, we also face risks from the inside, with users intentionally or unintentionally leaking critical data. In fact, most confirmed data breaches are due to weak or stolen passwords. Guess what the three most common passwords were in 2017? Surprise!

» 123456

» password

» 12345678

As a small business, you most likely do not have the budget to implement a highly complex security infrastructure to combat cyber-attacks. You probably also do not have the means to hire top security talents to manage your computing environment. These realities, however, do not mean that you're out of luck. With a shift in mindset, a commitment to adopting security best practices, and a cost-effective monthly subscription to Microsoft 365 Business, even a small business like yours can enhance its security posture just like the large enterprises do today.

In this chapter, you glean insights into the built-in security features in Microsoft 365 Business and how these features work across the different services. You can follow along with the step-by-step instructions on configuring security features and learn how to send encrypted emails to reduce your vulnerability to cyber-attacks.

Securing the Front Door

When you run a business, you have data and you collect data. Data can be in the form of proprietary information, employee data, customer data, or data from your vendors and partners. In today's digital age, data is the new currency. Hackers know that protecting data is a challenge for SMBs, so it is no surprise that hackers increasingly target small businesses. A few years ago, ransomware from hackers who wanted a quick buck started out at around $5,000. Nowadays, with the availability of ransomware-as-a-service, I have seen victims who were asked to pay $1,500 to get their data back.

Although you can't stop hackers from being hackers, you can stop them from making you their latest victim. The first step in protecting your environment is to assume that you will be attacked. With that mindset, you can begin securing your front door and letting hackers know they're not welcome.

Office 365 Advanced Threat Protection overview

Statista.com studies show that 48 percent of email traffic worldwide is spam. When you're using Office 365, the emails you see in your mailbox are mostly ones that have passed the cloud-based mail-filtering system for spam (unwanted mail) and malware (viruses and spywares). This filtering system is automatically configured in the subscription, but you, as an admin, can tweak the settings to fit your company's needs.

Hackers, however, have become smarter. To bypass these filters, they've resorted to social-engineering techniques to try to breach your environment. They employ deceptive techniques to manipulate you — for instance, to get you to give them your password.

Office 365 Advanced Threat Protection (ATP) is a cloud-based solution that employs a multilayered approach to protecting not just email but also data across the Microsoft 365 Business environment, including SharePoint Online, OneDrive for Business, and Microsoft Teams. In the Microsoft 365 Business subscription, Office 365 ATP comes with two features: ATP Safe Attachments, and ATP Safe Links.

ATP Safe Attachments

While traveling this year, I thought I'd use a 30-minute layover to be productive and check my email. I connected to the airport Wi-Fi and fired up Outlook; soon I was responding to emails and accomplishing a lot. As I was about to shut down my computer to start boarding my flight, I saw an email come in marked "Urgent." It was from a colleague, with an attachment and a note saying she needed my immediate approval or the project we were working on would be delayed by four weeks. In my rush, I didn't verify the email associated with the sender and immediately double-clicked the attachment. As it turns out, even someone aware of phishing tricks can still fall prey to social-engineering tactics. Lucky for me, ATP Safe Attachments is running on my system, so instead of the hacker wreaking havoc, I was presented with a notification that the attachment was blocked, as shown in Figure 6-1.

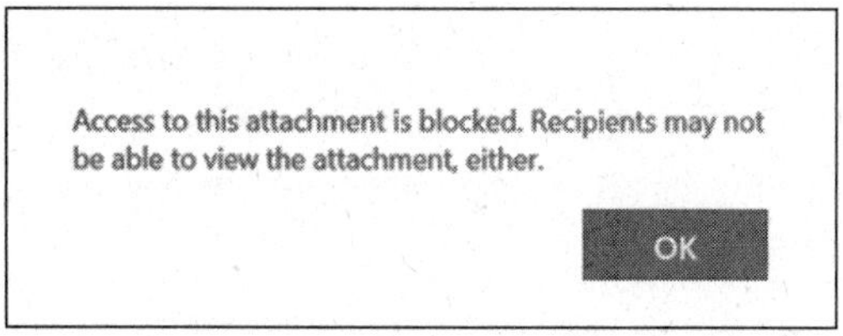

FIGURE 6-1:
Attachment blocked by Safe Attachments in Office 365 ATP.

Access to this attachment is blocked. Recipients may not be able to view the attachment, either.

OK

The ATP Safe Attachments feature took the appropriate action based on the policies I configured in Exchange Online. The policy allowed me to see the body of the email but blocked access to the malicious file. Sophisticated machine-learning technologies, artificial intelligence, and a host of other automated systems run in the background in real time to ensure that the policies are in effect — that is the beauty of cloud technologies. Imagine if you were to do this all by yourself. You'd have to spend a ton of money, time, brainpower, and — actually, you simply couldn't do what this technology does.

ATP Safe Attachments also works for files in SharePoint Online and OneDrive for Business document libraries. If someone loads malicious files in document libraries, the system detects them and prevents users from opening them.

Here's how to set up ATP Safe Attachments.

1. **Log in as a global administrator at** `https://admin.microsoft.com/.`

2. **In the left pane, under Admin Centers, select Security & Compliance.**

3. **In the left pane, in the Microsoft 365 Security & Compliance portal, expand Threat Management. Then select Policy, and click the ATP Safe Attachments card, as shown in Figure 6-2.**

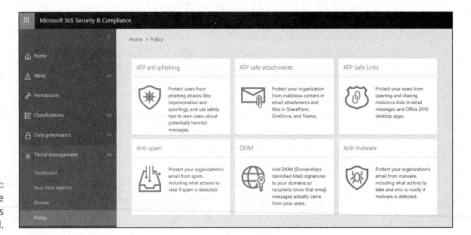

FIGURE 6-2:
ATP Safe
Attachments
card.

4. **On the Safe Attachments page, select the box to the left of Turn on ATP for SharePoint, OneDrive, and Microsoft Teams.**

   This action enables Safe Attachments in SharePoint Online, OneDrive for Business, and Microsoft Teams.

5. **Click the New button (+ sign) to create a new policy.**

6. **In the New Safe Attachments Policy window, specify the name and description.**

   In Figure 6-3, I named the policy Deliver Right Away.

FIGURE 6-3:
Creating a Safe Attachment policy.

7. **Choose the action that's appropriate for your organization.**

In my example in Figure 6-3, I chose Dynamic Delivery. This choice delivers an email that contains an attachment immediately to the recipient. While the attachment is being scanned, a placeholder attachment is attached, and the user is notified that the attachment is being analyzed. After the scanning is complete, if the attachment is deemed safe, the attachment is reattached to the email. If the attachment is determined to be malicious, it is sent to quarantine, where the global administrator of Microsoft 365 Admin Center can review and manage it.

8. **In the Redirect Attachment on Detection section, select the Enable Redirect option and enter an email address.**

This step is required if you want someone investigate malicious attachments.

9. **In the Applied To section, in the *If. . . box, select The Recipient Domain Is.**

10. **In the domain picker window that pops us, select the domain for your Microsoft 365 Business tenant that ends with .onmicrosoft.com, and then click the OK button.**

11. **Click the Save button.**

A Warning window appears, reminding you that Dynamic Email Delivery is only for mailboxes hosted in Office 365.

12. **Click OK to close the window.** You return to the Safe Attachments page, where you can see the Safe Attachment policy you just created.

13. **In the Save Attachments page, click Save to save your changes.**

If you're finished with creating policies for Safe Attachments, you can navigate away from the page by clicking any of the menus on the left or by closing the browser.

ATP Safe Links

Hackers are persistent. They will continue to find ways to try to breach your environment. If you close the door with attachments, they will try to open another door by tricking you into clicking a link in the body of an email or inside a document to take you to a malicious site. They may even make it so that the first time you click the link, it takes you to a legitimate website. If you click the link again, it redirects you to a malicious site!

ATP Safe Links, another security feature in Office 365 ATP, verifies the link each time you click it in real time. If the link is malicious, and ATP Safe Links is configured, a warning page will appear to notify the user that access to the website is blocked, as shown in Figure 6-4.

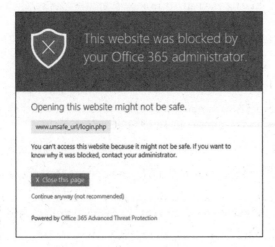

FIGURE 6-4:
ATP Safe
Links alert.

TIP

Office 365 ATP comes with a default policy for ATP Safe Links that blocks malicious links based on sophisticated machine-learning algorithms, artificial intelligence, and a bunch of automated processes. This service is constantly being updated, so stay current to align your policies based on what's new. To find out more about updates, visit https://docs.microsoft.com/en-us/office365/securitycompliance/office-365-atp#new-features-are-continually-being-added-to-atp.

As a cloud service, Office 365 ATP is updated regularly, so it's best to edit the default policy to ensure that all the new features are enabled for your company.

To edit the default ATP Safe Links policy, follow these steps:

1. **Log in as a global administrator at** https://admin.microsoft.com/.

2. **In the left pane, under Admin Centers, select Security & Compliance.**

3. **In the left pane, under the Microsoft 365 Security & Compliance portal, expand Threat Management. Then select Policy, and click the ATP Safe Links card.**

4. **On the Safe Links page, under the Policies that apply to the entire organization section, select Default and click the Edit icon (pencil).**

5. **In the Safe Links Policy for Your Organization window, add any URLs you want to block.**

6. **For added protection, select all boxes under Settings that apply to content except email heading.**

   This default policy does not apply to email messages. You can use this as a guide to create your own policy to apply to emails.

7. **Click the Save button to save your changes.**

   You return to the Safe Links page.

If you're finished with creating policies for Safe Links, you can navigate away from the page by clicking any of the menus on the left or by closing the browser.

Using Encryption to Protect Email

About 20 years ago, while working on some confidential projects, I had to use PGP (Pretty Good Privacy) to send encrypted email. I found the experience cumbersome, time-consuming, and sometimes maddening. First, I had to install the PGP software, generate a private key and public key, share my public key with others, get other people's public keys, and then get all these keys in one place. When I was finally ready to send an encrypted email, I'd have to encrypt the email with other people's public keys and send it over to them. Then they would have to decrypt the email using their private keys. If I forgot to encrypt the email with another person's public key, I'd have go through the steps all over again. A lot of times, people would complain that they couldn't open the email because it wasn't encrypted to them or it was encrypted with an old key. The process was a nightmare.

Today, sending encrypted emails in Office 365 involves a few clicks. There is no software to install or keys to generate or share with others. All the magic happens in the backend.

The IT admin doesn't even have to configure anything in the backend. That's because Microsoft 365 Business automatically comes with Office 365 Message Encryption as part of the Azure Information Protection service. Right out of the gate, licensed users can immediately take advantage of this security feature.

Azure Information Protection labels

As the name suggests, Azure Information Protection (AIP) is a cloud-based service designed to protect information. AIP includes a variety of features depending on the type of plan you subscribed to. One of the features of AIP is Office 365 Message Encryption (OME).

Microsoft 365 Business includes AIP Premium 1, which includes OME. OME in turn, comes with the following four default labels:

>> **Encrypt:** When this label is applied to an email, the entire email is encrypted and can be viewed only by the recipients of the email. Recipients can be people inside or outside your company. If the recipients of the encrypted email are using Microsoft cloud technologies such as Office 365 or Microsoft 365, no additional steps are required to decrypt and read the email. Recipients who are using another email system, such as Gmail or Yahoo, must complete a few simple steps to confirm their identity before the email is decrypted and becomes readable. Recipients of an encrypted email will not be able to remove the encryption.

>> **Do Not Forward:** If the Do Not Forward label is applied to an email, the email will be encrypted and the recipient will not be able to forward the email to anyone.

>> **Confidential:** The Confidential label allows anyone in your organization with a Microsoft 365 Business license to view, reply, forward, print, and copy the data. If an email labeled Confidential is accidentally sent to someone outside

the organization, the recipient will still receive the email but the content will not be readable. The sender of the email will be able to track and revoke access to the email at any time.

>> **Highly Confidential:** This label is similar to the Confidential label except that recipients will not be able to forward, print, or copy the data.

These labels are accessible from the Outlook desktop application as well as its cloud version, Outlook Online.

Sending an encrypted email

No software installation, no key generation or distribution, and no admin setup and configuration. That's the promise of Office 365 Message Encryption. Sending encrypted messages from Outlook or Outlook Online is quick and easy with a Microsoft 365 Business subscription.

To send an encrypted email:

1. **In Outlook Online, click New Message to create a new message.**

2. **Compose the email as you normally would.**

Enter the recipient's email address in the To line, the subject, and the message.

3. **In the top menu bar, click Encrypt, as shown in Figure 6-5.**

The Encrypt label is automatically applied to the email. You can apply a different label by clicking Click Change Permission in the gray bar above the recipient's name.

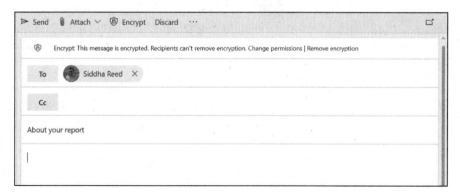

FIGURE 6-5:
Protect your
email with
encryption.

4. **Click Send.**

The email is sent and the screen reverts to Outlook's reading view.

If the recipient of the email uses Exchange Online in Office 365 of Microsoft 365, the email will automatically be readable. If the recipient uses another email system, such as Gmail, the email will include a button that shows the recipient how to read the encrypted email.

Figure 6-6 shows a recipient using Gmail. When the recipient clicks the Read the Message button, a new window opens. In the new window, the recipient is given two options for viewing the message: sign in with a Google account or use a one-time passcode. After one of these authentication requirements is met, the email is displayed.

FIGURE 6-6:
Email encryption in Gmail.

Chapter **7**

Getting Tactical with the Deployment

mplementing a new technology is never easy. Show me an IT admin who says his technology implementation is flawless and I'll show you someone who is stretching the truth. There will always be bumps in the road — some big and some small — especially when migrating from a legacy system. Whether you stumble and fall on those bumps depends on how much planning went into the endeavor and how well you prepared your organization.

Change is hard. Even in small organizations, I've seen pockets of people who resist change. I start talking to them about the cloud and the awesome features in the new version of Outlook, and they tell me how much they like their trusted Outlook 2003, thank you very much.

Too many times, I've seen IT leaders lose their jobs over a bad technology implementation. Most unsuccessful implementations share two common elements: a lack of planning and preparation.

As the IT admin rolling out Microsoft 365 Business in your organization, I don't want you to be a casualty of a bad implementation. In this chapter, I share a real-life experience implementing Microsoft 365 Business by a 20-year-old college freshman with no engineering background. You will hear about the issues he encountered and get a glimpse into the project plan he used for the deployment.

I realize that each organization is different, so I don't expect everything in this chapter to be 100 percent applicable to you. My hope, however, is that you will glean some valuable information here to help you on your cloud journey.

Peering into a Real-Life Deployment

In Chapter 3, I discuss the need for a road map when implementing Microsoft 365 Business and outline the approach in five phases: prep and plan, deploy, communicate, train and adopt, and manage and enhance.

Based on this road map, I created a project plan in Microsoft Project to help my then-20-year-old son (with no engineering background) migrate a customer to Microsoft 365 Business. The plan was based on my experience as a solutions architect for a company that has migrated over 500,000 mailboxes to Exchange Online.

My son decided to do the migration himself because his customer was a small business with a limited budget. I offered to assist as needed during my spare time because I knew it would be helpful to share a real-life example in this book.

Questions to ask before deployment

Before we started the deployment, my son and I needed answers to three key questions:

>> **What are we rolling out?** The answer would determine what feature sets to enable during the deployment.

>> **Why are we doing this deployment?** Knowing this would help us understand the customer's current pain points and determine the focus of the communications plan.

>> **Who will be affected by this implementation?** The answer would help us define the training and adoption activities and tailor the content to the technical ability of the end user.

REMEMBER

Microsoft 365 Business comes with several features, functionalities, and toolkits to drive productivity and enhance security. The productivity side includes Outlook, Yammer, SharePoint, Microsoft Teams, Groups, and Planner. On the security site, you could roll out self-service password reset, multi-factor authentication, and single sign on to SaaS apps, to name a few features. If you don't plan and leave everything enabled at the get-go, you run the risk of end users encountering unfamiliar feature sets, getting confused, and ultimately running to you for help.

Tales from the deployment trenches

For this deployment, I provided the training sessions and created the email templates for the communications plan. Meanwhile, my son did the setup and configuration. He experienced some hiccups along the way because this was his first deployment, but overall, the deployment went as planned.

The customer's environment and requirements included the following:

>> The firm has 20 employees, located in the same office.

>> Email system was on a hosted Exchange environment.

>> A cutover migration on a Friday night was acceptable.

>> No on-premises servers.

>> Devices are running Windows 10 Home.

>> The shared documents in Dropbox would be moved to a SharePoint Online document library.

>> The customer did not want to use Yammer and wanted to use Microsoft Teams for collaboration.

We encountered two issues with this deployment:

>> A couple of mailboxes had errors and Outlook wouldn't load. We ended up running the Support and Recovery Assistant (SARA) tool to resolve the issue. You can download the SARA tool at https://diagnostics.office.com/.

>> We chose not to use third-party tools for migrating data from Dropbox to the SharePoint Online document library for a variety of reasons. Although all the files were migrated successfully, the users ran into issues opening the documents. Some problems were due to unsupported characters or migration errors, but others were still unresolved two months later. Fortunately, we hadn't deleted the files from Dropbox, so we were able to re-upload them.

TIP

If you plan to migrate data to SharePoint Online or OneDrive for Business, check out the newly released and updated version of the SharePoint Migration tool. The tool is free and worth considering. You can read more at https://docs.microsoft.com/en-us/sharepointmigration/introducing-the-sharepoint-migration-tool.

Planning the Deployment

Although no two organizations deploying technology in the same way, there is value in considering what others have done so you don't reinvent the wheel. Table 7-1 outlines the tasks from the project plan I created. Please note that the information shared here is meant only as guidance. You should make revisions as needed to fit your implementation scenario.

TABLE 7-1   **Microsoft 365 Deployment Project Plan**

Prep and Plan

Microsoft 365 Admin Center

Provision the Microsoft 365 tenant

Add users to the tenant using .onmicrosoft.com domain

Purchase licenses and assign licenses to users

Disable Yammer from each user's license

Enable Self-Service Password Reset from Azure AD

Run the Setup wizard to configure device and application policies

Windows 10 Home Prep

Purchase Windows 10 Pro upgrade licenses

Update Windows 10 Home to the most recent version

Upgrade Windows 10 Home to Windows 10 Pro

Deploy

Migrate Email

Synchronize users from the source environment to the M365 tenant

Replicate mailboxes

Migrate mailboxes via Cutover Migration method

Update DNS records

Deploy Windows 10 Business

Upgrade Windows 10 Home to Pro

Update Windows 10 Pro to the most recent version

Join the Windows 10 Device to Azure AD

Verify that the device is connected to Azure AD
Verify that the device is upgraded to Windows 10 Business
Verify that Office 365 ProPlus is installed
Create Outlook Profile
Run Outlook and create a new profile
Test 5 mailboxes
Run the Support and Recovery Assistant tool for mailboxes with issues
Migrate Data from Dropbox
Log in to the OneDrive for Business desktop app
Drag files from the Dropbox folder to the OneDrive folder
Validate that all files have been successfully moved over
Cancel the Dropbox account to save cost
Create a Self-Service Training Portal
Provision communications site
Populate site with links and other training content
Create support requests list
Communicate
Email: We are moving to a modern workplace!
Email: Get ready for the move!
Email: We are moving in 5 days!
Email: We are moving tonight!
Email: Welcome to a modern workplace!
Train and Adopt
30 minutes: Microsoft 365 Overview
1 hour: Productivity and collaboration tools
1 hour: Staying secure
1 hour: Teams overview

A few notes about the project plan:

>> We ended up not sending the Communication emails as called out in the plan. Because we were in the same office with all the employees, it was easier to just verbally let them know what was happening.

>> For the Train and Adopt plan, we started with a two-hour immersion experience workshop in which the employees joined us in a conference room and, using their laptops, played with the features of the solution from a trial environment. The workshop was useful because we were able to see the users' technical level, which informed us of the content to use for follow-up trainings.

>> By having a deployment project plan to refer to, my novice IT admin son was able to accomplish a seemingly daunting task with my guidance. The experience built up his confidence and started him on a path to a career in the technology industry.

3
Driving Productivity and Collaboration

Get an overview of the key productivity tools in Office 365 and the purpose each serves.

Enhance collaboration with the help of machine learning and artificial intelligence.

Create an elegant communications site in SharePoint Online without learning how to code.

Understand how Microsoft Teams powers modern collaboration in the workplace.

Chapter **8**

Unlocking Enhanced Collaboration

A day in the life of an IT admin is typically focused on keeping everyone in the organization productive. From resetting passwords to resolving printer issues to fixing "broken" computers, IT admins are the underappreciated, forgettable team member in the workplace. In fact, there is no shortage of funny videos on the Internet about IT admins. Although some of these videos exaggerate, they have a common theme related to the stereotypical perception of an IT admin: nerdy, geeky, condescending, socially awkward, and usually a guy.

The reality in today's world, however, is that we all depend on our IT admins to get our jobs done. In their own way, they wield huge power that could make a difference in an organization's quest to realize its goals. Can you imagine what it would be like if there were no IT admin to help a marketing executive print a file to a network printer? Or think of the repercussions if there were no one to remotely wipe a CEO's lost laptop or mobile device. Business life without an IT admin would be catastrophic!

It's hard to find a company nowadays that does not use technology in some way to deliver its products or services, and the shared understanding is that every company is a technology company. The tide has shifted for the IT admin who has been the butt of jokes over the past several decades. TV shows such as *The Big Bang Theory* or *The IT Crowd* have helped make the geek culture mainstream and raised the profiles of these back-office geniuses. It has also made pursuing a career in IT desirable for women as well as men.

The timesaving collaboration features in Microsoft 365 Business are another opportunity for an IT admin to elevate the status of his or her field. Never mind that artificial intelligence and machine learning are already built into the solution; IT admins can still impart knowledge to their users as if they did all the complex programming and configuration.

In this chapter, you explore the advanced technologies that underpin the collaboration features in Microsoft 365 Business. You see these features come alive as you step through productivity scenarios using the collaboration toolkit in the solution. By the end of this chapter, you'll have learned so many cool things about the technology that you might just end up the office hero.

Understanding the Advanced Technologies in the Solution

Our world is exploding in data. From selfies on our mobile devices, to the number of steps recorded on our Fitbits, to the rants we post on Facebook, and all the way to the logs our Internet of Things (IoT) devices send to the cloud, data is everywhere.

The same is true in our workplace. We have emails, meeting notes, chats, presentations, and more. The challenge we face with this massive amount of data is finding the one bit of information we need at the right moment. Studies have shown that a big part of productivity loss in the workplace is looking for and not finding data.

The advanced technologies in Microsoft 365 Business are designed to solve this challenge. In this section, you learn more about the built-in artificial intelligence and machine learning that happens in the background to make collaboration a much better experience in Microsoft 365 Business.

All together as one with Groups

Office 365 Groups (or Groups for short) is a service in Microsoft 365 Business that enables end users to be part of a membership service. Those memberships then serve as the basis for access to the rest of the services in the solution. For example, suppose a marketing team has ten members. An IT admin can create a group called Marketing Team and use that group to grant access to company resources such as files and folders in SharePoint, device management in Intune, and more. This approach saves the IT admin time from having to enter ten users one at a time to all the different services in Microsoft 365.

Groups is the secret sauce for seamless collaboration because it provides a single identity for teams working together, whether in SharePoint Online, Office Apps, Yammer, or Microsoft Teams. In addition to its end user collaboration benefits, Groups is an important tool for IT admins when managing identities and devices.

Groups can be either private or public. In a *private group,* content can be accessed by only members of the group. Anyone wanting to join a private group will need to be approved by the group owner. In a *public group,* anyone in the organization can access the content of the group. Anyone can also join the group without needing group owner approval.

By default, Groups is enabled for external sharing, so a group member can invite people outside the organization to access and join the group. If you want to disable this feature, you must have global admin privileges for your Microsoft 365 tenant.

To disable external sharing for Groups, follow these steps:

1. **Navigate to** https://admin.microsoft.com/

2. **In the left pane, under Settings, select Services & Add-Ins.**

   The Services & Add-Ins page appears.

3. **Scroll down and select Office 365 Group.**

   The Office 365 Groups settings form appears on the right.

4. **Next to Let Group Members outside the Organization Access Group Content, toggle the switch to the off position, as shown in Figure 8-1.**

   This action also turns off the settings for Let Group Owners Add People outside the Organization to Groups.

5. **Click the Save button to save your changes.**

6. **Click the Close button to close the form.**

   You return to the Services & Add-Ins page.

Depending on how you plan to use Groups, you can create them in a few places. If you want to collaborate with others with a shared calendar and email, Outlook Online is an ideal place to create Groups. Simply click the new icon (+ sign) next to Groups, as shown at the bottom of Figure 8-2, and follow the prompts in the form that pops up.

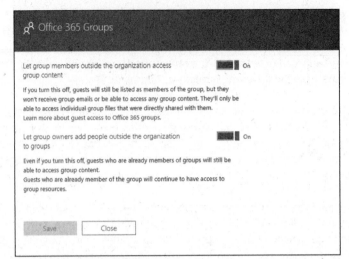

FIGURE 8-1:
Turning off
external sharing
for Groups.

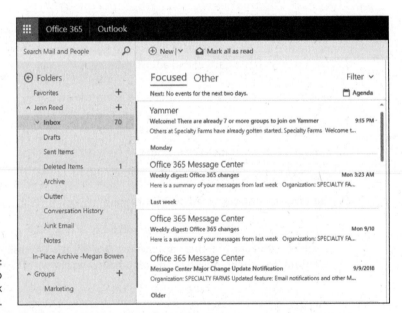

FIGURE 8-2:
Creating a Group
from Outlook
Online.

If you're aiming for a broader audience reach, such as company-wide communications, Yammer is a great place to create a Group. While logged in to Yammer, click the + Create a Group link (see Figure 8-3) in the left pane and then follow the prompts.

For a robust team collaboration with all the bells and whistles that come with team sites in SharePoint, you can create a Group at the same time you create a new SharePoint team site.

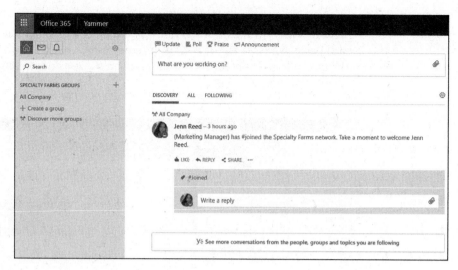

FIGURE 8-3:
Creating a Group
from Yammer.

And last but not least, if you want to have a chat-based collaboration workspace, you can create a Group from Microsoft Teams. I cover Teams in Chapter 9.

Connecting the dots with Office Graph

It may seem a bit like Big Brother, but all your interactions and behaviors in Microsoft 365 Business are captured, analyzed, and processed by machine-learning algorithms that are then fed into artificial intelligence experiences so that relevant information can be made available to you without lifting a finger. For example, if you send and receive a lot of emails from a colleague named John, meet with him regularly on Microsoft Teams, or share documents with him on OneDrive for Business, the system determines that your connection with John is very high. As a result, the system will let know what John is up to by displaying information such as the last document he worked on or articles he's published in SharePoint — granted, of course, that you have access to those documents.

The technology that makes all this magic happen is called Office Graph. It runs in the background and there is no need to configure it. Office Graph automatically maps your connections with people in your organization so you can discover relevant content and save time by prioritizing your focus.

Serving up content with Delve

One of the best ways to see Office Graph in action is through Delve. The more you interact with others in Microsoft 365 Business, and the more signals Office Graph has collected from those interactions, the richer the information in Delve becomes.

Delve is a page in Microsoft 365 Business that is available to all licensed users. Each Delve page (see Figure 8-4) is different from one user to another and shows the most relevant content for a user based on the user's interactions as captured by Office Graph.

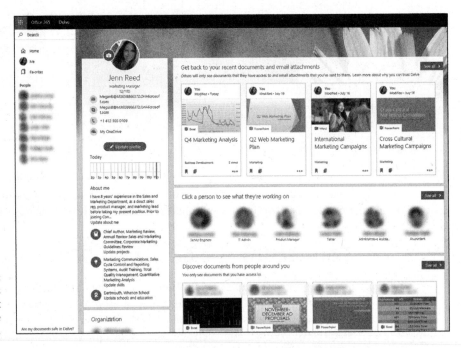

The top section of Delve, to the right of your profile summary, displays the documents you were working on last. I find this section helpful because I may have several documents open throughout the day. When I shut down my laptop to go to a meeting or start my commute, I close all open documents. When I'm back at my desk to start working again, it takes me a few minutes to remember what documents I had previously open. With Delve, I can see those documents and just pick up where I left off. Note, too, that the card for the document gives you tidbits of information, such as how many people viewed it.

TIP

If you haven't yet checked out Pinterest, please do. I'm seeing more apps taking inspiration from the way Pinterest displays information in a board. For example, Delve has a nifty feature that allows you to create a board similar to the ones on Pinterest. This feature is helpful when you want to organize documents into meaningful categories. I often find myself hunting for documents because they're saved in a folder that is meaningful only to the person who saved it.

Delve has a lot more to discover, so I encourage you to spend some time browsing around and clicking icons and buttons to see what they do.

Getting to Know Your Collaboration Toolkit

As individuals and as teams, we all work differently and therefore have different collaboration needs. In Microsoft 365 Business, we are not stuck with one cookie-cutter approach for teamwork. In this section, I touch on just two of the most commonly used services. After you gain an understanding of their capabilities, you should find it easy to learn how to use the rest of the collaboration tools in the solution. I don't cover Microsoft Teams in this section because a separate chapter, Chapter 9, is dedicated to the topic.

Creating a team site in SharePoint

Sometimes a shared calendar and mailbox is not enough to meet a team's collaboration needs. For example, you may be working on a project where you need a project schedule, or granular access permissions, or workflows to automate your team's work. In those situations, the answer to your collaboration needs is a SharePoint team site.

Creating a team site in SharePoint is easy. Here's how:

1. **Log in to the Office 365 portal at** https://portal.office.com.

2. **In the list of apps, click the SharePoint app icon.**

3. **On the SharePoint page, click the + Create Site button, as shown in Figure 8-5.**

   The Create a Site form appears on the right.

4. **Select Team Site.**

5. **In the form that appears to the right, complete the required information, as shown in Figure 8-6.**

6. **Click Next.**

   The Add Group Members form appears.

7. **In the box under Add Additional Owners, add a backup owner for the team site.**

8. **In the box below Add Members, add members to the site by adding their names.**

9. **Click Finish.**

   The form disappears and the home page for the new SharePoint site is displayed.

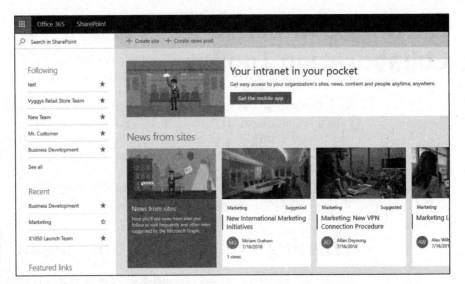

FIGURE 8-5:
The + Create Site
button in
SharePoint.

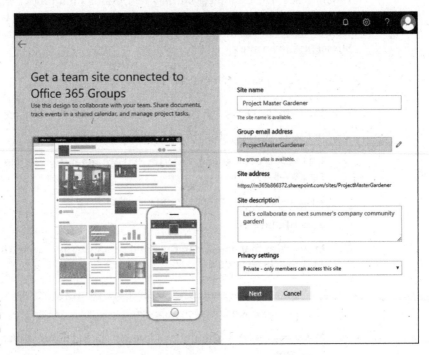

FIGURE 8-6:
Creating a team
site in
SharePoint.

From the landing page of the new SharePoint site, note on the top right the row of people icons representing the members of your site who are also members of your Office 365 Group.

Being social at work with Yammer

Yammer is similar to Facebook at work but better — professional without the annoying ads. It's a great solution for crowdsourcing ideas and connecting with everyone in the organization. You can create topics of interest, use hashtags and @mentions, and even collaborate with people outside your organizations.

In Yammer, you post updates, which can include *giphys* (images looped into a short video with no sound), files from SharePoint or Yammer itself, or a file from your computer, as shown in Figure 8-7.

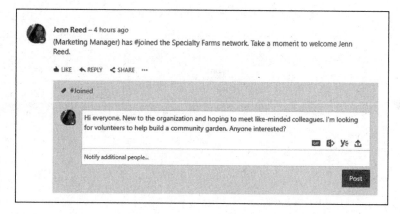

FIGURE 8-7:
Posting an update in Yammer.

If you really want to get into it, you can also conduct a poll, send someone a Praise or kudos, and broadcast an announcement to the entire organization (see Figure 8-8).

Yammer is best for onboarding new employees or a new team member. I once program-managed a global technology implementation project that went on for over a year. During the project, new team members from other countries would join the project. I saved a lot of time onboarding new team members by simply adding them to the Yammer group and encouraging them to read past posts and discussions to get up to speed.

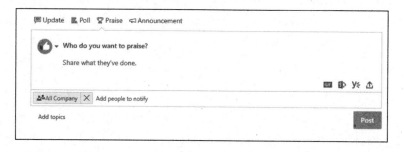

FIGURE 8-8:
Send a Praise through Yammer.

Chapter **9**

Teaming Up Digitally

Ten years ago, when I was a consultant working onsite on a project in Asia, meeting to collaborate with team members back in the United States meant we had to take turns either staying up late or starting work very early. We found it humorous when, in the middle of a phone meeting, we would hear snoring. Looking back, however, it's clear that was not the optimal way to run a project. If a team member missed a meeting, he or she could be working all day on tasks without knowing that they had been changed or deleted. Onboarding someone new was especially challenging for the team leader, who would spend hours getting a new team member up to speed on the process, the objectives, and the tasks, only to learn that the onboarding documents she used were out of date from changes I'd made during my work hours while the team lead was asleep.

Funny enough, my team members and I at that time thought we were cutting edge. We used Skype for phone conferencing, we adopted email, which was just starting to gain popularity, and I was tinkering with an earlier version of SharePoint to support our collaboration needs. It was an exciting time as a team and we felt that we accomplished a lot, even though we were not all sitting in the same office or even working in the same country.

In today's world, we would not share the same sense of accomplishment. For starters, if we used the same tools, we would probably be leaking sensitive data. Fortunately, Microsoft Teams, a service included in Microsoft 365 Business, is not only cutting edge but also has built-in security and compliance.

In this chapter, I outline the reasons why even a small business like yours should use Microsoft Teams. After you gain an understanding of the user interface, I help you plan the rollout of the service in your organization. That way, you'll have a high degree of confidence in the success of introducing your organization to a new, modern workplace.

Exploring Microsoft Team Capabilities

Microsoft Teams is a core technology in Microsoft 365 Business. It is the hub for teamwork for today's workforce. To begin to understand the power of Microsoft Teams, consider that within two years since its release, it has been adopted by more than 125,000 organizations in 181 markets in 29 languages with over 120 million active users. The number of companies using Microsoft Teams continues to grow, and I hope that you will become one of those taking advantage of this exciting technology.

Making the case for Microsoft Teams

Microsoft Teams can be accessed from a web browser, a desktop application, or a mobile app. You can conduct one-on-one or group audio and video calls, share screen during web conferencing, schedule meetings, record meetings, and use up to 1 TB of storage per user.

As an IT admin, you have tools to manage third-party applications that can be integrated with Microsoft Teams. Reports are available to glean usage, and you can configure settings with policies specific to your organization. For peace of mind, Microsoft Teams has a 99.9 percent financially backed service level agreement uptime from Microsoft. In other words, the service has a .1 percent (not 10 percent) chance of going down; if it were to exceed that, Microsoft would have to compensate its subscribers a certain amount.

So, what can you do with Microsoft Teams? In a nutshell:

>> **Communicate more efficiently and effectively — internally and externally.** You can chat or send an instant message, make a phone call, host a web conference, or share files. Team members can engage in private one-on-one chats or have group conversations that are persistent. (In a *persistent chat,* a new team member can read previous conversations, which helps with onboarding.) Microsoft Teams accommodates diverse communication styles and even allows you to include emojis, memes, and other fun graphics. If you have a

small business that employs a younger workforce, giving them a tool to express this communication style can be a hiring advantage.

>> **Simplify the flow of work for employees and increase their productivity.**
If you're in Microsoft Teams chatting with a co-worker and realize that you both have to collaborate on a document, you don't have to leave Microsoft Teams to go to OneDrive or SharePoint to find the file, run Word to open the document, and then start collaborating. Office Apps such as Word, PowerPoint, Excel, and SharePoint are integrated into Microsoft Teams. From a chat conversation, you can jump directly into document co-authoring without leaving Microsoft Teams.

Microsoft Teams has built-in integration with Exchange Online so users can forward emails from their Outlook mailbox into a Microsoft Teams channel. This feature is helpful if you have an email that could be valuable for current and future team members. Each channel in a Microsoft Teams hub has its own email address, which can be obtained by clicking the ellipsis next to the channel name as showing in Figure 9-1.

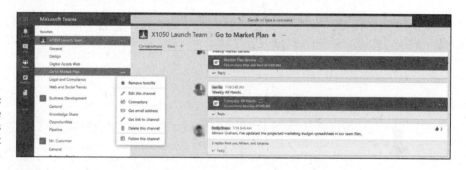

FIGURE 9-1:
Getting the email address for a Microsoft Teams channel.

>> **Empower users to be more productive.** Not all teams work the same way, so why not enable them to configure their workspace in a way that works for them without involving an IT admin? In Microsoft Teams, you can!

The technology is customizable, so users can tailor their workspace according to the way they work. For example, in a Microsoft Teams hub, users can create channels to have a more focused conversation on specific topics. Users can pin important file on tabs so others can quickly access the file in one click.

Microsoft Teams uses the intelligence capabilities of Microsoft Graph so you can increase productivity in your organization. For example, suppose you need help creating marketing material. Within Microsoft Teams, you ask Who-Bot for a list of people in your organization who have expertise in marketing, as shown in Figure 9-2.

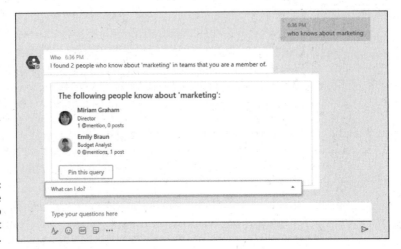

FIGURE 9-2:
Asking the
Who-Bot for help
in Microsoft
Teams.

» **Minimize data risks and stay compliant.** Microsoft Teams benefits from the enterprise-class security features in Microsoft 365. Data in Microsoft Teams is always encrypted, whether it's sitting in storage or being transmitted.

As an IT admin, you can go to the Security and Compliance Center and set an alert or search audit logs for all user and admin activities in Microsoft Teams. From Microsoft Teams, you can also conduct content searches of all data and export the data in to support compliance or litigation requests.

The Microsoft Teams user interface

Get ready to expand your vocabulary with words such as command bar, tabs, bot, @mentions, and red bangs when you roll out Microsoft Teams. Then add mainstream social-media-speak such as emoji, stickers, and Giphys.

The Microsoft Teams user interface is consistent whether you're using the web version or the desktop application. The key elements in the user interface are shown in Figure 9-3 and detailed in the following list:

» The **app bar** on the left has icons for Activity, Chat, Teams, Meetings, Files, More Apps (shown as an ellipsis), Get App (shown in the web version for downloading the desktop app), the Teams Store, and Feedback.

» The **Teams** section next to the app bar lists the teams and channels to which the logged-in user is a member.

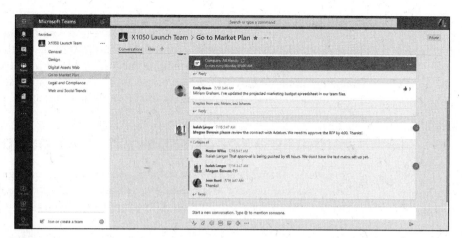

FIGURE 9-3:
The Microsoft
Teams user
interface.

>> The **Conversations** window next to the Microsoft Teams section displays all conversations in the selected channel. Chats can include visual indicators such as @mention, which indicates that the chat specifically mentions a user, or a red bang (!) to indicate high importance.

>> The **command bar**, at the top, is used to query apps or perform a search in Teams.

>> The **Conversation and Files tabs** is found just below the name of the team and channel. The Conversation tab is where you'll find chat or instant messages (IM). The Files tab displays the files in the folder for the channel. The + sign allows a user to add shortcuts to content in Microsoft Teams.

>> The **compose box,** at the bottom right, is where you type a message to start a conversation.

Planning Your Microsoft Teams Deployment

Now that you're familiar with what Microsoft Teams can do for you, it's time to start putting what you've learned into action. Although Microsoft Teams is intuitive and easy to use, letting it loose in your organization with no planning and preparation is not the best deployment approach — unless you find joy in dealing with a bunch of questions, support tickets from end users, and backend reconfiguration.

Planning a Microsoft Teams rollout is a great way for an IT admin to learn new skill sets. Unless you have the budget for a lot of resources, you'll most likely play the role of project manager, business analyst, solution architect, and systems engineer. Don't worry. The work you put into planning a Microsoft Teams rollout will make you more valuable and marketable in the IT industry.

Building a roadmap with your people

There is no shame is asking for help, so ask people in your organization to help define the roadmap for Microsoft Teams. They will feel that they are part of the journey and will be more invested in the success of the project.

As an IT admin for a small business, you probably don't have a big budget for adoption consultants. You'll need to go outside your comfort zone and put together a group of people to act as your project team in rolling out Teams.

Here are some of the questions your project team should seek to answer when building the roadmap for your deployment:

>> *How do people in the organization currently collaborate?* Do they IM? Text? Email? Do they use their laptops more than their phones? Do they currently use web conferencing? Do people share video during the web conferences? The answers to these questions will help you determine your network requirements.

>> *Who should be responsible for creating a Microsoft Teams hub?* Only certain people or everyone in the organization? In my opinion, everyone should be allowed to create a Microsoft Teams hub under certain guidelines, but there may be a compelling reason why you would limit that capability in your organization.

>> *How should Microsoft Teams be organized?* Should Microsoft Teams be created for each department or by project? The information you glean from these questions will inform your Microsoft Teams guidelines or governance.

>> *Should Microsoft Teams be opened for external users?* There are many scenarios in which Microsoft Teams may invite users outside an organization. A marketing team, for example, might want to invite a freelance graphic designer or a social media guru into its channel conversation. If you want a similar capability, you'll need to enable external sharing in Microsoft Teams.

Getting your network ready

Nothing is worse than having the latest technology for productivity only to be hampered by a network that doesn't support the bandwidth requirements for audio and video conferencing and application sharing. In addition to the network, devices used for real-time media sessions, such as headsets and webcams, also affect the overall audio and video quality in web conferences.

Many details are involved in network readiness for Microsoft Teams, so I recommend reading what Microsoft recommends at https://docs.microsoft.com/en-us/MicrosoftTeams/prepare-network.

You can install on the computers in your organization a Network Assessment tool to perform a simple test for network performance and connectivity. In that way, you'll know what the experience will be like for a Microsoft Teams call. You can download the tool at www.microsoft.com/en-us/download/details.aspx?id=53885.

TIP

If you find that the effort required to get your network ready for Microsoft Teams is outside your area of expertise, it's best to engage a Microsoft partner to help you with a network assessment and implementation guidance. Companies such as Softchoice (www.softchoice.com) have experts who can help ensure that your organization is set up for Microsoft Teams success. The investment you make on hiring experts will pay big dividends down the road. I have seen companies who skimped on hiring professionals and tried to do the network readiness themselves, only to end up with a bunch of unhappy end users and angry executives who couldn't complete a call or join a video conference due to network issues. If you need introductions to Microsoft Partners, please send your request to info@cloud611.com.

Getting your users ready for Microsoft Teams

If you were able to get some people involved in building the roadmap for Microsoft Teams, reach out to them and ask for their help getting the rest of the organization ready for the deployment. Give this group early access to the service so they can practice what they've learned and then teach others when the technology is rolled out. They can watch a ton of videos for end users at https://docs.microsoft.com/en-us/MicrosoftTeams/enduser-training.

For videos designed for IT admins, visit https://docs.microsoft.com/en-us/MicrosoftTeams/itadmin-readiness.

TIP

Don't reinvent the wheel when sending emails to your end users about the Microsoft Teams rollout. I recommend downloading the sample email templates, quick start guides, and posters at www.microsoft.com/en-us/download/56505 and customizing the materials to fit your needs.

Configuring Microsoft Teams

As a cloud service, Microsoft 365 Business is constantly evolving. Similarly, Microsoft Teams will continue to evolve and expand its feature sets. I mention this because some of the instructions for configuration in this section might change as the features and functionalities of the service grow.

Currently, users with a Microsoft 365 Business license are automatically assigned a Microsoft Teams license. If you want to disable Microsoft Teams for a specific user, do the following:

1. Navigate to https://admin.microsoft.com.

2. Log in with your global admin credentials for Microsoft 365 Business.

3. On the left menu, click Users, and then select Active Users.

The right pane displays all the users in your Microsoft 365 tenant.

4. Select the user for whom you want to disable the Microsoft Teams license.

A form displays more details about the user.

5. Click Edit to the far right of Product Licenses, as shown in Figure 9-4.

The form displays all the licenses assigned to the user.

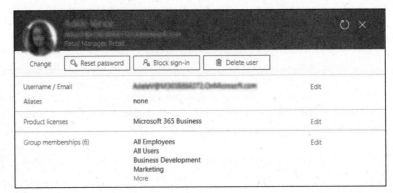

FIGURE 9-4: Editing the license assigned to an active user.

6. **Look for Microsoft Teams and toggle the switch to Off.**

7. **Click the Save button and, in the next window, click Close.**

The form reverts to the user's detail form.

8. **Click the Close button to close the form.**

You are taken back to the Home ⇨ Active Users window.

To enable external sharing for Microsoft Teams, do the following:

1. **From the left menu in Microsoft 365 Admin Center at** `http://admin.microsoft.com`**, click Settings and then select Services & Add-Ins.**

The Services & Add-Ins page appears.

2. **Scroll down the page and select Microsoft Teams.**

The Microsoft Teams form appears on the right.

3. **In the Settings by User/License Type section, next to Select the User/License Type You Want to Configure, click the drop-down arrow and select Guest (see Figure 9-5).**

You see a new form with a toggle switch for the Guest option.

FIGURE 9-5:
Selecting a user.

4. **Next to Turn Microsoft Teams On or Off for All Users of This Type, toggle the switch to On.**

   The previous form appears.

5. **Click the Save button to save your changes, and then click Close the close the form.**

   You return to the Home ⇨ Services & Add-Ins page.

Microsoft is currently building out a robust admin center for Microsoft Teams at `https://admin.teams.microsoft.com/dashboard`. At some point, all the configuration options for Microsoft Teams in the Services & Add-ins page will be moved over to Microsoft Teams & Skype for Business Admin Center.

Figure 9-6 shows the meeting settings that you can configure from the new admin center. On the same page, you can also update with your logo the branding for the email invitation for Teams meetings as well as set up how Teams handles real-time media traffic during meetings.

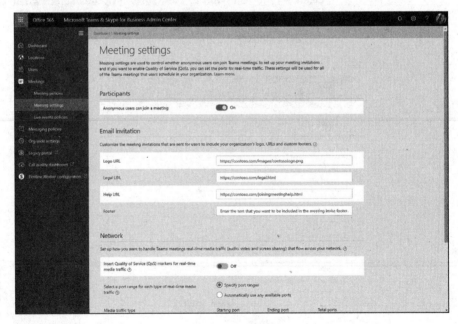

FIGURE 9-6: Configuring Teams Meetings settings.

Integrating Microsoft Teams with Office 365 Services

For many years, a typical information worker would rely on email as the bread and butter for performing daily tasks. Microsoft Word or Excel usually comes next to Outlook in terms of heavy usage in the Office suite. It's very common for a person to have several windows open in a PC throughout the day while switching from Outlook, to Excel, to Word, to a browser, and then back again in Outlook.

With Microsoft Teams, such switching back and forth is no longer necessary. You can be communicating with a co-worker on the Channel Conversation window when you both decide to work together on a document. If the document is already saved in Microsoft Teams, neither of you will need to leave the service to go to Word. Both of you will simply navigate to the Files tab (or click the document if it has been pinned to the tab) and start co-authoring in real time.

Another nifty feature in Microsoft Teams is the capability to record meetings by clicking the More Actions (shown as an ellipses) icon that displays along with other call controls. The recording of the meeting is automatically saved in Microsoft Stream, yet another cloud service that's included in the Microsoft 365 Business license. Stream is like a private version of YouTube. Videos stored in Stream are automatically transcribed, providing you with closed captioning without having to deploy complicated systems and infrastructure.

It's easy to understand why Microsoft is investing heavily in Microsoft Teams. After you start using the service, I think you'll agree that it is truly the digital hub for teamwork.

4

Building a Culture of Security

Chapter **10**

Managing Passwords

As the IT admin for a small business, you wield great power. In your capable hands lies the future of a modern workplace and a productive workforce as the result of the technology you make available for your end users. But as Uncle Ben in *Spiderman* so wisely said: "With great power comes great responsibility."

That wisdom is particularly apt for IT admins in today's security landscape. Cyberattacks, data leakage, and security breaches are the realities we must deal with daily. According to a study released by Microsoft and YouGov in April 2018, one in four SMBs are targeted by hackers. The average loss for these breaches is almost $80,000. Want to know what's worse? In the study, 33 percent of the companies admitted that they spent more money solving the problems caused by the attack than it would have cost to prevent it.

Although these sobering statistics can be enough to make IT admins retreat into their obscure server room, there is good news! Microsoft 365 Business has built-in security functionalities to help IT admins perform the tasks necessary to secure their IT environment and minimize risks. Note that I used the word *minimize*. No matter what anyone might say, no security solution can guarantee that your company will never be attacked. Therefore, as an IT admin, you should operate under the assumption that your IT environment is currently under attack. Only with that mindset will you be able to responsibly take measures to protect your users and your company data.

In this chapter, I cover the tasks you need to complete to secure the most common attack vector: stolen passwords. Be prepared to rethink your approach to password policies because what you are doing today may be out of date. I also walk you through the steps to enable end users to reset their own passwords, thus relieving you of this repetitive but time-consuming task.

Knowing What You're Up Against

You've heard of software as a service (SaaS), platform as a service (PaaS), infrastructure as a service (IaaS), and a whole bunch of cloud-based services using the as-a-service model. This model is great news for SMBs because it has leveled the playing field and allowed small businesses to compete with large enterprises.

The bad news is that bad actors are also using this model. Did you know that anyone with access to bitcoins can also buy ransomware as a service (RaaS)? Do a search online — you don't even have to be in on the dark web — and you'll find entrepreneurial hackers offering their services to the public for as low as $39 for a lifetime license. Some of them even offer technical support!

Imagine what the call must be like to these guys from some shady person who's trying to hack a small business. "Hey man, I'm trying to hack this company and I'm running into issues trying to get someone to click a phishing email. Any ideas?"

As you can see, the barrier for entry into the hacking business has become very low. As an IT admin, you must be on high alert for cyberattacks. Fortunately, with the advancements in cloud technologies, you don't need 20 years of infrastructure experience and tons of money to build a perimeter of protection around your organization. With a few tasks based on current best practices, you can start securing your organization and minimizing the risk of a breach.

Today's common attacks

Unless you've been living under a rock the last couple of years, you most likely have been affected directly or indirectly with a cyberattack. Whether you had the credentials from your favorite online store stolen, or had your Facebook data exposed in the Cambridge Analytica scandal, or received an email from a "prince" in Nigeria wanting to transfer a million dollars into your account, most of us have been attacked.

You are not alone. Here are the top three attacks Microsoft is seeing in their ecosystem.

>> **Password spray:** In August 2018 alone, more than 200,000 accounts were compromised by this type of attack. In a *password spray,* attackers use a common password such as 123456 or password against many accounts, hoping to find a few users who didn't get the memo about using stronger passwords.

And even a user who did get the memo and is diligent about updating passwords every 90 days will most likely recycle old passwords and simply add an exclamation point at the end. Hackers count on this behavior when they do a password spray. After they get a hit on just one account, they will have the ability to access the company's address book, which can then be used for a phishing campaign.

>> **Phishing:** Attackers using this tactic usually try to lure users into giving up personal information after following a link in an email. In 2018, Office 365 blocked about 5 billion phish emails and analyzed approximately 300,000 phish campaigns. Microsoft's logs show that 20 percent of users will click phish email within five minutes of receipt.

This blunder happened to TalkTalk, the United Kingdom's leading business-to-business telecom provider, and landed them in a high-profile data breach. The breach started when a user clicked a malicious link in an email that started encrypting the data on the machine. The user then forwarded the email to the manager, writing something like "Something weird happened to my machine when I clicked this link. What happens when you do it?" Of course, the manager clicked the link. The company ended up paying a record fine for security failings leading to the theft of personal data for almost 157,000 customers.

>> **Breach replay:** Microsoft processed 2 billion credentials in 2018 and were able to match 650,000 accounts with leaked credentials. A *breach replay* happens when a user uses the same username and password on many sites.

Admit it, most of us have done it. In fact, even smart people in Washington, DC do it, as we learned from the Ashley Madison scandal, in which 15,000 government officials accessed the extramarital dating site by using email addresses registered to the White House, top federal agencies, and military branches.

If any company is well positioned to address security challenges in today's computing environment, it is Microsoft. Every month, Microsoft scans 400 billion emails for malware and phishing attacks from Office 365 and Outlook, and processes 450 billion authentications every month from their 200-plus cloud consumer and commercial services globally. In addition, Microsoft has scanned 18 billion-plus Bing web pages and collected data from a billion Windows devices. These insights provide Microsoft with visibility into the current threat landscape like no other company. And that bodes well for an IT admin for a small business with no budget or expertise to maintain a security infrastructure.

Applying the latest password guidance

If you're looking for the latest guidance for password best practices, you should check out the following two resources:

» National Institute of Standards and Technology (NIST) Digital Identity Guidelines at https://pages.nist.gov/800-63-3/sp800-63b.html

» Microsoft Password Guidance White Paper at https://www.microsoft.com/en-us/research/publication/password-guidance/

TIP

Although both documents are written in different styles (the NIST document is more official looking and wordy), they are aligned on best practices. I recommend using the white paper from Microsoft as a reference if you want to skip the formal talk.

As an IT admin, you can complete two action items today to make your environment secure with your Microsoft 365 Business license: enabling multi-factor authentication and eliminating mandatory password resets.

I cover multi-factor authentication in a separate chapter (Chapter 11) because the topic requires a thorough discussion to ensure a good experience for your end users if you roll it out.

I had initially thought eliminating mandatory password resets was counter to driving a more secure environment. The argument presented in the guidance from Microsoft, however, does make sense. Their experiment showed that users who are asked to update passwords often do not create a new, independent password. Rather, they update an old one. Full disclosure: I have done that myself but will no longer do so, now that I have read these new guidelines.

Want a remember or tip icon for the preceding paragraph?

To eliminate mandatory password resets, do the following:

1. **Log in with your global admin credentials for Microsoft 365 Business at** `http://admin.microsoft.com`.

   You will need your Microsoft 365 Global Admin credentials.

2. **From the left menu, click Settings and then select Security & Privacy.**

   The Security & Privacy page appears, as shown in Figure 10-1.

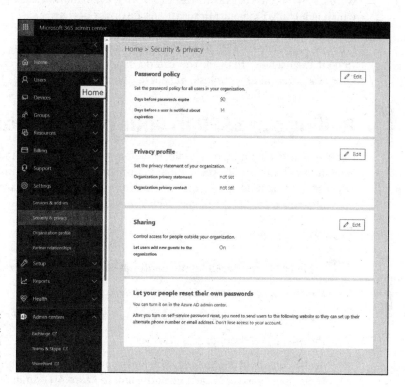

FIGURE 10-1:
The Security &
Privacy page in
Microsoft 365
Admin Center.

3. **In the Password Policy section, click Edit.**

   A form appears on the right.

4. **In the Password Policy form, toggle On the switch next to Set Users Passwords to Never Expire.**

5. **Click the Save button and then click the Close button.**

   Your changes are saved and you return to the Security & Privacy page.

CHAPTER 10 **Managing Passwords**   115

Enabling Self-Service Password Reset (SSPR)

According to the Gartner Group, 20 to 50 percent of calls to the IT help desk are for password resets. Forrester Research estimates that the labor cost for a single password reset is about $70. If you have a small IT team or are the only IT team for your organization, you might want to let your end users reset their own passwords. Self-service password reset (SSPR) is available in Azure Active Directory, which is included in your Microsoft 365 Business license.

Why get bogged down with password reset tasks when you can empower your users to do it themselves? Instead, you can do many other tasks to proactively manage your IT environment — unless, of course, the reset request comes from your CEO.

Rolling out SSPR in your organization

Change is difficult for some people, so before you roll out SSPR in your organization, be sure to let people know about your plans. If you want to minimize the risk of people getting mad at you for implementing yet another newfangled thing, first do a pilot rollout of SSPR to a few receptive folks.

To enable SSPR, follow these steps:

1. **Log in to Microsoft 365 Admin Center at** http://admin.microsoft.com.

    You need your Microsoft 365 Global Admin credentials.

2. **On the left menu, click Settings, and then select Security & Privacy.**

    The Security & Privacy page is displayed.

3. **At the bottom of the Security & Privacy page, in the Let Your Users Reset Their Own Passwords card, click the link to Azure AD Admin Center.**

    A new browser window opens and the Azure Active Directory Admin Center page is displayed. Alternatively, you can reach the same page by going to https://aad.portal.azure.com.

4. **On the left side of Azure Active Directory Admin Center, shown in Figure 10-2, click Users.**

    The Users — All Users blade is displayed.

5. **In the Users — All Users blade, click Password Reset, as shown in Figure 10-3.**

    The Password Reset — Properties blade is displayed.

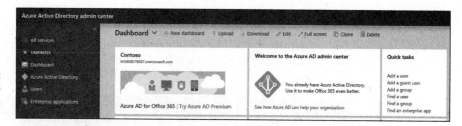

FIGURE 10-2:
Azure Active
Directory Admin
Center.

FIGURE 10-3:
Password Reset
option in the
Users — All Users
blade.

6. **In the Properties page, click All to enable SSPR for all users in your organization, and then click the Save button (see Figure 10-4).**

The system processes your changes. After your changes are saved, the Save button appears dimmed.

FIGURE 10-4:
Enabling SSPR for
all users.

After SSPR is enabled, users will be prompted to provide additional contact information the next time they log in to Office 365 so that the system can verify their identity should they reset their password on their own.

By default, users will be asked to provide two methods of verification if they reset their password. Two is the recommended setting, but you can change it to one from the Authentication Methods blade, as shown in Figure 10-5.

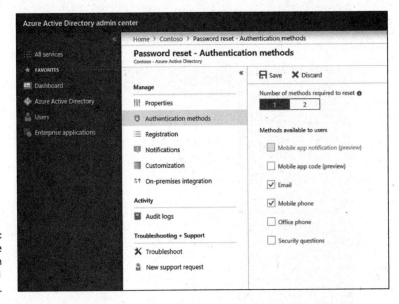

FIGURE 10-5:
Change the verification method to 1 instead of 2.

The end user's experience in SSPR

When end users log in to Office 365 after SSPR is enabled, they enter their username and password as usual. After they successfully enter their credentials, the More Information Required window will appear to prompt the user to provide additional information. Figure 10-6 shows the user interface for a non-admin end user. Note that an admin user may have a slightly different user interface.

FIGURE 10-6:
End user login experience after SSPR is enabled.

After clicking Next, the end user will be guided through the process of providing additional information. After the process is finished, the end user can now reset his or her password at any time.

For example, let's say that a user forgot her password. Here are the steps the user should follow to reset the password:

1. **Navigate to** `https://portal.office.com`**, enter the username, and then click Next.**

   The Enter password window is displayed.

2. **Click Forgot My Password, as shown in Figure 10-7.**

   The Get Back Into Your Account page appears.

FIGURE 10-7: Selecting Forgot my password to reset the password.

3. **Enter the characters in the box above the phrase** *Enter the Characters in the Picture or the Words in the Audio,* **and then click Next.**

   You see the first verification step.

4. **Choose the contact method for verification.**

   To follow along with the example, choose Email.

5. **Click the Email button.**

   The system sends an email to the email address provided during the end user SSPR setup.

6. **Enter the code from the email in the box, and then click Next.**

   The next verification step is displayed.

7. **Enter the code received from the secondary verification method (a text message, for example) and then click Next.**

   The Choose a Password page is displayed.

8. **Enter the new password twice and then click Finish.**

   The Your Password Has Been Reset page appears.

9. **Sign in to Office 365 with your new password by clicking the Click Here link and following the prompts.**

   The sign in page is displayed, prompting the user to enter his or her username. The rest of the login process proceeds as usual.

Changing passwords from the MyApps portal

Sometimes users need to change their password even though they know the current password. You can complete this task in the MyApps portal.

The MyApps portal is a web-based portal for users who are licensed for Azure Active Directory through their Office 365 or Microsoft 365 Business subscription. In this portal, users can reset passwords, view the apps to which they have access, view their account details, set up multi-factor authentication, and more. It's best to bookmark the portal and visit it often because new features may show up as the service evolves.

To change an existing password, follow these steps:

1. **Navigate to** `https://myapps.microsoft.com` **and log in in with your Microsoft 365 Business credentials.**

   The MyApps page is displayed.

2. **Click your profile photo (at the top right of the page) and then select Profile, as shown in Figure 10-8.**

   The Profile page appears.

3. **On the right, under Manage Account, click Change Password.**

   The Change Password page is displayed.

4. **Enter the old password, enter the new password twice, and then click Submit.**

   You return to your profile page.

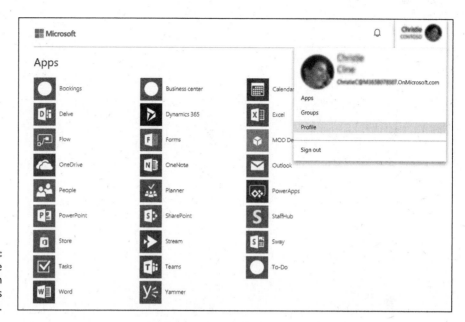

WARNING

One of the highly recommended tasks for securing the IT environment is to enable multi-factor authentication (MFA). I cover that subject in the next chapter. For now, note that the end user is also required to set up MFA from the MyApps portal.

Living in a Password-Less World

One of the exciting things coming up in Azure Active Directory is the notion of a world where a password is not required. The idea is that all you need to access your Microsoft 365 Business services is your phone and your fingerprint. Your phone would have the Microsoft Authenticator app, which is the gateway to your cloud services. Instead of entering a password after entering the username, users would see a message in the Microsoft Authenticator app, asking them to tap a number and then swipe a fingerprint to complete the authentication.

This feature is currently in Preview and is slated for global availability sometime in 2019. This solution holds great promise because it would render password breaches useless. Imagine a world where there is no password spray, no phishing, and no breach replay!

Chapter **11**

Configuring Multi-Factor Authentication

"Have you tried turning it off and on again?"

As an IT admin, you most likely have uttered those words at some point while providing support for your end users. I know I have. In fact, I have been at the other end of a support call with an irate customer who was very unhappy with the "broken" printer we delivered because it only worked for one day. After trying several troubleshooting steps, including flicking the switch on and off, it occurred to me to ask the customer to check if the printer was plugged in. It was not. Someone had unplugged it while rearranging the workstation and forgotten to plug it back in.

In today's threat landscape, we can only hope that the support calls we get are as simple to fix as turning a device of and on again. The harsh reality is that IT admins today need to be prepared to support a user whose device or identity has been hacked. Only when an IT admin operates with the mindset of assumed breach will an organization be best positioned to minimize security risks.

Microsoft 365 Business has built-in security features including multi-factor authentication (MFA), which greatly enhances an organization's security posture. Although industry experts recommend enabling this feature as a security best practice, some IT admins are hesitant to turn on this feature. I can understand why. I have seen MFA implementations in which the IT team bore the brunt of the backlash from unhappy end users who had trouble logging in from a poorly planned rollout.

In this chapter, you explore the security capabilities of MFA, understand how to plan its implementation for the best end-user experience, step through the MFA tasks an IT admin needs to perform, and experience MFA from the lens of an end user.

Getting Grounded on Authentication

Although the phrase "multi-factor authentication" may not be something that comes up in your everyday water-cooler conversations, the concept has been around for a while and is widely adopted without people even knowing it.

Multi-factor authentication (MFA) is the process by which a user confirms his or her identity by presenting at least two forms of proof before being granted access to online or electronic resources.

If you've ever used an ATM where you had to provide your card number plus a PIN, you've used MFA. If your end users have used Facebook or Gmail, they most likely have also encountered MFA, especially if they've signed on to those services from a new or unknown location. With that background, you can take advantage of your end users' prior experience with MFA to successfully implement this security feature in your organization.

MFA in the Microsoft ecosystem

In this chapter, I cover the implementation of MFA only for users whose identities are managed in the cloud through Azure Active Directory (AAD). To avoid confusion, however, I go into a little more detail on the different versions of MFA because not all features in the full version of MFA are available in Office 365 and, ultimately, Microsoft 365 Business.

Three versions of multi-factor authentication are available:

>> **MFA for Office 365:** This version is included in Office 365, which is one of the services in Microsoft 365 Business. It allows for two forms of verification for a user to authenticate. In this chapter, I cover this version of MFA.

>> **MFA for Azure Active Directory Administrators:** This free version of MFA is given only to a global administrator for an Azure Active Directory tenant.

Anyone can go to `http://portal.azure.com` and create an Azure Active Directory tenant and pay for the standalone service without purchasing a Microsoft 365 Business license.

>> **Azure MFA:** This full version of MFA is available when you purchase Azure Active Directory Premium licenses. Larger organizations that run an on-premises environment typically need this version because it enables both cloud and on-premises deployment. It also has robust reporting and configuration capabilities.

Best practices from the trenches

Anyone with global admin privileges in the Microsoft 365 tenant needs to have MFA enabled. That's because a breach of a user with admin privileges opens the door for hackers to do anything they want in your tenant.

For end users with no admin privileges, MFA should still be enabled because passwords are no longer enough. As described in the preceding chapter, hackers can obtain a user's password in several ways.

Enforcing MFA for global admins with a systems engineering background is usually not a big deal. But when you roll out a new process for end users, you can sow a lot of confusion and end up with a bad user experience if you don't see things from a non-IT person's perspective. I know of an implementation that ended up badly for the IT admin because the end user negatively affected was an executive. I hope that the following best practices will keep you from experiencing that nightmare:

>> **Communicate the change** to your organization and the reasons for the change. It's best to get sponsorship from leaders in your organization and even better if one of the leaders communicates the change.

>> **Pilot MFA to tech-savvy users** first before rolling it out to the rest of the organization. Learn from the pilot and use that intelligence to form the basis of your rollout plan and communication.

>> **Create a training portal** replete with how-to videos using Stream, a video service that comes with your Microsoft 365 Business subscription. Try to keep your videos to a minute or less so they're easily consumable.

>> **Choose a preferred authentication factor** that you think will work for at least 80 percent of your users and encourage its adoption. If you're using MFA for Office 365, your users have four options for the second authentication factor:

- *Phone call:* The end user answers the call and presses the pound (#) key to authenticate.

- *Verification code from a mobile app such as Microsoft Authenticator:* The app generates a verification code every 30 seconds. The end user enters the code into the sign-in interface to authenticate.

- *Notification from a mobile app:* The system sends a notification to a registered mobile device to which the end user selects Approve to authenticate. I find this method the most seamless. It does require a few minutes to set up, but the time investment is worth it in the long run. This method is especially helpful when I'm traveling internationally and don't want to pay international roaming charges for phone call authentication. I simply use the hotel's Wi-Fi to receive the notification in the Microsoft Authenticator app to authenticate.

- *Verification code sent in a text message:* The end user needs to enter the code received via text message into the sign-in interface to authenticate.

>> **Deploy the latest version of the Office desktop applications** because versions older than Office 2016 require additional admin tasks to enable modern authentication required for MFA. Microsoft 365 Business comes with Office ProPlus, which is always the latest version of Office, so it's best to standardize on that version to reduce implementation complexity.

>> **Define the support and escalation model** before the roll out. Make sure end users understand where to go for help if they get stuck. Obviously, you also need to ensure that your support staff is ready when you roll out MFA.

Deploying MFA

Generally, people don't object to providing second-factor authentication when using ATM machines to withdraw cash. Train end users that their identities are just as valuable as the cash in their bank accounts and, as a result, the same security precautions should be followed.

Microsoft processes billions of authentications monthly and the cloud intelligence they gather from such a scale allows them to detect and block tens of millions of attacks every day. As new types of attacks are detected in various parts of the world, Microsoft's systems automatically protect customers, such as those in your organization. For organizations that have implemented risk policies, Microsoft has seen compromises reduced by 96 percent. For those who implement MFA specifically, they see a 99.9 percent risk reduction. If you have any doubt as to whether you should embrace MFA, I hope those statistics are convincing.

Admin tasks for setting up MFA

By default, Microsoft 365 Business tenants are enabled for modern authentication, a protocol required for MFA. If you're running a version of Office older than Office 2016 or have users who check email using Apple Mail, however, end users will need to create MFA app passwords because those legacy systems do not support two-step verification. You step through creating app passwords in the next section.

To configure MFA service settings, follow these steps:

1. **Log in to Microsoft 365 Admin Center at** `http://admin.microsoft.com`.

   You need your Microsoft 365 Global Admin credentials.

2. **On the left, Under Users, click Active Users.**

   The Active Users page is displayed.

3. **Click the More Settings icon (. . .) and then select Setup Multifactor Authentication from the drop-down menu that appears, as shown in Figure 11-1.**

   The Users tab of the Multi-Factor Authentication page appears.

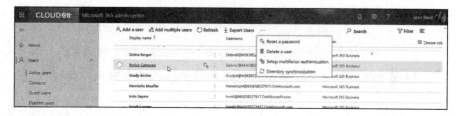

FIGURE 11-1:
Navigating to the Multifactor Authentication setup page.

4. **Click Service Settings.**

   The Service Settings page appears, as shown in Figure 11-2.

5. **Ensure that the options appropriate for your organization are selected, and then click the Save button.**

   The system saves the changes and displays a validation window to confirm that the updates were successful.

6. **From the Updates Successful window, click the Close button.**

   The validation window disappears, and the Service Settings page is displayed.

FIGURE 11-2:
The MFA Service
Settings page.

Enabling end users for MFA

To enable MFA for a user licensed for Microsoft 365 Business:

1. **Log in to Microsoft 365 Admin Center at** `http://admin.microsoft.com`.

   You need your Microsoft 365 Global Admin credentials.

2. **From the left menu, Under Users, click Active Users.**

   The Active Users page appears.

3. **Click the More Settings icon (. . .) and then select Setup Multifactor Authentication from the drop-down menu that appears**

   The Users tab of the Multi-Factor Authentication page appears.

4. **In the list of users, select the box to the left of the user you want to enable for MFA.**

   The right pane displays additional information about the user and actions you can take for the user.

5. **On the right pane below the end user's contact information, click Enable, as shown in Figure 11-3.**

   The system displays a validation window to confirm your intent to enable MFA for the user.

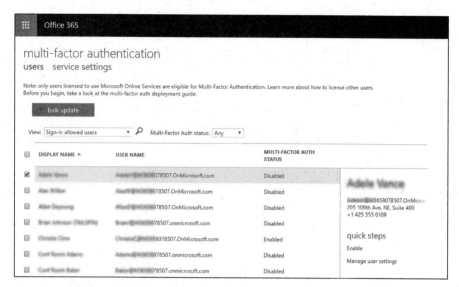

FIGURE 11-3:
Enabling MFA for
an end user.

6. **Click the Enable Multi-Factor Auth button**.

   The system processes the changes and displays the Updates Successful window.

7. **Click the Close button.**

   The Users tab of the Multi-Factor Authentication page is displayed.

WARNING

In the Service Settings page (refer to Figure 11-2) is an option to enable the Remember Multi-Factor Authentication feature. This handy feature allows end users to bypass second-factor authentications on trusted devices for a certain number of days after they've successfully signed in using MFA. Although this is a great experience for end users, Microsoft recommends NOT enabling this feature, and I agree. Otherwise, the device will pose a security risk if it is compromised. If you decide to enable this feature and a device is compromised, you must perform a task to restore MFA on all devices on which users have logged in with MFA. I cover this task in the "Managing MFA" section in this chapter.

TIP

You can enable MFA for multiple users at the same time by selecting more than one user from the list. For large organizations, a bulk update option is available to save the IT admin from clicking thousands of users. To enable MFA for a large number of users, click the Bulk Update button, upload a file in .csv format with all the users to be enabled for MFA, and then follow the prompts to complete the process. From the same window, you can download a sample file to ensure that your .csv file follows the required format.

End-user MFA experience

You've done your due diligence and have communicated that MFA will be implemented in your organization. It's now time for your end users to do their part.

The first step an end user needs to take is to register other methods for authentication. It is not enough that an end user is enabled for MFA; the end user also needs to complete the registration process. Here's the fastest way for an end user to register for MFA:

1. **Navigate to** `https://aka.ms/proofup`.

The sign-in page is displayed.

2. **Enter your username and click Next.**

The Enter Password window appears.

3. **Enter your password and click the Sign In button.**

The More Information Is Required window is displayed.

4. **Click the Next button.**

The Additional Security Verification page is displayed.

5. **Choose the appropriate option under Step 1, as shown in Figure 11-4.**

To follow along with the example, choose Mobile App.

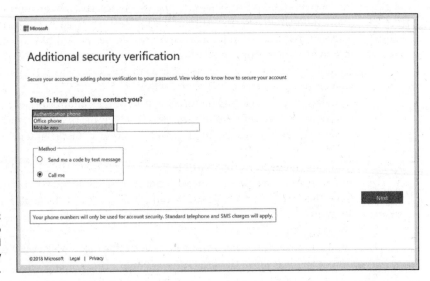

FIGURE 11-4: Setting up additional security verification.

6. Select Use Verification Code under How Do You Want To Use the Mobile App? section, and then click the Set Up button.

The Configure Mobile App window appears, as shown in Figure 11-5.

Configure mobile app

Complete the following steps to configure your mobile app.

1. Install the Microsoft authenticator app for Windows Phone, Android or iOS.

2. In the app, add an account and choose "Work or school account".

3. Scan the image below.

Configure app without notifications

If you are unable to scan the image, enter the following information in your app.
Code: 196 928 055
Url: https://cys01pfpad16.phonefactor.net/pad/602306309

If the app displays a six-digit code, choose "Next".

Next   cancel

FIGURE 11-5:
Configuring the
mobile app
for MFA.

7. Follow the instructions and then click the Next button.

In this example, I am using the Microsoft Authenticator app. After the app displays the six-digit code, the system displays the Verifying App window and a notification appears on the Authenticator app asking me to Approve or Deny the sign-in request.

8. On your mobile device, in the Authenticator app, tap Approve, as shown in Figure 11-6.

The Additional Security Verification page appears.

9. Click the Save button.

The system processes the changes and then displays the Updates Successful window.

10. Click the Close button.

The user's Account page appears.

TIP

If you're like me, you don't like reinventing the wheel. So here's a link from Microsoft you can use in your communication email to prepare your end users for the MFA implementation: `https://docs.microsoft.com/en-us/azure/active-directory/user-help/multi-factor-authentication-end-user`.

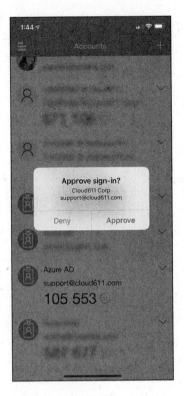

FIGURE 11-6:
Approving the
verification
request from the
Authenticator
app.

Managing MFA

It happens. No matter how much you empower your end users to self-serve, they'll invariably reach out to you for help with requests related to MFA. Or you may need to take action to mitigate a risk from a compromised device.

You manage user settings for MFA in the same location that you enabled MFA: the Multi-Factor Authentication page.

To get to the page, follow Steps 1 through 3 in the preceding section. But wait, there's a shortcut! You can reach the same destination by simply navigating to the following link: `https://account.activedirectory.windowsazure.com/UserManagement/MultifactorVerification.aspx`.

From the Users tab of the Multi-Factor Authentication page, note the three statuses in the Multi-Factor Auth Status column:

» **Enabled:** The user is enabled for MFA but has not yet completed the registration.

» **Enforced:** The user is enabled for MFA and has completed the registration.

» **Disabled:** The user is not enabled for MFA.

If for some reason you need to remove the MFA feature for a user, select the enabled user from the list, and then click Disable under Quick Steps in the right pane.

If an enabled user's device is compromised, click Manage User Settings under Quick Steps in the right pane. In the Manage User Settings window that appears, select one or more options, as shown in Figure 11-7. Then click the Save button.

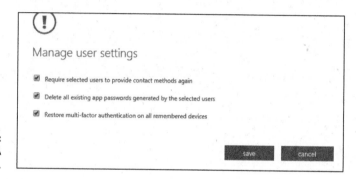

FIGURE 11-7:
Managing MFA
user settings.

Chapter **12**

Demystifying Information Protection

People can say anything they want about robots taking over IT jobs, but as far as I'm concerned, the job of an IT admin is still relevant and much needed today and in the future. If you think about how social media has encouraged people to loosen up about sharing personal information — what they had for lunch, the car they just bought, or their upcoming trip to Cabo while their home will be unattended — it's not hard to imagine that the same loose attitude could spill over into the workplace.

Consider the hapless lawyer who responded to a colleague with details about their pending case only to realize that by clicking the Reply to All button, he had shared that information with the opposing counsel. Or the police officer in the UK who sent a spreadsheet of criminal record checks to a newspaper instead of to an internal recipient because of Outlook's auto-complete feature.

These scenarios are just two of many illustrating why IT admins should feel secure about their jobs. Without proper data and information protection in place, businesses can be put in an embarrassing situation or face litigation or, worse, lose their competitive advantage. With the right toolset and access to the latest industry best practices, IT admins can protect their organization from data leakage and prevent data loss.

Microsoft 365 Business includes a robust set of functionalities for protecting company data through the recent addition of the Azure Information Protection Premium P1 license. This is great news for SMBs because these features have traditionally required purchasing more expensive enterprise licenses.

In this chapter, I break down the concept behind Azure Information Protection (AIP), describe data classification and labeling, explain how documents can be protected, and show you the AIP experience from the end user's perspective. The information presented in this chapter is designed to solidify the important role an IT admin plays in securing company data. If you're an IT admin, this chapter is a validation of your relevance and value.

Configuring AIP

The term *information protection*, or IP, is generally used to encompass industry standards and best practices for protecting information from unauthorized access. In the Microsoft ecosystem, *Azure Information Protection*, or *AIP*, is a cloud service that allows organizations to classify data with labels to control access. AIP can be purchased as a stand-alone license or bundled into a solution such as Microsoft 365 Business.

A breakdown of the features included in each of the four versions of AIP is available at this link: https://azure.microsoft.com/en-us/pricing/details/information-protection/. The AIP Premium P1 license is included in Microsoft 365 Business.

The evolution of AIP

AIP has gone through an evolution in the last few years, and you may have encountered this technology under a different name. Some of the technology's old names are Azure Rights Management Service (Azure RMS), Azure Active Directory Rights Management (AADRM), Windows Azure Active Directory Rights Managements, Information Rights Management (IRM), or to some, simply "The New Microsoft RMS." You'll do yourself and Microsoft a great favor by forgetting all those old names and just sticking with *AIP*.

The latest iteration of this cloud technology now offers classification and labeling capabilities that can, in turn, apply rights management to protect files. At a high level, AIP protects your data in three key steps:

1. **First, data is classified and labeled**. For example, if a document is classified as confidential and should be available only to the recipients of the email, the label might be *Confidential — Recipients Only."*

2. **Next, data is protected through encryption, access control, and policies based on the label.** Continuing with the preceding example, a document marked with the *Confidential — Recipients Only* label will be encrypted so that only the recipients can read it.

3. **Finally, documents can be tracked, and access can be revoked if necessary.** From the preceding example, the sender of the email may decide that one of the recipients should no longer have access to the document. In that case, the sender can revoke access for a specific user.

Office 365 Message Encryption, or *OME,* is one of the features in AIP. In Chapter 6, I cover the details of OME and provide step-by-step instructions for sending encrypted email by using Outlook. In this chapter, I focus on AIP features you can use in Office applications such as Word and Excel.

If you have the AIP Premium P2 license, you can avail yourself of additional functionalities, such as automatic classification for cloud and on-premises data. In this chapter, however, I cover the features available in the AIP Premium P1 license.

Activating AIP

To start using AIP, the first thing you need to do as an IT admin is to activate the service in your Microsoft 365 Business tenant. Even if you think the service is already enabled, it doesn't hurt to verify. Here's how:

1. **Log in to** `https://admin.microsoft.com` **with your global admin credentials.**

2. **In the left navigation, under the Settings group, click Services & Add-ins.**

   The Services & Add-ins page is displayed, as shown in Figure 12-1.

3. **Select Microsoft Azure Information Protection.**

   The Microsoft Azure Information Protection window is displayed on the right.

4. **In the Microsoft Azure Information Protection window, click Manage Microsoft Azure Information protection settings.**

   The Rights Management page is displayed, as shown in Figure 12-2.

5. **Confirm that Rights Management is activated. If it isn't, click the Activate button.**

   In this example, the tenant is already activated for AIP.

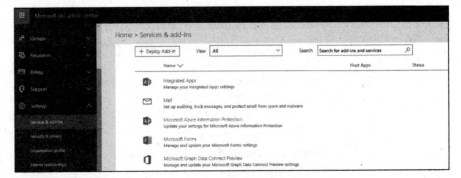

FIGURE 12-1:
Navigating to the
Microsoft Azure
Information
Protection
settings.

FIGURE 12-1:
Navigating to the
Microsoft Azure
Information
Protection
settings.

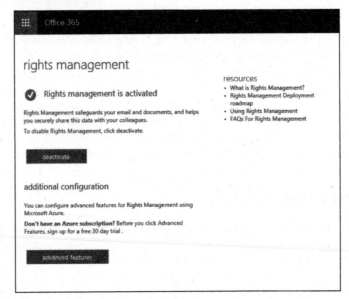

FIGURE 12-2:
A tenant with
Rights
Management
activated.

After you've confirmed the status of your AIP settings, you can safely close the browser window or navigate back to Microsoft 365 Admin Center from the app launcher.

Getting familiar with labels

TIP

AIP comes preconfigured with default policies and labels that are applicable for most organizations, including small businesses. Before you start thinking about configuring custom labels and policies for your organization, take the time to become familiar with the default settings. You might save yourself a lot of work creating and testing custom policies.

If your tenant was provisioned after February 2018, the following labels and corresponding descriptions are already available:

>> **Personal:** Non-business data, for personal use only.

>> **Public:** Business data that is specifically prepared and approved for public consumption.

>> **General:** Business data that is not intended for public consumption but can be shared with external partners as required. Examples include a company internal telephone directory, organizational charts, internal standards, and most internal communication.

>> **Confidential:** Sensitive business data that could cause damage to the business if shared with unauthorized people. Examples include contracts, security reports, forecast summaries, and sales account data. The Confidential label is further broken down into two sub-labels:

  • **Recipients Only:** Confidential data that requires protection and that can be viewed only by the recipients. This label will only appear in Outlook and will apply the Do Not Forward policy.

  • **All Employees:** Confidential data that requires protection that allows all employees full permissions. Data owners can track and revoke content.

  • **Anyone (not protected):** Data that does not require protection. Use this option with care and with appropriate business justification.

>> **Highly Confidential.** Very sensitive business data that would cause damage to the business if it was shared with unauthorized people. Examples include employee and customer information, passwords, source code, and pre-announced financial reports. The Highly Confidential label is further broken down into three sub-labels:

  • **Recipients Only:** Highly confidential data that requires protection and that can be viewed only by the recipients. This label will only appear in Outlook and will apply the Do Not Forward policy.

  • **All Employees:** Highly confidential data that allows all employees to view, edit, and reply permissions to this content. Data owners can track and revoke content.

  • **Anyone (not protected):** Data that does not require protection. Use this option with care and with appropriate business justification.

If your Office 365 tenant was provisioned before March 21, 2017, you'll find that the General and Highly Confidential labels are missing. Their equivalent in the older tenants are Internal and Secret, respectively.

To further explore these labels and corresponding policies, you need to navigate to the Azure portal and access the Azure Information Protection service settings. Here's how:

1. **Follow Steps 1-4 in the preceding section ("Activating AIP").**

2. **On the Rights Management page, click the Advanced Features button.**

    A new browser window launches and the Azure Information Protection — Labels page is displayed, as shown in Figure 12-3.

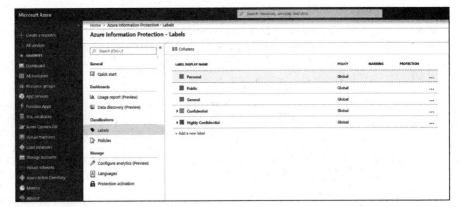

FIGURE 12-3: Azure Information Protection — Labels page in Azure.

The Confidential and Highly Confidential labels are collapsed by default. To view their sublabels, click the arrow to the left of the label to expand the selection.

A few words about policies

On the Azure Information Protection — Labels page, referenced in the preceding section, note that the labels all have *Global* under the Policy column. By default, AIP comes with a Global policy that is applied to all users in the tenant. You can edit this policy, but you can't delete it. You can also create new policies and configure them to your heart's content, but the Global policy will always be there.

To view the details of the Global policy, follow these steps:

1. **Follow Steps 1-4 in the previous section ("Activating AIP").**

2. **On the Rights Management page, click the Advanced Features button.**

    A new browser window launches and the Azure Information Protection — Labels page is displayed (refer to Figure 12-3).

3. **In the left menu, under the Classifications group, click Policies.**

On the right, the Configure Administrative Name and Description for Each Policy blade is displayed.

4. **In the Policy column, click Global.**

The Policy: Global blade is displayed, as shown in Figure 12-4.

FIGURE 12-4:
The Policy: Global blade in Azure Information Protection.

WARNING

Be careful about changing the default settings in the Global policy because it is applicable to everyone in your organization. You might want to create another policy first and test it out. If you decide to change the Global policy, make sure to save your changes. (If you forget and simply close the blade, the system will prompt you to save your changes.)

Putting AIP Into Action

Implementing Azure Information Protection is not something you would do without thoughtful planning and the involvement of keys stakeholders in your organization. You need to make sure that the rollout is communicated to end users, training is delivered, and support is planned.

As an IT admin, you should perform some testing and become familiar with the process before you implement AIP for the entire organization. After you've explored the Azure Information Protection service in Microsoft Azure, the next step is to put what you know into action. In this phase, you need your end users to participate.

Installing the AIP client

You can have the greatest policies and labels for AIP in Azure, but they'll be no good if your end users can't see and apply them. The *AIP client*, a program that is run on the end users' devices, solves this problem.

Before you install the AIP client, make sure Office ProPlus is already installed but not running on the device. When you're ready to install the AIP client, do the following:

1. **Navigate to the AIP client download page at** `https://www.microsoft.com/en-us/download/details.aspx?id=53018`.

   The Microsoft Download Center appears.

2. **Click the Download button.**

   The Choose the Download You Want window is displayed.

3. **Select AzInfoProtection.exe by selecting the box, as shown in Figure 12-5, and then click Next.**

4. **From the notification that pops up at the bottom of your screen, click (or double-click) Run.**

   The system performs a security check on the download. When the check is complete, the Microsoft Azure Information Protection window pops up, as shown in Figure 12-6.

5. **Click the I Agree button.**

   You can opt to install a demo policy (not recommended because it will clutter your user interface) or send usage statistics to Microsoft or both.

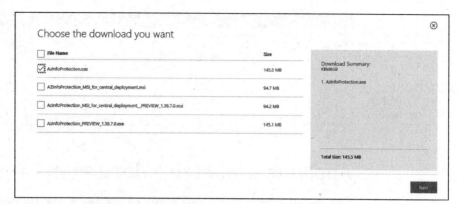

FIGURE 12-5:
Downloading the
AIP client.

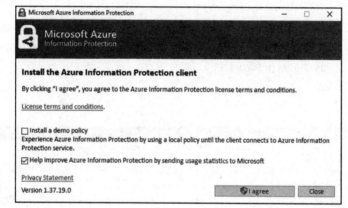

FIGURE 12-6:
Installation
window for AIP.

6. **In the User Account Control window that displays, click Yes to start the installation.**

   You see the progress of the installation.

7. **When the Microsoft Azure Information Protection window displays** *Completed Successfully,* **click the Close button.**

   The installation window disappears, and you're now ready to check that the AIP client was successfully installed.

To verify the installation, open a blank document in Word. You see the labels below the ribbon, as shown in Figure 12-7.

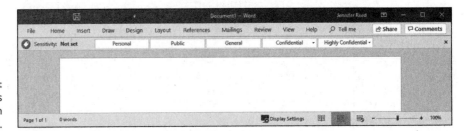

FIGURE 12-7:
AIP labels
displayed in
Word.

Applying a label to a document

Now that the AIP client is installed, and the labels are displayed in the Office applications, it's time to put it to the test.

1. **Create a Word document and pretend that it's highly confidential.**

2. **On the Sensitivity bar, click Highly Confidential and select All Employees as shown in Figure 12-8.**

   The label is applied, and the other labels will disappear.

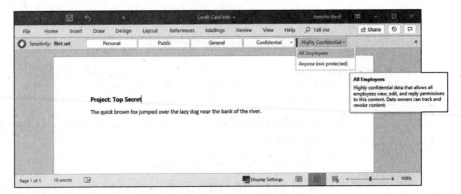

FIGURE 12-8:
Applying
the Highly
Confidential/All
Employees label.

3. **Run Outlook, start a new email, and attach the Word document.**

   Note that Outlook displays the Sensitivity bar with the same labels you saw in Word.

4. **Enter the email address of a user in your organization.**

5. **Enter an email address outside your organization, and then click Send.**

   Outlook sends the email to the recipients with the Highly Confidential/All Employees label.

In this exercise, the email will still go out to both the internal and external user. The internal user will be able to open and read the document from the sharing invitation. The external user, however, will be blocked from opening the document and will be presented with the message shown in Figure 12-9.

FIGURE 12-9:
An external user blocked from a sensitive document.

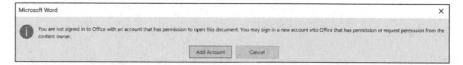

Revoking access to information

As illustrated in the preceding section, AIP protects your company information from falling into the wrong hands — even after it has fallen into the wrong hands.

For example, suppose you realize that you accidentally sent a document to the wrong people and want to remedy the situation by revoking all access to the document. Here's what you can do, continuing from the example in the preceding section:

1. **Open the protected Word document from the preceding exercise.**

   A yellow bar appears, indicating the sensitivity of the document and containing a button to view the permissions for the document.

2. **On the Ribbon, click Home, and then click the Protect button.**

   A submenu appears below the Protect button, as shown in Figure 12-10.

FIGURE 12-10:
Accessing the document-tracking site.

3. **On the submenu, click Track and Revoke to launch the document-tracking site.**

   Your browser launches to take you to the document-tracking site.

4. **If this is the first time you've visited the site, log in with your Microsoft 365 Business credentials.**

   After a successful login, the document-tracking site displays a summary of views of your document, as shown in Figure 12-11. Explore the tabs to see the robust features in AIP.

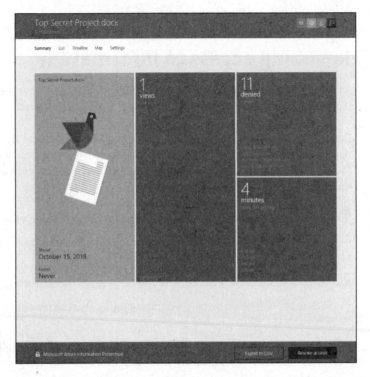

FIGURE 12-11:
The document-tracking site.

5. **At the bottom of the document-tracking site, click the Revoke access button.**

   The Revoke access page is displayed.

6. **Click the Confirm button at the bottom of the page.**

   The Revoke Complete window is displayed.

7. **Click Continue to go back to the document-tracking page.**

   In the Summary view, the document displays the Revoked stamp.

One of the features I find amazing in this solution is that in the Map tab, you can see where around the world users tried to access your document! So, if you ever find that someone from, say, Russia or Timbuktu tried to open your document even though all your users are in the United States, you'll know that access to the document should be revoked.

Chapter **13**

Measuring Your Security Posture

We've all heard about the importance of maintaining a good credit score. The higher the score, the better interest rates you'll be qualified for when applying for a home loan or car loan. If you're starting a small business, a high credit score opens the door for financial assistance. If you're applying for a job in the financial industry or the government sector, a high credit score could influence whether or not you get hired. For most people, their credit score is a measure of their financial well-being.

A security report from Symantec, a cybersecurity firm, reveals that 43 percent of cyberattacks target small businesses. Yes, the small business whose IT environment you're administering or managing. The same business you don't want to see become the next victim of a WannaCry or NotPetya ransomware attack.

Imagine yourself in front of your manager or your organization's leadership team and having to answer the question: "How secure is our organization from cyber-attacks?" Do you think you could provide an answer that's quantifiable? Do you think you'll be able to provide a number to measure your organization's security well-being?

With Microsoft 365 Business, the answer is yes. Your subscription to the cloud service includes access to Microsoft Secure Score, which provides a dashboard with a number that indicates your organization's security posture. And just like a credit score, your secure score is a good way to measure your organization's security well-being.

In this chapter, I review the Microsoft Secure Score dashboard, compare your score with average scores for industries similar to yours, and walk you through the interactive guide for improving your score as well and review your historical score to understand how your actions have influenced your security posture.

Exploring the Secure Score Dashboard

Microsoft Secure Score analyzes the security settings in your Microsoft 365 Business environment to calculate a score that indicates your organization's security posture. Daily user activities in Exchange Online, SharePoint Online, and OneDrive for Business also contribute to the score.

REMEMBER

Currently, a global admin account is required to access the Secure Score dashboard. The admin, however, can share results from the tool with other users in the organization.

Getting to the dashboard

You can get to the Secure Score dashboard in two ways. The quickest route is to navigate to `https://securescore.microsoft.com` and log in with your global admin credentials.

The other way to get to the dashboard is to do the following:

1. **Log in with your global admin credentials at** `https://admin.microsoft.com`.

2. **On the left menu, under the Admin Centers group, select Security & Compliance.**

   A new browser tab launches the Microsoft 365 Security & Compliance page.

3. **Look for the Microsoft Secure Score widget, shown in Figure 13-1, and then click the Microsoft Secure Score link below the number indicating your score.**

   A new browser tab launches the Secure Score page.

In the Secure Score dashboard, a slide show of cards, or a carousel, provides overview cards to orient you to the dashboard, as shown in in Figure 13-2. After you've reviewed the cards, you can remove them by clicking the close icon (X) at the top right to gain more real estate on the page.

FIGURE 13-1:
The Microsoft
Secure Score
widget.

FIGURE 13-2:
Secure Score
dashboard
carousel.

Understanding your score

After you're logged in to the Microsoft Secure Score dashboard, it's time to brush up on your fractions because we're going to be discussing numerators and denominators. In our grade school math class, we learned that the numerator is the top part of the fraction and the denominator is the bottom part of the fraction.

Similarly, in Microsoft Secure Score, the top bigger number you see in the Secure Score Summary is the numerator and the bottom, smaller number is the denominator, as shown in Figure 13-3. Both numbers represent your overall score. This number gets updated every 24 hours at around 1 AM Pacific Standard Time.

The numerator is the total points you have achieved based on the security features enabled in your tenant. The denominator is the maximum number of points you can achieve if all the security features available in your subscription are enabled.

Note that the denominator you see in your environment may differ from someone else's environment. That's because some Office 365 or Microsoft 365 subscriptions have additional security functionalities not included in the Microsoft 365 Business subscription.

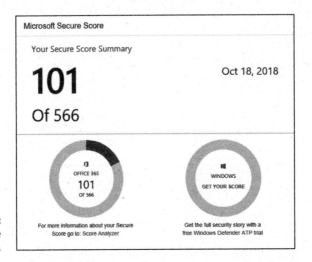

FIGURE 13-3:
Secure Score
summary.

Below the Secure Score Summary are two donut charts. The chart on the left is a visual representation of your secure score based on Office 365 data. The chart on the right represents the secure score for Windows based on data from the Windows Defender Advanced Threat Protection service. This service is not included in the Microsoft 365 Business subscription but can be purchased separately.

Taking action to improve your score

Below the Secure Score Summary widget is the Take Action, Improve your Microsoft Secure Score widget. Note that the target score recommended by the system in a balanced approach between security and productivity, as shown in Figure 13-4. The target score represents what your secure score could be if you were to take the recommended actions to increase your score.

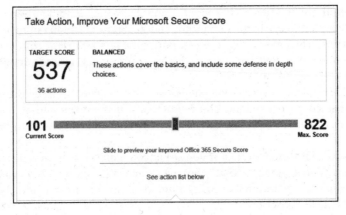

FIGURE 13-4:
Target score in a
balanced security
approach.

In Figure 13-4, the target score is 537. To get to that number from the current score of 101, 36 actions must be taken, as noted by the 36 Actions link below the target score.

The slider dynamically changes as you move the toggle from left to right. If you move the slider to the left or right from the middle, which indicates the balanced approach to security, the target score and the corresponding number of actions to achieve the target score will change.

A variety of factors determine an organization's ideal target — no magic target number applies to everyone. Fortunately, you can easily change your target if you feel that the current number is not meeting your needs.

If you click the 36 Actions link, the screen will scroll down to display the queued list of actions to take to achieve the target score. Clicking an item in the list will give you an expanded view with more details about the item. In Figure 13-5, for example, enabling multi-factor authentication (MFA) for Azure Active Directory privileged roles will increase the score by 50 points, as noted by the Action Score number.

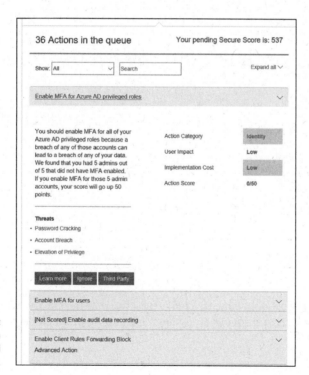

FIGURE 13-5: Action items with a description and other details.

The expanded view also provides more details about the action, why it should be enabled, and what threats it addresses.

Clicking the Learn More button opens a window on the right so you can discover more details about the action.

If you're using third-party solutions to take care of the security feature described in the item, you can click the Third-Party button and then the Save button to exclude it from the calculation. The Ignore button, as of this writing, achieves the same purpose.

In the list of actions to take, you'll find the Show box which allows you to filter the list of actions. Next to the Show box is the Search box if you just want to do a keyword search.

Clicking the drop-down arrow next to the Show box displays the different ways by which the action items can be filtered, as shown in Figure 13-6.

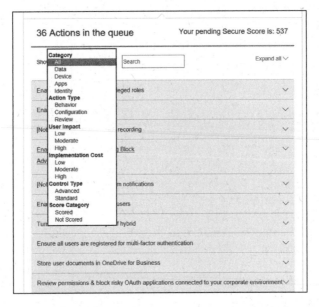

FIGURE 13-6:
Filtering the list of action items.

For example, if you want to enable features that have a low effect on your end users, select Low from the drop-down menu under User Impact.

Comparing your score

As mentioned, no one magic number applies to all organizations because different organizations have different needs. A large enterprise might need more features than a small business, for example.

The Compare Your Score widget is a great way to get insights into the secure scores of other organizations, which might help inform your own organization's target score.

As shown in Figure 13-7, the first bar on the left is the current secure score for the organization. For example, Figure 13-7 shows the results for an example organization with 25 users. The first bar on the left is the organization's current secure score

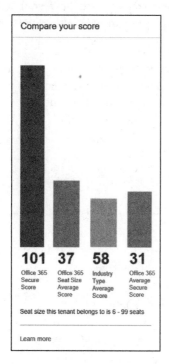

Next to the organization's current score is the average active seat size score, which is 37. Below the score, you can see that the organization's 25 users place it in the 6 to 99 seats category. In this example, our company with a secure score of 101 is doing well compared to other companies with a similar seat size, whose average score is 37.

The third bar from the left represents the average score for companies like the example organization in the industry as a whole. When you first visit Secure Score, the Industry Type Average Score bar is zero. You need to set this up for the system to start reporting the score. Simply click the Please Select Industry Type link below the bar and follow the prompts. When you're finished, it will take at least 48 hours to take effect.

The final bar represents the average score for all Office 365 tenants in the world, be they small or large companies.

Reviewing the Score Analyzer

The Score Analyzer page is where you can see how your actions over time has affected your security posture. You can view and export up to 90 days of scoring data.

Score Analyzer, shown in Figure 13-8, includes several parts. At the top is a line that shows how your secure score has trended over time. The line on the bottom represents the average secure score for Office 365 tenants.

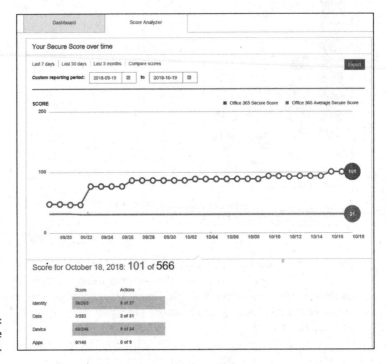

FIGURE 13-8:
Secure Score
Analyzer.

You can change the view for the chart in Score Analyzer by clicking one of the tabs just below the Your Secure Score Over Time label. The options are Last 7 Days, Last 30 Days, and Last 3 Months. The Compare Scores tab enables you to compare scores between dates based on actions that have been taken in the environment.

Like all the other services in Microsoft 365 Business, Secure Score is continuously evolving. Make a habit of checking the Secure Score dashboard for updates to the system and to stay current on the latest best practices for data security.

5

Managing Mobile Devices and Apps

Chapter **14**

Introducing Microsoft Intune

I n my household, I manage four laptops and one desktop running Windows 10, a MacBook Pro, an iMac, two iPhones, one Android smartphone, an iPad, and an Android tablet. And that's not all. We have smart TVs, gaming devices, routers, smart watches, and IoT devices. Did I mention my husband and I are recent empty nesters?

Imagine what it would be like for an IT admin who has to manage desktops, laptops, tablets, and mobile devices for an entire organization, deal with users who have diverse needs and technical abilities, and to add more pressure, be the gatekeeper for the company's data security and privacy. How do you balance pleasing your end users and making sure you don't get in the way of their productivity while ensuring that the right controls are in place to minimize risk?

In today's security landscape, companies of all sizes need a mobile device management (MDM) and mobile application management (MAM) strategy. Without such a strategy, you could end up with an employee calling you from the airport and freaking out because he has lost his phone, where he has saved confidential, personally identifiable information (PII) from one of your customers. You, as the IT admin, are sitting in your cubicle sweating, trying to figure how to get out of this mess smelling like a rose. Hint: You may not.

In this chapter, I introduce you to Microsoft Intune, a cloud-based mobile device and mobile application management solution designed to help your users stay productive while keeping your company data protected. Don't be dissuaded if you've heard that Intune is applicable only in the enterprise environment. Intune very much applies to small business — and even a high-tech household like mine!

Getting to Know Intune

As a cloud service, Microsoft 365 Business is an ever-evolving solution. Don't be surprised if you're looking at Microsoft 365 Business Admin Center one day and realize that new features have been added to your service while the cost of your service has stayed the same. That is the nature of a software-as-a-service (SaaS) model and the reason why small businesses benefit from this type of solution.

Similarly, the features and functionalities of Intune that are available in the Microsoft 365 Business license are also evolving. While the current list of Intune device and application management features included in the license is robust, expect to see more features added or enhanced based on industry requirements and feedback from customers like you. You can view the latest list of features for the service at `https://docs.microsoft.com/en-us/office365/servicedescriptions/ microsoft-365-business-service-description`.

Better together with Intune and AAD

Intune and Azure Active Directory (AAD) are perfect together, like peanut butter and jelly in a sandwich. Intune uses the identity and access control features in AAD to effectively carry out its purpose, Without AAD, Intune would be a bit lost.

At a high level, the Intune/AAD combo in Microsoft 365 Business offers three key features that can help an IT admin run a tight operation:

>> **Managing mobile devices:** Whether it's a company-supplied device or a bring your own device (BYOD) approach, keep control of company data in mobile devices used by employees on different platforms.

>> **Managing mobile applications:** Whether a mobile device is managed by a company or not, Intune enables the management of apps running on devices used to access company information.

>> **Protecting company data:** Imagine the effect on your company's reputation if a disgruntled employee were to cut and paste an embarrassing detail about your organization and circulate it via email or Twitter. With app protection policies in Intune, you won't have to imagine digging yourself out of such a nightmare.

These features are included in the pricing for the Microsoft 365 Business license currently starting at $20/user/month. They can be implemented in both company-owned mobile devices and an employee-owned device (*bring your own device, or BYOD*).

Although these Intune features are typically enough to meet the needs of a small business, it's helpful to understand that they do not represent the complete capabilities in the full version of Intune, which can be purchased as a stand-alone service for as low as $6 per user per month all the way up to $14.50 per user per month as part of the Enterprise Mobility + Security suite.

REMEMBER

There are many third-party mobile device and mobile application management solutions on the market, but I've found some to be overkill for small business needs and too expensive. With Microsoft 365 Business, you get more bang for your buck, especially if you're just starting to implement device management and security policies for your organization.

Toggle switch revelations

Confession time. Without knowing it, you've been fed the Intune/AAD sandwich earlier in this book. In Chapter 5, I walk you through the Setup wizard for protecting work files on mobile devices. Although the process required only a few clicks on some toggle switches, you were creating complex policies in Intune worthy of a seasoned systems engineer!

Let's get a refresher on what you did in Chapter 5 when you followed the steps for protecting working files on mobile devices. In the following, you review the policies created during this process:

1. **Navigate to** `https://admin.microsoft.com` **and log in with your global admin credentials.**

2. **On the left menu, under the Devices group, click Policies.**

   A list of policies is displayed in the Device Policies page, as shown in Figure 14-1.

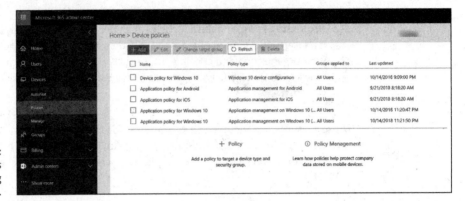

FIGURE 14-1:
Device policies
created during
the Setup wizard.

3. **Select the Application Policy for iOS row, and note the settings for this policy displayed in the Edit Policy window on the right, as shown in Figure 14-2.**

FIGURE 14-2:
Device policies
created during
the Setup wizard.

4. **Click the Close button to close the window and return to the Devices Policies page.**

Now that you've seen what the policies look like in Microsoft 365 Admin Center, let's see what they look like in Intune:

1. **Navigate to** `https://portal.azure.com`.

   If you've already signed in to Microsoft 365 Admin Center, you should be automatically signed in to Azure. If not, enter your Microsoft 365 global admin credentials.

2. **In the Search box at the top, type** Intune, **and then click Intune in the list that appears, as shown in Figure 14-3.**

   The Microsoft Intune page appears.

FIGURE 14-3:
Searching
for Intune.

3. **On the left menu, click Client Apps.**

   The Client Apps blade is displayed.

4. **In the Client Apps blade, under the Manage group, click App Protection Policies.**

   The same application protection policies found in Microsoft 365 Admin Center Device Policies page are displayed, as shown in Figure 14-4.

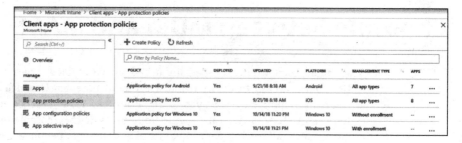

FIGURE 14-4:
Application
policies in Intune.

5. **Click the Application Policy for iOS row.**

   The Intune App Protection blade is displayed.

6. **On the left menu, click Properties.**

   The Properties blade appears with three settings.

7. **Click the Access Requirements Configure Settings row.**

   The Access Requirements blade is displayed, as shown in Figure 14-5.

As you can see, the toggle switch you clicked during the Setup wizard controls several settings in Intune! When you've finished reviewing the magic you unknowingly created, click the Microsoft Intune link in the top breadcrumb navigation (see the top row in Figure 14-5) to go back to the Intune Overview page.

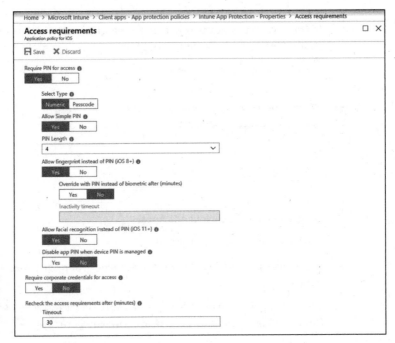

FIGURE 14-5:
Access
Requirements
settings for
application policy
for iOS.

Choosing Between MDM and MAM

We're all about choices. Especially in today's workplace, where younger generations have access to devices that are much more feature-rich and nicer than company-supplied devices, you as an IT admin need to balance end user productivity and security. If you provide your users with a completely secure phone (some call it a "brick") with all kinds of restrictions, people are not going to like it and may not use it. If you let people use their own mobile devices, you run the risk of exposing your company to security breaches.

Fortunately, a happy medium exists. With Intune, you can implement just a mobile device management (MDM) or a mobile application management (MAM) strategy or a combination. You'll find that with the capabilities in your Microsoft 365 Business subscription, you can delight your end users without giving up your responsibility to secure company data.

Making the case for MDM

Unbeknownst to you, in addition to the complex policies configured during the Setup wizard in Chapter 5, you also created a robust Windows 10 device management policy with a few clicks to secure your Windows 10 device. If you're curious to see what it is, follow these steps:

1. **Log in to Microsoft 365 Admin Center at** `http://admin.microsoft.com`.

   You need your Microsoft 365 Global Admin credentials.

2. **On the left menu, under the Devices group, click Policies.**

   A list of policies is displayed in the Device Policies page (refer to Figure 14-1).

3. **In the Policies page, click the Device Policy for Windows 10 row.**

   The Edit Policy window is displayed on the right.

4. **Click Edit next to the line that reads Windows 10 Device Protection, Some Settings are ON.**

   The Change Setting window is displayed.

5. **Click the drop-down arrow to the left of Secure Windows 10 Devices to display the toggle switches for this policy, as shown in Figure 14-6.**

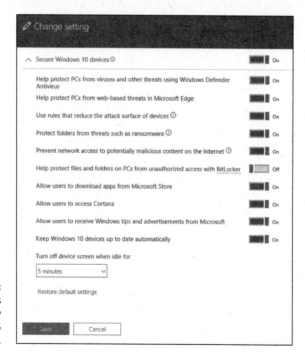

FIGURE 14-6:
Secure Windows
10 Devices policy
in Microsoft 365
Admin Center.

6. **Review the settings.**

7. **Click the Cancel button, and in the next window, click Close.**

If you want to see the configuration of this policy in Intune, follow these steps:

1. **Navigate to** `https://portal.azure.com`.

If you've already signed in to Microsoft 365 Admin Center, you should be automatically signed in to Azure. If not, enter your Microsoft 365 global admin credentials.

2. **In the Search box at the top, type** Intune **and click Intune in the list that appears (refer to Figure 14-3).**

The Microsoft Intune page appears.

3. **On the left menu, click Device Configuration.**

The Device Configuration — Profiles blade is displayed.

4. **Under the Manage group, click Profiles. On the right, click Device Policy for Windows 10.**

5. **In the Device Policy for Windows 10 blade, click Properties, and then click Settings 5 Configured.**

The Device Restrictions blade is displayed, as shown in Figure 14-7.

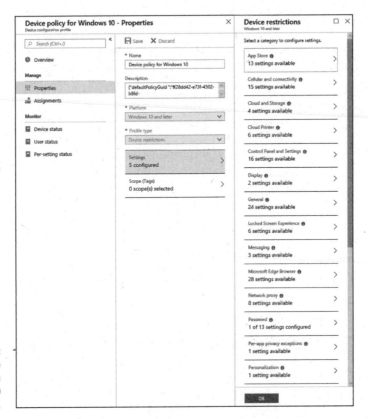

FIGURE 14-7: Device restrictions on Windows 10 device settings.

166   PART 5 Managing Mobile Devices and Apps

6. **Review the settings.**

7. **Click the OK button, and in the next window, click Close.**

As you can see from the various configuration options available in Intune, you can manage devices at a granular level. For example, you can manage multiple devices owned by one user. Managing devices starts with the users enrolling their devices in Azure Active Directory (AAD). The process for enrolling mobile devices for management is covered in Chapter 15

After mobile devices are enrolled, you can have control over those devices by remotely wiping corporate data from a device without affecting the user's personal data. You can also prevent a user from accessing company data from mobile devices that are jailbroken; a device with restrictions removed could create a security hole.

If you purchase additional higher-end Intune licenses, you can also configure Wi-Fi or VPN on the devices, push apps to be automatically installed, and run additional controls to meet certain regulatory requirements.

Choosing MAM

If you have millennials in your organization walking around with their latest gadget and using your company-supplied laptop as a doorstop, that might be a signal for you to implement a mobile application management (MAM) strategy.

MAM is a great way to have a BYOD (bring your own device) strategy. If you choose this option, you'll make your end users happy because they'll be allowed to use their own swanky devices. On top of that, you'll be saving them from a few warning prompts, which may lead to confusion and frustration.

You may also choose MAM over MDM if you have specific requirements to comply with regulations related to management of data on personal devices. Note that in MDM, you can remove all the data from a mobile device, whereas in MAM, you can remove only company data, leaving the user's personal data untouched.

You can implement MAM by itself or on top of MDM policies. The app protection policies you create can stand on their own and do not have dependencies on any MDM policies. In fact, MAM can even be implemented alongside other third-party MDM solutions.

Chapter **15**

Managing Mobile Devices

A few years ago, implementing a mobile device management (MDM) strategy for a small business — especially those with a bring your own device (BYOD) policy — was challenging. The process was much more complex and required highly skilled IT staff whose salaries were out of reach for SMBs. Additionally, the solutions available at that time didn't have the flexibility to manage only the data that belongs to the company. Therefore, if mobile devices were enrolled in MDM, the device owners would lose all of their personal files if the devices were wiped for one reason or another.

Fast forward to today, and we find that SMBs no longer have the luxury of not managing mobile devices in their organization. The question a small business needs to address today is whether they should manage just devices, or just the apps running on devices, or a combination of devices and apps.

Think of Dave, a millennial, who works in the sales department for an organization similar to yours. Dave has the latest smartphone, a tablet at home that he uses to stream his favorite TV shows and movies, and a generic company-supplied laptop that he hates because he can't even use it to watch and comment on YouTube videos. If you have a Dave in your organization, you should ensure that his smartphone is secured with a PIN if he's using it to access company resources and data. You probably also want to have the ability to remotely wipe his device in case of loss or theft.

Luckily for you, Microsoft 365 Business is full of features and capabilities to help an IT admin for a small business implement an MDM strategy, an MAM (mobile application management) strategy, or a combination of both.

In this chapter, I walk you through the concepts behind mobile device management to lay the foundation for implementing the solution. I help you prepare your environment for mobile device management, show you basic tasks for managing mobile devices, and walk you through the device enrollment experience from the end user's point of view.

With the knowledge you'll gain from this chapter, you can keep the Daves in your organization happy and productive while protecting company data and minimizing security risks.

Understanding Device Management

Small businesses have always been at the forefront of the BYOD approach for a lot of reasons, one of which is cost. When you don't have a huge IT budget for company-supplied laptops and smartphones, it makes sense to allow employees to use their existing devices to access work-related documents and resources.

Industry research validates the existence of the Dave persona just mentioned. According to Forrester research, 52 percent of information workers across 17 countries use three or more devices for work. To compound the complexity of what an IT admin must manage, those three devices are not necessarily running the same operating system. Dave's laptop might be running Windows 10, his smartphone might be running iOS, and his tablet might be an Android device. But wait! The life of an IT admin is even more complicated. Studies have shown that 80 percent of employees admit to using non-approved software-as-a-service (SaaS) apps on their jobs!

Mobility is the new normal for all types of businesses, especially small businesses. Enabling employees to freely move around, take their data with them, and have easy but secure access to company data is fast becoming a standard expectation. SMBs can no longer look the other way and pretend that everything will be alright even if the devices their employees are using are not centrally managed. A company simply faces too much risk without a sound MDM strategy in place, especially in today's cybersecurity landscape.

Although the idea of device management may sound daunting, it is good news for an IT admin. You are now more valuable than ever — especially if you know how to implement MDM.

Stepping through the device lifecycle

The device management capabilities in Microsoft 365 Business support the most common mobile environments, including iOS, Android, Windows, and macOS. These environments can be managed either through a BYOD approach or a company-owned device approach.

In Chapter 5, you step through the deployment of Windows 10 devices in your organization through a manual or a Windows 10 AutoPilot deployment process. In either instance, the Windows 10 device is automatically enrolled as a mobile device in MDM. Don't be alarmed if you see Windows 10 devices treated like mobile devices instead of regular PCs. This concept is by design because the Windows 10 operating system has built-in capabilities for a cloud-based modern device management scenario.

Regardless of the operating system, a managed device in MDM goes through the following *device lifecycle* (key stages):

>> **Enroll.** In this stage, the mobile device is enrolled or registered for management. The enrollment process can be done by the end user individually or by the IT admin for company-owned devices. The IT admin must complete some tasks to enable the enrollment process (covered in the next section).

>> **Configure.** After a device is enrolled for management, the door is opened for the IT admin to configure policies that get pushed to the mobile device. For example, you can require that a mobile device accessing company data must have a PIN. You can even configure iOS devices to disable the use of the camera. App restrictions can also be configured at this point to prevent data leakage.

>> **Manage and protect.** In this stage, the configuration policies that have been pushed to the mobile device becomes reality. For example, suppose you configured a policy whereby a jailbroken device is restricted from accessing company data. If the system detects that this policy has been violated, the policy is applied.

>> **Retire.** If a mobile device being managed is lost or stolen, you can immediately retire or wipe the device to remove all company data and reset the device. If an employee leaves the organization, you can also remove the device from management in addition to wiping the data.

REMEMBER

For BYOD devices, be sure to let the end user know that only company data will be wiped from the device. The process will not delete their personal files, pictures, or any data that's not owned or managed by the company.

The device lifecycle typically ends in the retire stage in a BYOD scenario. For company-owned devices, a mobile device may be put back into circulation after it has been reset so that another employee can use the device.

Preparing for device management

Before implementing an MDM strategy, an IT admin must be mindful of certain prerequisites. Some of the tasks associated with these prerequisites may have been completed as part of the initial tenant setup for Microsoft 365 Business, during the user setup and configuration, or during the MDM policy configuration. Regardless of when these tasks were completed, it's helpful to get an understanding of their interdependencies in the overall MDM deployment process.

WARNING

If you are already using mobile management solutions such as Mobile Iron or AirWatch, be aware that a device can be managed by only one solution at a time. If you plan to take advantage of MDM capabilities in Microsoft 365 Business, make sure to remove devices from management by third-party device management solutions.

To prepare for device management, take note of the following key tasks: setting up users and setting up groups, both described next.

Setting up users

The identity of the users in your organization serves as basis for securing access to your data and resources. By managing identities, an IT admin can find the right balance between security and productivity for the end user.

Users in the Microsoft 365 Business tenant are managed in Admin Center under the Users group, as shown in Figure 15-1.

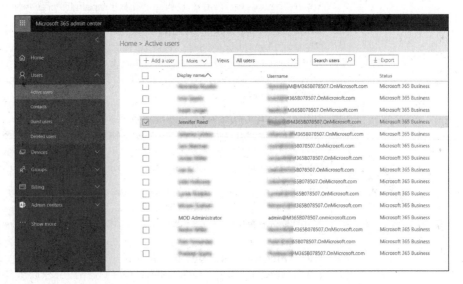

FIGURE 15-1:
Managing users in Microsoft 365 Admin Center.

For users to be able to enroll devices for MDM, they must have the right license. A Microsoft 365 Business license entitles a user to consume services required for MDM, such as Microsoft Intune.

To validate that a user has the right license to enroll mobile devices in MDM, do the following:

If the figures in the following instructions look slightly different from what you're seeing on your screen, most likely you're reading this book after the new admin center experience has become generally available. Don't fret. These instructions are still relevant, but you might be able to skip a step or two as the services are enhanced to make management by a novice IT admin even easier.

1. **Navigate to** `https://admin.microsoft.com` **and log in with your global admin credentials.**

2. **In the left menu, under the Users group, click Active Users.**

3. **Select a user to see the details about that user.**

4. **Next to Product Licenses, click Edit.**

   The panel displays the list of services associated with the Microsoft 365 Business license, as shown in the snippet in Figure 15-2.

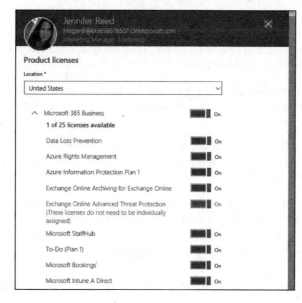

FIGURE 15-2:
Snippet of the services associated with the Microsoft 365 Business license.

5. In the list of services, find Microsoft Intune A Direct and ensure that the toggle switch is set to On.

6. Click the close button (X) twice to go back to the Active Users page.

Remember how I said that users are managed in Microsoft 365 Admin Center? Well, users can be managed in two other places: from the Azure portal in Azure Active Directory or in Microsoft Intune. I purposely didn't lead you down the complicated path first. For the most part, the admin task you'll be performing to administer Microsoft 365 Business can be completed in the more user-friendly Admin Center interface. Later in this chapter, you get an opportunity to play in Azure when you configure policies for MDM.

Setting up groups

I have never met an IT admin who did not want to take advantage of shortcuts to get things done faster. When configuring MDM, the Groups feature is an IT admin's best friend for managing tasks at scale. You can create groups by department or by location and then create policies specific to a group. For example, the accounting group could have MDM policies that require an accounting mobile app to be deployed in addition to the Office Apps everyone else is getting.

You can create four types of groups in Admin Center. At a high level, the differences between these four types of groups are as follows:

>> **Office 365 group:** Typically used for team collaboration which gives members of a group a shared workspace for persistent chat, shared documents and calendars, and a group email.

>> **Distribution list, or DL:** A great way for a group of users to receive and reply to the same email coming from internal users as well as people from outside the organization.

>> **Mail-enabled security group:** Similar to distribution list but with the added capability of granting access to resources in OneDrive for Business and SharePoint Online.

>> **Security group:** Allows users who are members of the group to access resources in OneDrive for Business and SharePoint Online. It also enables policies created for MDM to be pushed to the devices enrolled by the members of the security group.

REMEMBER

When creating a group to be used for MDM, be sure to choose a security group.

To create a new security group:

1. **Navigate to** `https://admin.microsoft.com` **and log in with your global admin credentials.**

2. **In the left menu, under the Groups group, click Groups.**

   The Groups page is displayed.

3. **Click the + Add a group button to open the New Group panel.**

4. **In the New Group panel, under Type, click the arrow next to Office 365.**

   The submenu displays the four different types of groups, as shown in Figure 15-3.

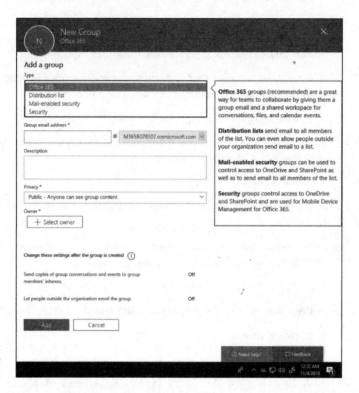

FIGURE 15-3:
Creating a new security group.

5. **Select Security in the list of options.**

   The panel updates to display the required information for the security group.

6. **Enter the name and description of the security group in the appropriate boxes, and then click the Add button.**

   The system creates the group, and the panel displays a validation that the group was added.

7. **In the validation panel, click the close (X) button.**

The panel closes, and the Groups page is displayed.

8. **In the Groups page, select the newly created group.**

The new group panel is displayed.

9. **Next to Owners, click Edit, and then click the + Add Owners button.**

A list of the users in the organization is displayed.

10. **In the list of users, select the name of the user, and then click the Save button.**

The system displays a validation that your changes were successfully updated.

REMEMBER

At least one owner is required for a group. Designating an owner allows the IT admin to share the responsibility of managing the group. The owner can add or remove users and even delete the group.

11. **In the validation page that is displayed, click the close (X) button, and then click the close button in the Add Owners panel.**

The panel displays the settings for the newly-created group.

12. **In the panel for the Security group, next to Members, click Edit, and then click the + Add members button.**

A list of the users in the organization is displayed.

13. **In the list of users, select the name of the user, and then click the Save button.**

14. **In the validation page that appears, click the close (X) button, and then click the close button in the Add Members panel.**

The panel displays the settings for the newly-created group.

15. **In the panel for the Security group, click the close (X) button.**

The Groups page is displayed.

Like managing users, groups can be created also in Azure Active Directory and Microsoft Intune from the Azure portal. Regardless of where the group was created, the system will sync the group, so you'll be able to see it in all three locations.

Working in the Device Management Portal

I obviously believe in Microsoft cloud technologies and am passionate about sharing the value proposition of these technologies — that's why I wrote this book and co-authored the *Office 365 for Dummies* book. But although I'm a fan, I am the first to point out that Microsoft has not necessarily made it easy for admins to manage different aspects of the service. As I pointed out in the preceding section, you can manage users and groups in more than one location. Similarly, device management became confusing because you could perform configuration and implementation tasks in various places.

At the Ignite 2018 conference in September 2018, Microsoft announced the simplification of the admin centers by consolidating all standalone portals into one starting point: Microsoft 365 Admin Center. For device management, a link will take you to Device Management from the Admin Centers group in Microsoft 365 Admin Center. However, the link has not been implemented as of this writing, so in this section you follow a URL to go directly to the Device Management portal.

The Device Management portal is accessed by navigating to `https://device management.microsoft.com` and logging in with your global admin credentials. The portal, shown in Figure 15-4, is your one-stop-shop for managing devices, monitoring them, and taking actions when needed to protect your environment.

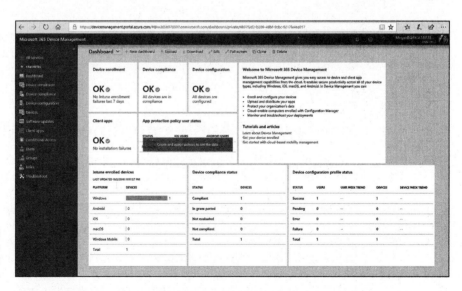

FIGURE 15-4:
The Device Management portal.

The actions you take in the Device Management portal can also be performed in the Microsoft Intune portal in Azure, but the dashboard for the former gives you a better sense of your MDM environment.

Preparing for device enrollment

If you've completed the prep work in creating users, assigning licenses to users, and creating groups from the preceding section, you are ready to start setting up your organization for enrolling mobile devices.

Whether managing an iOS or an Android device, you need to determine your device management strategy. Will you allow BYOD? Or are you deploying company-owned devices to your users? Or will you be doing a combination of both? The answers to these questions will inform your deployment scenario.

If you will allow BYOD in your environment, will you be asking your users to enroll their devices, so you can manage them? Or are you okay with just managing the apps running on the devices? If the latter, the user does not need to enroll the device for management and your scope of control as an IT admin is limited to company-managed apps. In this scenario, you would not, for example, be able to prevent the user from using the device's camera.

In this chapter, we focus on mobile device enrollment in a BYOD scenario because this is the most common scenario for SMBs with a small or nonexistent IT department. Application management is covered in more detail in the next chapter, so I only touch on the subject here. Another aspect for device enrollment I do not cover in this chapter is the Windows 10 AutoPilot scenario because I covered that in Chapter 5.

I further focus this chapter by setting up Apple enrollment by using the Apple MDM push certificate. After you go through the process of configuring Apple enrollment, setting up Android enrollment will be intuitive, with tooltips and guidance to help you along the way.

Configuring Apple enrollment for MDM

Setting up Apple enrollment requires an Apple MDM push certificate from the Apple Push Certificates portal, which, in turn, requires an Apple ID.

TIP

To log into the Apple Push Certificates portal, I highly recommend creating a company-owned Apple ID versus using a personal Apple ID. The push certificate is valid for only a year and must be renewed annually. If you use someone's personal Apple ID to create the certificate and that person leaves the company, you will not be able to renew the certificate without getting that person's personal Apple ID credentials. An expired certificate with produce errors and result in a poor user experience.

To configure Apple enrollment, follow these steps.

1. **Navigate to the Microsoft 365 Device Management portal at** `https://devicemanagement.microsoft.com` **and log in with your global admin credentials.**

2. **In the left menu, click Device Enrollment.**

3. **In the Device Enrollment blade, click Apple Enrollment.**

   The Apple enrollment blade is displayed, as shown in Figure 15-5.

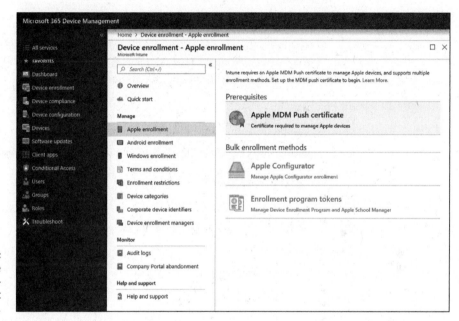

FIGURE 15-5:
Device
enrollment —
Apple enrollment
blade.

4. **Click Apple MDM Push Certificate.**

   The Configure MDM Push Certificate blade appears.

You're now ready to configure the Apple MDM push certificate.

In the Configure MDM Push Certificate blade, follow these steps in the order listed in the blade:

1. **Select the box under "I grant Microsoft permission to send both user and device information to Apple to indicate your agreement."**

2. **Click the Download Your CSR link, and save the IntuneCSR.csr file to your computer at a location you can go back to later.**

   You will need to navigate to this location later in Step 4e.

3. **Under Create an Apple MDM Push Certificate, click the Create Your MDM Push Certificate link.**

   A new browser tab launches and takes you to the Apple Push Certificates portal.

4. **Enter your Apple ID and password and provide additional authentication if needed:**

   a. *Sign in with a company-owned Apple ID and then click the Sign In button.*

   b. *If two-factor authentication is configured for the Apple ID, follow the instructions to verify your identity.* After your identity is verified, you will be logged in to the Apple Push Certificates portal, as shown in Figure 15-6.

FIGURE 15-6: Apple Push Certificates portal.

   c. *Click the Create a Certificate button.* The Terms of Use page is displayed.

   d. *Read the content, select the box next to "I have read and agree to these terms and conditions," and then click the Accept button.* The Create a New Push Certificate page displays.

e. *Click the Browse button and navigate to and select the IntuneCSR.csr file, and then click the Open button.*

f. *Back in the Create a New Push Certificate page, click the Upload button.* After a successful upload, the Confirmation page appears.

g. *Click the Download button (see Figure 15-7) and save the MDM_Microsoft Corporation_Certificate.pem file in your computer at a location you can go back to later.* You need to navigate to this location in Step 6.

h. *Sign out of the Apple Push Certificates portal.*

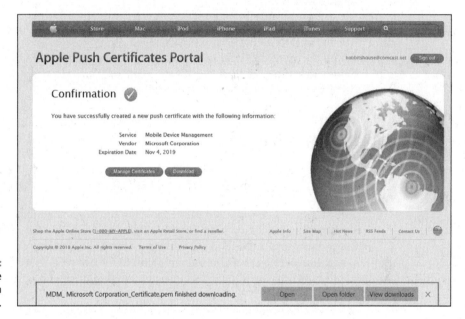

FIGURE 15-7:
Downloading the Apple MDM push certificate.

5. **Navigate back to the Configure MDM Push Certificate tab on your browser, and under the Apple ID in Step 4 heading, enter the company-owned Apple ID.**

6. **Under the Apple MDM Push Certificate in Step 5 heading, click Select a File, navigate to and select the MDM_Microsoft Corporation_Certificate. pem file, and then click the Open button.**

   The box under Apple MDM Push Certificate is populated with the name of the file.

7. **Click the Upload button.**

   The system processes your changes and displays a confirmation.

After you've successfully configured the certificate, the Configure MDM Push Certificate blade will display the status of your certificate, as shown in Figure 15-8.

FIGURE 15-8: MDM Push Certificate successfully configured.

REMEMBER

The expiration date will also be displayed — set up a calendar reminder a week before the certificate expires to ensure that you remember to renew the certificate before it expires. If your certificate expires, your end users will have trouble accessing company data from their iOS devices.

With the Apple enrollment task completed, you're ready to set up device compliance policies for MDM.

Setting up a device compliance policy

After a device is enrolled in MDM, policies can be pushed to the device to meet your organization's requirements. Example policies might be: require a PIN code, encryption, or a minimum OS version allowed. Or a policy might even prevent jailbroken devices from enrolling in MDM. To ensure that these policies are applied, device compliance policies must be configured and pushed to the device.

If a device does not meet the device compliance policies, it will be marked as non-compliant. The compliance status of devices provides IT admins with a quick view when taking appropriate actions on non-compliant devices.

To set up a basic device compliance policy for an iOS device, you start by picking up from where you left off in the preceding section:

1. **Navigate to the Microsoft 365 Device Management portal at** `https://devicemanagement.microsoft.com` **and log in with your global admin credentials.**

2. **In the left menu, click Device Compliance. Then in the Policies blade, click Policies.**

    The Device Compliance — Policies blade appears.

3. **In the Device Compliance — Policies blade, click +Create Policy in the top bar.**

   The Create Policy blade appears.

4. **In the Create Policy blade, enter the name and description.**

5. **Under Platform, click the blank box and then select iOS.**

   The iOS Compliance Policy blade appears.

6. **In the iOS Compliance Policy blade, click the Device Health category and do the following:**

   a. *In the Device Health blade that appears, find Jailbroken Devices and then select Block.*

   b. *Click OK.* The Device Health blade closes, and the iOS Compliance Policy blade is restored.

7. **In the iOS Compliance Policy blade, click the Device Properties category and do the following:**

   a. *In the Device Properties blade that appears, set the minimum and maximum OS versions.* Note the tooltip that appears when setting the minimum and maximum OS versions. In Figure 15-9, I set the minimum to 8 and left the maximum blank.

   b. *Click OK.* The Device Properties blade closes, and the iOS Compliance Policy blade is restored.

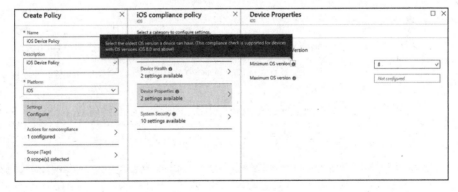

FIGURE 15-9: Setting the minimum OS version for device properties.

8. **In the iOS Compliance Policy blade, click the System Security category and do the following:**

   a. In *the System Security blade that appears, select the appropriate settings for your organization.* In Figure 15-10, I set Password Is Required to unlock the mobile device, blocked simple passwords, set the minimum password length to 6 characters, and required numeric characters.

b. *Click OK.* The System Security blade closes, and the iOS Compliance Policy blade is restored.

FIGURE 15-10:
Setting the
System Security
policies.

9. **Back in the iOS Compliance Policy blade, click the OK button.**

   The iOS Compliance Policy blade closes, and the Create Policy blade is restored.

10. **In the Create Policy blade, click the Create button to save your settings.**

    The Create Policy blade closes, and the iOS Device Policy blade is restored.

Congratulations! You're one step closer to applying the policies you've created.

Assigning device compliance polices

Now that you've set up the enrollment policies and device compliance policies, the next step is to assign the compliance policies to a group. Here's how:

1. **In the Device Management portal's left navigation, click Device Compliance.**

2. **In the list of policies, select the iOS device policy you created in the preceding section.**

3. **In the iOS Device Policy blade, under the Manage group, click Assignments.**

4. **In the Assignments blade, under the Include tab, ensure that Selected Groups is displayed.**

   Alternatively, you can assign the policy to All Users, but I don't recommend doing this unless you've tested the policies and tweaked them to fit your organization's needs.

5. **to display the list of groups available, click Select Groups to Include, select a group, and then click the Select button.**

   In this example, I chose the MDM Pilot Group I created in the "Setting up Groups" section earlier in this chapter.

6. **Back in the iOS Device Policy — Assignments blade, click Save, and then close the blade by clicking the close (X) button at the top right.**

   The Device Compliance — Policies blade is restored.

With that step completed, you now have the ability to manage and monitor your MDM environment for compliance.

Creating a device configuration profile

So far you've enabled MDM for Apple enrollment and configured the device compliance policies for iOS devices. The next step is to configure a device configuration profile for devices managed in MDM.

Device configuration profiles are settings that allow you to standardize the features and functionalities that users in a group can use on their enrolled devices. The standardization could mean that a certain group will have a profile that does not allow them to use their phone's camera or another group with a profile that does not allow them to take screen captures.

To get familiar with the process, navigate to Device Configuration from the left menu in the Device Management portal. In the Device Configuration blade, click Profiles under the Manage group.

Right off the bat, note that two device configuration profiles are already set up for Windows 10 devices, as shown in Figure 15-11.

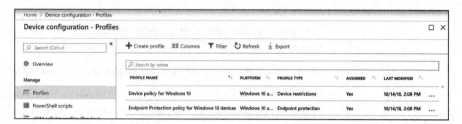

FIGURE 15-11:
Windows device
configuration
profiles.

Remember in Chapter 5 when you went through the Setup wizard and the Windows 10 deployment process? Unbeknownst to you, by clicking a few toggle options, the system automatically took the guesswork out of configuring the basic device policies for Windows 10 devices!

If you click the properties for those profiles, you'll notice a bunch of options that, to a novice, are daunting and downright scary. You can thank the engineers at Microsoft for sparing SMBs the gory task of figuring out which security settings to configure or block.

Back to the task of setting up MDM for iOS devices. Let's create a basic device configuration policy for iOS devices that blocks a user from taking screen captures.

In the Device Configuration blade, do the following:

1. **Click the +Create a Profile button.**

2. **In the Create Profile blade, enter the name and description of the profile.**

   I typed *iOS Device Config* in both fields.

3. **Under Platform, select iOS, and then under Profile Type, select Device Restrictions.**

   The Device Restrictions blade appears.

4. **In the Device Restrictions blade, click the General category.**

   The General blade displays.

5. **In the General blade, next to Screen Capture, select Block, and then click OK.**

   This setting blocks enrolled devices from taking a screen capture of their phone's screen.

6. **In the Device Restrictions blade, click OK.**

7. **In the Create Profile blade, click the Create button.**

   The system saves the settings and the iOS Device Config blade appears.

8. **In the iOS Device Config blade, under the Manage group, click Assignments.**

9. **In the blade that appears on the right, click Select Groups to Include.**

10. **In the Select Groups to Include blade, click the group you want to assign the profile to, and then click the Select button.**

    In this example, I selected the MDM Pilot group. The Select Groups to Include blade closes, and the iOS Device Config — Assignment blade appears.

11. **In the iOS Device Config — Assignments blade, click the Save button.**

12. **After you see a validation that your settings have been saved, click the close (X) button.**

    The Assignments blade closes, and the Device Configuration — Profiles page appears.

Now that you've created and assigned the device configuration profile, a user who enrolls a device to MDM will no longer be able to use the screen capture option on his or her device.

Feel free to do a happy dance because you just completed a task that in the past would have required a steep learning curve and years of experience implementing MDM. I highly encourage exploring the other settings for device configuration to find the right settings for your organization.

Administering an enrolled device

If you did the happy dance as I recommended in the preceding section, just remember that your work is not done. Now you need to make sure you manage and monitor your environment for potential threats. You also need to take actions on enrolled devices depending on the lifecycle stage of the device.

Let's say, for example, that a user lost an enrolled device at the airport and you want to wipe the device. Here's what you need to do:

1. **In the Device Management portal's left navigation, click Devices.**

2. **In the Devices blade, under Manage, click All Devices.**

3. **Select the device from the list.**

    A new blade with more details about the device appears, as shown in Figure 15-12.

FIGURE 15-12:
Managing an
enrolled device.

4. **In the top menu, select the action you want to take on the device. Heed the warnings, follow the guidance, and then click OK.**

5. **When you're finished with your task, close the device's blade by clicking the close (X) button in the top right.**

TIP

I highly recommend exploring all the menu items in the Devices blade to become familiar with the management and monitoring capabilities available in your Microsoft 365 Business subscription. If you have the budget, you can pay for a TeamViewer subscription, a third-party tool that allows IT admins to provide remote assistance to Intune-managed Android or Windows devices.

Walking in the End User's Shoes

Let's face it. Everything that you do as an IT admin is not just about security but also about delighting your end users. After all, the investments you made in Microsoft 365 Business are only as good as the end users adopting it.

Now that you've configured the MDM policies for iOS devices, let's put it into action and see what the experience is like from the end user's perspective.

We start by enrolling an iPhone 7 for MDM in the organization. In this scenario, the iPhone is owned by the employee who wants to enroll his device for MDM. (The installation of Office applications is covered in the next chapter.)

1. The end user goes to the App Store on his or her iPhone and downloads the Company Portal app.

2. After the app is installed, the end user taps the app to run it.

3. The end user taps the Sign In button shown in Figure 15-13.

   The Sign In page appears.

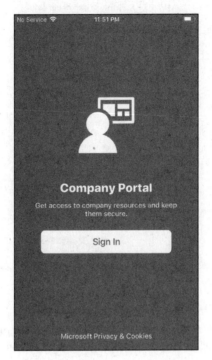

FIGURE 15-13: Company Portal app sign-in screen.

4. The user enters the email address for Microsoft 365 Business, and then taps the Next button.

   The Enter password screen appears.

5. The user enters the password, and then taps the Sign In button.

   The Company Portal checks with Microsoft Intune to see whether the user has been configured for device enrollment. If the user is assigned to a group licensed for MDM, the user is taken to the Set Up [Company Name] Access screen shown in Figure 15-14, left.

   In this example, the company name is Contoso, and I refer to that name for the rest of the instructions.

6. In the Set Up Contoso Access screen, the user taps the Continue button.

   The next screen displays What Can Contoso See? so the user knows what his or her company can never see and may see on the user's iPhone, as shown in Figure 15-14, right.

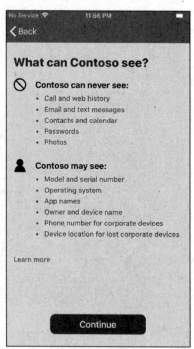

FIGURE 15-14:
Set up Contoso
access screen.

7. The user taps the Continue button.

   The device starts to communicate with Microsoft Intune and prompts the user to allow the website to open the phone's settings to display a configuration profile.

8. The user taps Allow.

   The user is taken to Management Profile in Settings.

9. The user taps the Install button, as shown in Figure 15-15, left.

   The next screen displays information about the mobile device management profile that's about to be installed on the phone. A Remote Management notification pops up on the screen, asking the user to trust the remote management profile (see Figure 15-15, right).

10. The user taps Trust.

    The next screen asks the user to install the profile.

11. The user taps Install.

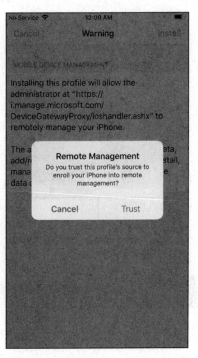

FIGURE 15-15:
Installing the
management
profile.

12. In the Enter Passcode screen, the user enters the PIN code for the device and then clicks the Install button.

    Intune starts to install the device profile created in the previous section ("Creating a device configuration profile").

13. In the Warning screen, the user taps Install.

14. In the Remote Management notification, the user taps Trust again.

15. In the Profile Installed screen, the user taps Done.

16. In the Open This Page in Company Portal? notification, the user taps Open.

    The next screen displays a confirmation that the device is now enrolled in MDM, as shown in Figure 15-16.

17. The user clicks the Done button and is taken to the Company Portal app's home screen.

From the Company Portal's home screen, the user can download apps managed by the company. I cover this topic in the next chapter.

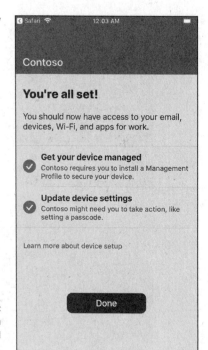

FIGURE 15-16:
The confirmation screen for MDM enrollment.

Chapter **16**

Managing Mobile Applications

What do teen idol Justin Bieber, Japanese astronaut Aki Hoshide, and someone you know have in common? Hint: One regularly takes his shirt off when he does it, the other uses a robotic arm to do it, and another one uses an app to perfect it.

I think the last description there probably gave the answer away, but in case you didn't guess it, all three above have taken selfies! The selfie has become a such global phenomenon that it has spawned an entire industry of selfie cameras, selfie sticks, and selfie apps that ensure your friend's doe-eyed stare and messy hair make her look like she just woke up. And then there's the totally amazing selfie taken by Aki Hoshide that gives you a glimpse of the sun, the Earth, and the infiniteness of outer space from the reflection of the astronaut's spacesuit. It's published by NASA at this link: `https://apod.nasa.gov/apod/ap120918.html`.

It may surprise you, but as an someone managing a small business IT environment, a lot about selfies affect your work. Imagine telling someone whose smartphone has hundreds of selfies that have not been synced to an online storage yet that you have to wipe the device — including the selfies — because you think the device is compromised. Or imagine telling your users that they must enroll their device for management and, when they do, they can no longer use their smartphone's camera app. You'll could end up dealing with a mutiny or worse — a workplace where no one trusts you.

You don't want to find yourself in any of those scenarios, so in this chapter, I show you how to win your users over by implementing mobile application management (MAM) policies with or without mobile device management (MDM). I review the out-of-the-box protection policies automatically enabled when you go through the setup configuration wizard in Chapter 5, and then dive deeper into configuring policies in the Device Management portal. The chapter concludes with a walkthrough of how an end user would experience MAM.

Laying the Groundwork for MAM

It always worries me when I see my adult son assembling furniture without reading the manual. I have this image of a bookshelf he put together coming apart suddenly because he put one screw in the wrong place. Fortunately, I'm quite handy, so when something he's assembled breaks, I can figure out how to fix it.

As an IT admin, you may not have the same luxury as my son has. If you don't configure your MAM policies right and articulate how they work, you'll end up with unhappy end users who have no clue how to fix the mess you created.

Not all MAMs are created equal. A basic understanding of the technology and the different flavors of MAM that you can implement in Microsoft 365 Business is an ideal first step in figuring out which MAM is right for your organization.

Understanding app protection policies

In Chapter 15, I walk you through the process of configuring device compliance policies, so you can manage non-compliant devices enrolled in your organization's MDM. The idea is that you set the rules by which your users should abide by; if they don't, there are consequences.

In mobile application management (MAM), you still must configure policies, but the policies are set at the app level and are appropriately called *app protection policies*. When these policies are implemented, they serve as guardrails to protect end users — and ultimately the company — from data leakage and exposure to breaches.

When end users perform non-compliant actions on the app, the policies will simply not allow the action to happen. For example, suppose you have an app policy that prohibits a user from saving a work document in a cloud storage other than OneDrive for Business. If a user attempts to save a document in Dropbox, the app protection policy will not save the document in Dropbox and the mobile device will display a warning notification, as shown in Figure 16-1.

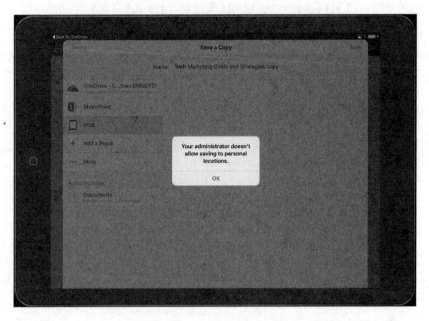

FIGURE 16-1:
MAM policy
prohibiting users
from saving files
in personal
locations.

App protection policies are driven by the identity of the end user, not the device. As such, you can protect company data in managed apps without needing a user to enroll devices into MDM. The policies do not affect the end user's personal data because the policy is applied only to company data.

To illustrate the difference and similarities of MAM and MDM, consider the following scenario. Sarah, the millennial social media manager, has an Android smartphone she uses to access company data and resources. She takes the phone with her wherever she goes so he can work anytime, anywhere. Sarah's Android phone is enrolled in MDM, giving the IT admin the ability to push the latest apps to Sarah's phone without touching the device. On top of MDM, the IT admin also applied MAM policies on Sarah's smartphone so that she won't accidentally cut and paste company data into her personal Twitter account.

At home, Sarah has an old iPad she uses to watch Netflix. When she gets bored watching a movie, she scans through work emails. For this device, the Outlook app running on the iPad is managed through MAM. The iPad does not need to be enrolled in MDM because Sarah doesn't regularly use it for work (and besides, the operating system running on the device is too old to be supported by MDM).

Different ways to do MAM

In Microsoft 365 Business, you're not stuck with just one way of implementing MAM. You can configure app protection policies that can be applied for different scenarios as follows:

>> MAM for devices owned by the company and enrolled in MDM using Microsoft Intune

>> MAM for devices owned by the company and enrolled in MDM using a third-party solution

>> MAM for devices owned by the employee and enrolled in MDM using Microsoft Intune

>> MAM for devices owned by the employee and not enrolled in MDM using Microsoft Intune

In this chapter, we focus only on the scenarios configured in Microsoft Intune, which is included in the Microsoft 365 Business license.

REMEMBER

MAM has no dependency on MDM. You can protect apps on mobile devices even if that mobile device isn't managed. However, implementing MAM on top of MDM has its advantages. As illustrated in Sarah's first scenario in the preceding section, the app protection policies on Sarah's enrolled device give the added protection of preventing her from cutting and pasting content from managed company apps into her personal apps.

Reviewing the Default App Policies

The few mouse clicks you take when you go through the Setup wizard in Chapter 5 to set up Microsoft 365 Business create a few app protection policies in your tenant. Although those policies are created without you even thinking about it, the underlying configuration in Microsoft Intune for those policies is involved. That's the gift Microsoft 365 Business gives you. The solution has given valuable time back to the IT admin by taking the guesswork out of configuring the basic policy settings applicable to SMBs.

Application policy for Window 10

A Microsoft 365 Business license entitles a user to upgrade a Windows 10 Pro device to Windows 10 Business as part of the setup process when connecting the device to Azure Active Directory.

Separately, in setting up the Microsoft 365 tenant, a few device and app policies are created during the Setup wizard process. These policies are captured in Microsoft Intune.

Between Azure Active Directory, which manages the user's identity, and Microsoft Intune, which manages the policies, you end up with a robust set of out-of-the-box policies. Two of those policies are application policies targeted for Windows 10 devices, as shown in the last two policies in Figure 16-2.

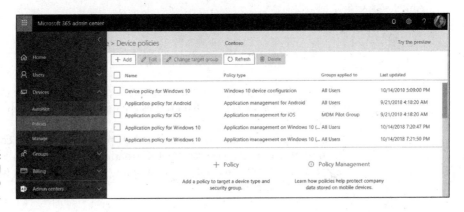

FIGURE 16-2:
Policies created during Setup wizard process.

Although the last two application policies look similar, one is designed for personal devices and the other is designed for company-owned devices. The former will protect company data on personal devices that are not managed in Microsoft Intune. The latter protects data on company-owned devices that are managed in Microsoft Intune.

Both policies have the same settings. In the following, you look at the policy for company-owned devices:

1. **Navigate to** `https://admin.microsoft.com` **and log in with global admin credentials.**

2. **From the left navigation, under Devices, select Policies.**

   The Device policies page appears.

3. **Click the second Application Policy for Windows 10 entry.**

   The Edit policy pane is displayed, as shown in Figure 16-3.

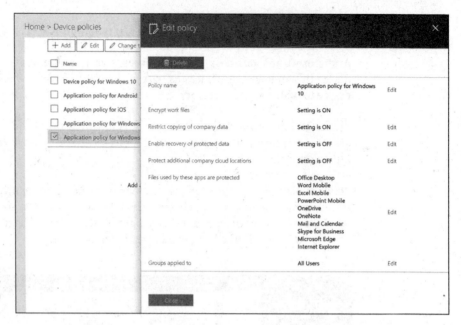

FIGURE 16-3:
Application policy
for Windows 10
settings.

In the Edit Policy pane, note that Restrict Copying of Company Data is set to On. You also see a list of apps in which files created by using the apps are protected.

The technology that distinguishes between personal data and company data on Windows devices is called Windows Information Protection (WIP). With this technology, an IT admin can safely wipe company data from devices without touching an end user's personal data.

Application policy for iOS

The out-of-the-box application policy for iOS in Microsoft 365 Admin Center is an easy way for an IT admin to get started implementing application policies for iOS devices. With this policy, end users do not need to enroll their devices for management. For some employees, this approach gives them a higher degree of confidence that they still control their devices and the personal data on the devices, such as their selfies.

You can view the application policy for iOS in Microsoft 365 Admin Center. In the left menu, under the Devices Group, click Policies to display the screen shown in Figure 16-4.

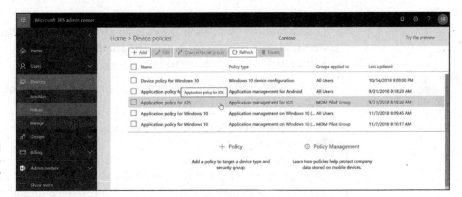

FIGURE 16-4:
Accessing the
application policy
for iOS.

Clicking Application Management for iOS opens the Edit policy pane, which displays the settings that you can change to suit your needs. In Figure 16-5, for Groups Applied To, I edited the group from All Users to MDM Pilot Group because I want to test the policy first before I roll it out to all the users.

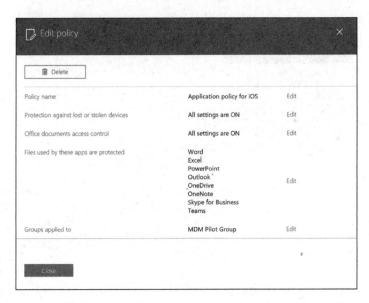

FIGURE 16-5:
Editing the
application policy
for iOS.

Let's test this policy on an iPhone 7 to see what the end user experiences:

1. **From the Edit policy pane (refer to Figure 16-5), click Edit next to Office Documents Access Control.**

2. **Click Manage How Users Access Office Files on Mobile Devices to expand the policy and view the settings.**

3. **Ensure that the Don't Allow Users to Copy Content from Office Apps into Personal Apps is set to On, and then click the Cancel button to retain the setting.**

   If the toggle switch is set to Off, set it to On and then click the Save button to save your settings.

4. **Back in the Edit policy pane, click the Close button to return to the Device Policies page.**

Let's say I downloaded the Outlook app from the App Store to an iPhone 7. I then set up my company email in Outlook following the setup instructions when I run the app. After my work email is configured in Outlook, I see an email that seems interesting, and I want to cut and paste the contents of that email into my Notes app. I start selecting the text in the email, as shown in Figure 16-6, left. I tap the Copy button.

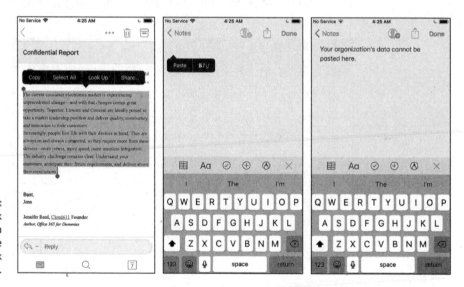

FIGURE 16-6: Copying a block of text from an email in the Outlook mobile app.

I then run the Notes app on my iPhone and compose a new note. I tap inside the new note and the Paste menu appears, as shown in Figure 16-6, center.

When I tap the Paste button, the app protection policy is applied, and instead of the copied text, I see a message saying "Your organization data cannot be pasted here," as shown in Figure 16-6, right.

An application policy for Android is also preconfigured in the Device Policies page of Microsoft 365 Admin Center. The settings are the same as the application policies for iOS. I encourage you to explore the settings and test the functionalities to find the configuration that meets your organization's needs.

Going Beyond the Basics

In Chapter 15, you went through the process of configuring MDM policies and walked through enrolling an iPhone 7 through the Company Portal app. Picking up from where you left off at the end of that chapter, you'll add the Microsoft Excel app to the Company Portal app.

Adding an app to the Company Portal app

After you finish with the following steps, the Excel app will be available as a managed app. Managed apps are easy for end users to install, and IT admins can manage the app from Intune or Microsoft Admin Center.

To add the Excel app to the Company Portal app, follow these steps:

1. **Navigate to** `https://devicemanagement.microsoft.com` **and log in with your global admin credentials.**

2. **In the left menu, click Client Apps.**

3. **In the Client Apps blade, under the Manage group, click Apps (see Figure 16-7).**

   Note that I have already added a few apps in the Company Portal app.

FIGURE 16-7:
Displaying the
Client Apps blade.

4. **Click the + Add button in the top navigation.**

5. **In the Add App blade, click the box under App Type, and select iOS.**

6. **Below Search the App Store, click Select App.**

7. **In the Search the App Store blade's search box, enter** Excel **and press Enter.**

8. **In the search results, click the Microsoft Excel icon (see Figure 16-8), and then click the Select button at the bottom.**

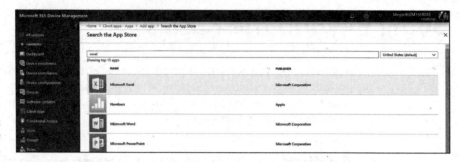

FIGURE 16-8:
Adding the
Excel app.

9. **Back in the Add App blade, click the Add button at the bottom.**

   The system saves the changes and closes the Add App blade.

10. **In the Microsoft Excel blade that appears, under the Manage group, click Assignments, and then click the Add Group button on the right.**

11. **In the Add Group blade, under Assignment Type, click Select Assignment Type, and then select Available with or without Enrollment.**

12. **Click Included Groups.**

13. **In the Assign blade that appears, select Yes next to Make This App Available to All Users, Regardless of Whether Their Devices Are Enrolled in Intune.**

14. **Under Selected groups, click Select Groups to Include, select the appropriate group from the Select Groups blade, and then click the Select button.**

15. **Back in the Assign blade, click the OK button.**

16. **Back in the Add group blade, click the OK button.**

17. **Back in the Microsoft Excel — Assignments blade, click the Save button.**

   The system saves the changes.

18. **Click Close (X) to go back to the Client Apps blade.**

   Microsoft Excel appears in the list of apps that will be pushed to the Company Portal app all for iOS devices.

Downloading the Excel app from the Company Portal app

Now that the Excel app has been configured to be available in the Company Portal app for iOS devices, I'll walk you through the end user's experience when access-ing the Excel app:

1. From the same iOS device enrolled in MDM in Chapter 15, the user navigates to the Company Portal app.

   In the Home screen, the user sees the newly added Excel app, as shown in Figure 16-9, left.

2. The user taps the Excel app icon, and then taps the Install button in the next screen.

   The user's smartphone communicates with Intune, and Intune sends a notification to the phone about the app installation process and prompts the user to tap the Install button, as shown in Figure 16-9, right.

3. The user taps the Install button.

   The Company Portal app starts downloading the Excel app to the user's device.

4. After the app has finished downloading, the user simply taps the Excel icon on the screen.

   The app runs without prompting the user to enter credentials.

From this point on, the same application policies you tested in the preceding section will apply to Excel data.

Chapter **17**

Browsing with the Edge Mobile App

I n the early 1800s, a young child was playing in his father's workshop with an awl, a tool that punches holes in leather. While pressing the tool down hard on a piece of leather, the three-year-old somehow struck his eyes with the tool. This accident led to an eye infection and, ultimately, complete blindness in both eyes by the time he was five years old.

It's fair to feel sorry for this young child and to assume that for the rest of his life, his disability would prevent him from achieving great things. But such is not the case for Louis Braille. Through his determination, creativity, intelligence, and the love and support of his parents, Braille went on to become a professor, a musician, and most importantly, the inventor of a system that, more than 200 years later, is still widely used today: braille.

Braille is a system for reading and writing for people who are blind or visually impaired. Although it has been adapted to many languages around the world, the system has remained largely unchanged from the version Louis Braille developed at the age of fifteen.

I am sharing this story not to tout the accessibility capabilities of the Edge browser but rather to encourage you, the IT admin, to adapt a growth mindset, the same mindset Louis Braille had.

Carol Dweck, a pioneer researcher in the field of motivation, describes growth mindset as "the belief that your abilities can grow with effort and persistence, that goals are opportunities to grow, and the purpose of what you do every day is to improve."

That is exactly the mindset you need when you roll out the Edge mobile app to your organization because you will undoubtedly be met with pushback, skepticism, and criticism. I hope no one will send you a link to a Mashable article entitled "Microsoft has a new mobile browser for you to download and probably never use" when people learn that you'll be pushing the Edge mobile app as a managed browser as part of your organization's mobility strategy.

In this chapter, I explain the benefit of deploying the Edge mobile app from the point of view of the two groups of people you answer to: management and end users. I walk you through the process of configuring the Edge app for MAM. And together, we experience the mobile browser as an end user. I hope the knowledge you glean from this chapter will allow you, just like Louis Braille, to triumph over objections, pessimism, and even ridicule.

Driving Users to (the) Edge Is Good

Let's face it: Mashable, in the article just mentioned, has a point. (You can find the article here: https://mashable.com/2017/11/30/microsoft-edge-mobile-app-ios-android/#MQ7QBTzvjOqN.) Although the numbers have changed a bit from when the article was published in November 2017, Google Chrome still reigns as the king of browsers, with a 76 percent market share as of October 2018, according to Trendcounter (www.trendcounter.com/research/).

You might ruffle some feathers when you go down the path of deploying the Edge app. You might even drive your end users to the edge (pun intended). This section provides you with information to justify the smart move to implementing the Edge app as a managed mobile browser.

Value for the organization

Your Microsoft 365 Business subscription already give you the capabilities for MAM protection and conditional access at no additional cost. The combination of those two capabilities enables you to further enhance your organization's security posture by managing the browser on your mobile devices. The Edge mobile browser for iOS and Android can be easily integrated into your mobile strategy with or without enrollment.

When the Edge app is deployed as a managed browser, you enable the same security policies available in other apps, thus preventing cutting, copying, and pasting to personal apps, blocking screen captures, and making sure company links are opened using only the managed apps and browser.

Productive employees give companies a competitive edge. As a managed browser, the Edge app enables information worker to access company information in a streamlined process with a single sign-on. An employee can even switch from company use to personal use seamlessly within the same browser app!

In terms of manageability, you can make it so that all end users in the organization have the same experience with the Edge mobile browser. You can program the Favorites links, so they show up the same for everyone. Users won't be able to delete or edit the Favorites you programmed. You can even prevent users from using the browser to access certain sites by blocking them.

Between driving productivity and enhancing security, rolling out Edge as a managed browser in your organization has a lot of positives. Unless your management team's goal is to run the business into the ground, you have a good chance of convincing your leaders of the value proposition of the Edge app.

Value for the end user

Imagine a fast and secure browser that has a split personality, allowing you to use it both for personal and work purposes. Now imagine that browser with a built-in camera that allows you to take pictures that then trigger an artificial intelligence to find related images of the picture you just took. Let's take this scenario even further and imagine not having to install yet another app for scanning QR and bar codes because you already have that capability built-in in your browser.

Imagine no more because all those functionalities are now available in the Edge mobile app, which you can roll out without forcing end users to give up their preferred smartphones and mobile devices. And while your end users are happily switching between their personal account and work account as they browse the web, you can put controls in place to prevent data leakage and security breaches.

Although the mobile version of Edge does not enjoy 100 percent parity with its desktop version, it is chockful of productivity features that not only help get work done faster but can also be fun! Confession time. I used a two-minute downtime at work to take a photo of my sick indoor lemon tree to find out what was wrong with it. According to my Edge app, I was overfertilizing the poor plant! I managed to find a site with tips on how to save the plant, which I then bookmarked using my personal Microsoft account rather than mixing the bookmark with my work account. That way, if my IT admin should ever decide to wipe my device or remove the browser, I will still have that link in my personal account.

How would you like instant results? Turns out, Edge comes with that too! This morning, I was in a hurry to get ready for work and wanted to know the weather. By simply typing the word *weather*, Edge immediately gave me the weather icon and the current temperature. I wasn't sure if the data was relevant to my location, so I followed the link. Sure enough, the weather forecast was indeed for my area, as shown in Figure 17-1. Thank you, artificial intelligence!

FIGURE 17-1:
Instant search results in the Edge mobile app.

These are just some of the features you'll find in the Edge app for iOS and Android devices. Microsoft continues to invest heavily in the technology, so there are plenty of features to get your end users excited and drive them to the Edge of their seats.

Deploying Edge as Managed App

Data is today's currency. It is also a hackers' ticket to big money. One of the easiest ways for a hacker to get to your data is through a browser. Hacking browsers has become so mainstream that you can buy how-to guides on the subject.

As an IT admin, it's your responsibility to keep the hackers as far away as possible from your company data. You should start by implementing a managed mobile browser in your organization. In this section, I walk you through the steps in implementing Edge as a managed app.

Creating the Edge app configuration policy

When you add the Edge mobile app as a managed app in Microsoft Intune, you can configure standardized policies for your users. For example, you can set bookmarks in the Edge app in addition to the default MyApps bookmarks generated by Azure Active Directory.

End users can't delete bookmarks that the IT admin has configured in the Edge mobile app. However, they can add their own bookmarks.

Configuring company bookmarks for the Edge mobile app starts with creating an app configuration policy. Here's how:

1. **Navigate to** `https://devicemanagement.microsoft.com` **and log in with global admin credentials.**

2. **In the left navigation, click Client Apps.**

3. **In the Client Apps blade, click App Configuration Policies.**

4. **Click the +Add button.**

   The Add Configuration Policy blade appears.

5. **In the Add Configuration Policy blade, enter the name of the policy and a description. Then, under Device Enrollment Type, select Managed Apps.**

   Additional configuration options appear below Managed Apps, as shown in Figure 17-2.

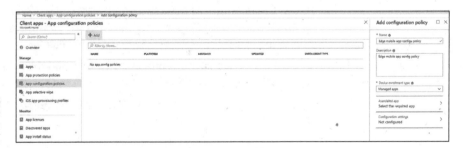

FIGURE 17-2:
Adding the Edge app configuration policy.

6. Under Associated App, click Select the Required App.

7. In the Targeted Apps list, select the box to the left of the Edge app for both Android and iOS (see Figure 17-3), and then click the OK button.

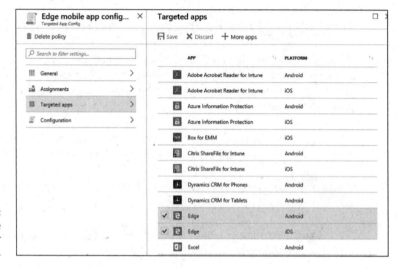

FIGURE 17-3:
Selecting the
Edge app for
Android and iOS.

8. Back in the Add Configuration Policy blade, under Configuration Settings, click Not Configured.

The Configuration blade appears, so you can add key-value pairs.

9. Add two bookmarks, https://bing.com and https://cloud611.com:, by entering the following key-value pair in the blank boxes:

Name: com.microsoft.intune.mam.managedbrowser.bookmarks

Value: Bing|https://www.bing.com||Cloud611|https://cloud611.com

Note that the title and the URL are separated by a pipe character (|) and that the two URLs are separated by double pipe characters (||). The pipe character is usually the uppercase key above the backslash, as shown in Figure 17-4. (The pipe/backslash key is below the Backspace key in the figure.)

10. Click the Save button in the Configuration blade, and then close the Edge Mobile App Config Policy blade by clicking the close (X) button.

The Client Apps — App Configuration Policies blade is restored.

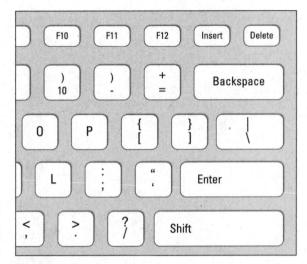

FIGURE 17-4:
Finding the pipe
character on your
keyboard.

Assigning the Edge app configuration policy

Now that an app policy is created, the next step is to assign the policy to users or groups. Using the policy created from the preceding section, let's assign the Edge mobile app config policy:

1. **In the Client Apps — App Configuration Policies blade, click Edge Mobile App Config Policy.**

2. **In the Edge Mobile App Config Policy blade, click Assignments.**

3. **In the Assignments blade, under the Include tab, click Select Groups to Include.**

4. **In the Select Groups to Include blade, select the appropriate group and then click the Select button.**

    In the example, I am selecting MDM Pilot Group, as shown in Figure 17-5. The Assignments blade's Include tab will displays the group you selected.

5. **Click the close (X) button to close the Assignments blade, and then click the close button again to close the Edge Mobile App Config Policy blade.**

You have now set up the Edge mobile app configuration policy.

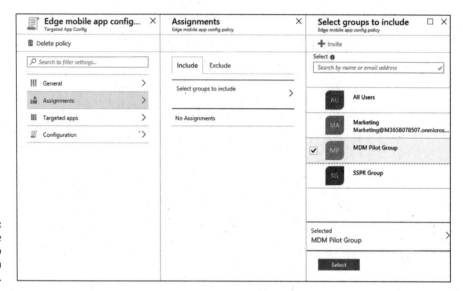

FIGURE 17-5:
Assigning the
Edge mobile app
config policy to a
group.

Adding the Edge app to the Company Portal app

In Chapter 16, you went beyond the basics by adding an app to the Company Portal app to make it easy for end users who enrolled their device for MDM to download and configure apps on their devices. You can follow the same steps to add the Edge mobile app to the Company Portal app.

In this example, I added the Edge mobile app for iOS devices, required iOS 8.0 as the minimum operating system, made the application device type applicable for iPad, iPhone, and iPod, set the category for the app under Productivity, and selected the Yes button to display the app as a featured app in the Company Portal app. Figure 17-6 shows these settings.

I want to assign this app to my MDM Pilot Group and make it available with or without enrollment. I follow the instructions in Chapter 16 for assigning an app to a user or group. Figure 17-7 displays the setting I configured.

Installing the Edge mobile app

Now that you've configured the policies for standardizing bookmarks in the Edge app, let's experience the app from the end user's point of view.

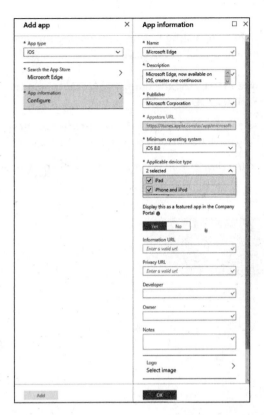

FIGURE 17-6:
Settings for the Edge mobile app.

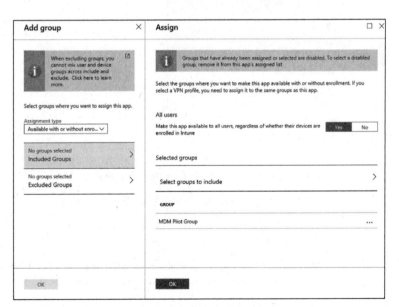

FIGURE 17-7:
Assigning the policy to a group.

To test the Edge mobile app configuration policy using the device you enrolled in Chapter 16, I performed the following tasks:

1. **From my iPhone 7 Plus, I tap the Company Portal app and sign in with my Microsoft 365 credentials.**

2. **Because it takes about 5-10 minutes for the policies to show up on my device, I sync my device to Intune to pull down the latest policies.**

   To do that, I tap the Devices icon at the bottom of the screen, as shown in Figure 17-8.

3. **In the list of devices, I tap Jennifer's iPhone.**

4. **In the Jennifer's iPhone screen, I tap Check Settings.**

   The phone communicates with Microsoft Intune and pulls down the latest policies.

5. **After the device has finished checking the settings, I tap the Apps icon at the bottom of the screen, and then I tap the View button.**

   The Edge app is now in my list of apps.

6. **I tap the Edge app, and then tap the Install button.**

7. **In the App Installation notification screen (see Figure 17-9), I tap Install.**

FIGURE 17-9:
Installing the
Edge mobile app.

Testing the Edge mobile app policy

Depending on your Internet connection, downloading and installing the Edge mobile app can take 3 to 5 minutes. After the app has finished installing, I can now run the app and test the policy:

1. **I tap the Edge app.**

   Because my device is enrolled in MDM, the device automatically recognizes my credentials in the sign-in screen, as shown in Figure 17-10.

2. **In the See Browsing History across Devices screen I tap my login name and click Yes.**

3. **In the warning screen, I tap Allow.**

   The warning reads *Edge would like to send you notifications.*

4. **In the next warning screen, I tap OK.**

The warning reads *Your organization is now protecting its data in this app. You need to restart the app to continue.* The Edge app closes after I tap OK.

5. **I tap the Edge app again to run the app.**

6. **I tap the Favorites icon (star) in the top-right corner, as shown in Figure 17-11, left).**

The screen displays the Favorites list for my company, Contoso.

7. **I tap Contoso to display to default apps configured by my IT admin, as shown in Figure 17-11, right.**

I see Bing and Cloud611 in addition to MyApps.

8. **I tap < Favorites in the top-left corner to return to the Favorites list.**

9. **In the Favorites list, I tap Edit at the bottom-right corner, and then I tap the Contoso folder.**

The screen displays a *Can't Edit* notification, as shown in Figure 17-12, because end users can't edit company bookmarks that the IT admin has set.

10. **I tap Close.**

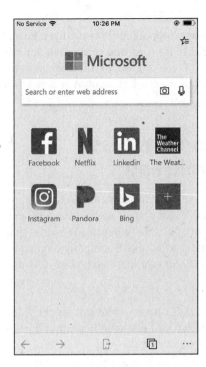

FIGURE 17-11:
Edge app home
page (left) and
Favorites list
(right).

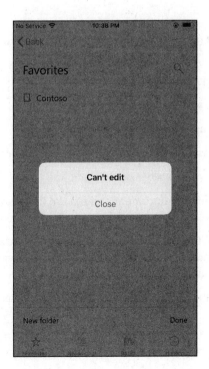

FIGURE 17-12:
Favorites list can't
be edited by the
end user per the
app config policy.

Managed apps like the Edge app support multi-identities, so an end user can use the same Edge mobile app for more than one credential. For example, if I have a personal Microsoft account, I can log in to that account in addition to my Microsoft 365 account. Depending on what account is active, I may see different bookmarks.

Testing conditional access in the Edge mobile app

One of the benefits of deploying the Edge app as a managed app is the added layer of security you get from conditional access. Azure Active Directory and Microsoft Intune make conditional access possible. What this means is that an IT admin can set conditions for how an end user accesses company data and resources. Conditions may be in the form of MFA or requiring that a device is managed or enrolled in Azure Active Directory.

Let's see if a user really can set up two identities in the Edge app: a personal account and a work account. You will test whether cut and paste is allowed from the work account to the personal account.

To test conditional access:

1. **I tap my work account (MeganB@M365. . .nMicrosoft.com) to activate my work account.**

2. **I tap the Favorites icon in the top right.**

3. **I tap My Organization, and then I tap MyApps.**

4. **In the list of company apps I have access to, I tap Word.**

5. **In the list of documents in the Recent tab, I tap Contoso Electronic Sales.**

   The document opens in Word Online.

6. **I select a paragraph from the document and tap the Copy button, as shown in Figure 17-13.**

7. **I tap the profile icon in the top left of the screen to display the accounts running on the app, and then I tap my personal account,** MeganB@M365. onMicrosoft.com, **as shown in Figure 17-14.**

   The Edge app switches the active account running on the browser.

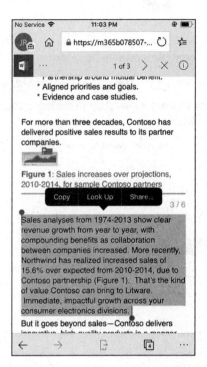

FIGURE 17-13:
Copying a paragraph from Word Online in the Edge app.

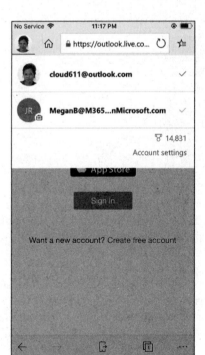

FIGURE 17-14:
Multiple identities set up in the Edge app.

8. With my personal account active, I type outlook.com in the URL bar, and then I sign in to my personal Outlook.com account.

9. In Outlook, I compose a new email, and tap inside the body of the email.

10. I tap the Paste button to paste the paragraph I copied in Step 6, and am told that copy/paste is not allowed.

As shown in Figure 17-15, the screen displays *Your organization's data cannot be pasted here.*

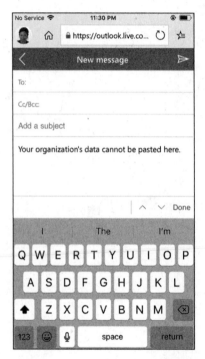

So far, you've seen the value of deploying the Edge mobile app as a managed app in the Company Portal app. There are other controls you can configure to manage the mobile apps in your environment in Intune. You've also seen that Edge, even with the initial set of features available today, can enhance your security posture.

When you make the move to deploy the Edge app for your company, you'll be prepared to address any concerns and reservations your end users may raise. And if they give you a hard time, keep at it and find someone in your organization who can champion your cause. With a growth mindset, you're bound to find someone who will see the value of what you're trying to achieve.

6

Administering the Service

IN THIS PART . . .

Get to know the Microsoft 365 Admin Center and the specialist workspaces in the portal.

Stay on top of your Microsoft 365 services with reports and alerts.

Understand how teamwork happens across the different services in Microsoft 365.

Manage your SharePoint Online environment from a one-stop-shop portal.

Chapter **18**

Working in Microsoft 365 Admin Center

n 500 BC, the Greek philosopher Heraclitus said, "Change is the only constant in life." More than 2,500 years later, that observation could not be more spot on, especially when it comes to cloud computing.

Ever-changing cloud technology has afforded small businesses the capability to use the same enterprise-class tools that Fortune 500 companies use through a software-as-a-service (SaaS) model. In this model, it's easy to scale software licenses up or down, enabling SMBs to pay for only the services they need at any given time, like using electricity. There is no need to invest in expensive infrastructure up front or hire a full staff of skilled IT professionals to manage the IT environment.

Aside from the reduced cost, SaaS users get to enjoy the improvements to the service at a faster clip than before, often at no additional cost. Such is the case for Microsoft 365 Business and other SaaS solutions from Microsoft. If you visit the Microsoft 365 Roadmap web page at www.microsoft.com/en-us/microsoft-365/roadmap, you'll find that since the service was announced in the middle of 2017, more than 600 updates have been announced, with more than half already launched. So, to paraphrase Heraclitus, "The only constant thing in Microsoft 365 Business is change."

In this chapter, you get insight into the changes being rolled out in Microsoft 365 Admin Center that help IT admins like you simplify the management of your tenant. You learn how to customize the Admin Center landing page to fit your needs so you can quickly act on tasks that matter most to you. While changes are constantly being rolled out to your tenant, you can stay on top of administering your services and continue to provide value to your organization.

Modernizing IT Management

Microsoft 365 Business is the convergence of three unique but integrated products: Office 365, Enterprise Mobility + Security, and Windows 10. Although this convergence is a good thing, having three complex products rolled into one presents challenges. You need to log into many portals to Managing your environment and administering the different services in Microsoft 365 Business requires 23 portals, each with its own look and feel.

For example, suppose you're the IT admin for a construction firm. In the middle of dealing with ten support tickets, you get a call from your project manager, who is working onsite, to say he's lost his phone. You drop everything you're doing and log into `https://portal.office365.com` to reset the user's password. Then you log into `https://portal.azure.com` to find the user's device and wipe it. Although the tasks themselves are not that difficult, completing them is overly complicated.

This scenario is one of the reasons why the Microsoft 365 Admin Center experience has been updated. As of October 2018, admins who are in the Targeted Release ring may review the new Admin Center experience (the current interface is called the classic Admin Center experience). The first set of features rolled out in the Preview are focused on the most common tasks IT admins perform, based on telemetry data gathered from the millions of Office 365 and Microsoft 365 tenants around the world. All the features in Preview are slated to be rolled out for general availability in the middle of 2019.

Experiencing the new Admin Center

If you're still logging into `https://portal.office365.com` to administer your tenant, now is a good time to update your link and go directly to `https://admin.microsoft.com`. In previous chapters, I started training you to go the new link whenever there are instructions requiring access to Admin Center.

If you're reading this book before the general availability of the new admin experience, I highly recommend clicking the Try the Preview button. If you don't see the button at the top right of the page, it means you're not in the Targeted Release ring.

Assuming you're still viewing Microsoft 365 Admin Center in the classic experience, follow these steps to participate in the Targeted Release ring:

1. **While logged in to Microsoft 365 Admin Center, click your company name below the navigation bar.**

2. **In the Organization profile page, click the Edit button next to Release Preferences, as shown in Figure 18-1.**

   The Release Preferences window appears.

FIGURE 18-1: Editing the Release preferences.

3. **Select either Targeted Release for Everyone or Targeted Release for Selected Users, and then click the Next button.**

4. **If you select Targeted Release for Selected Users, you can add people by following these steps:**

   a. *Click Next.*

   b. *In the Release Preferences window, click Yes.*

   c. *Click the Add people button.*

   d. *Tick the boxes to the left of the users you want to add and then click the Save button.*

   e. *Click the Close button, and then click the Close button again to go back to the Organization Profile page.*

5. **Click the Close button to save your changes.**

When Preview is enabled, you immediately see the new, streamlined look and feel. Don't be fooled by appearances. Whether you're viewing the new experience as a Preview or the default view when it becomes generally available, Microsoft 365 Admin Center is designed to make your life as an IT admin more efficient. You can customize it to fit your role in the organization and act on smart recommendations based on intelligent services running under the hood. Best of all, you have one place to administer the services in your subscription versus going to different portals!

You heard that right. Instead of 23 different portals, you can now log into Microsoft 365 Admin Center and do a variety of tasks in Admin Center or through seven specialist workspaces that can be accessed from Admin Center. In these workspaces, you do granular configurations, view detailed reports, and take advanced actions. The specialist workspaces are as follows:

>> SharePoint

>> Teams & Skype

>> Exchange

>> Security

>> Compliance

>> Device Management

>> Azure Active Directory (AAD)

Figure 18-2 is a great illustration of the consolidation of the portals into a single portal with specialist workspaces, courtesy of the marketing folks at Microsoft from the Ignite 2018 conference.

Personalizing the experience

Microsoft 365 Admin Center was designed to simplify your tasks as an IT admin. In a small-business scenario, an IT admin might perform most if not all admin roles. For larger companies, the different aspects of the administration might fall under different IT roles. For example, you might have an IT staff who is the global admin, another staff whose responsibility is related to only security and compliance, another IT staff who just administers SharePoint, and so on.

Each IT staff obviously has different tasks and different work styles. As a result, you want to empower them to customize Admin Center to make it their own. In the new Admin Center experience, you can do just that. Here's how.

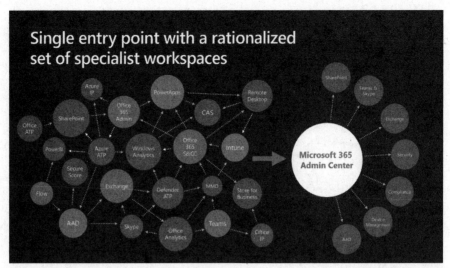

Microsoft Ignite 2018 Presentation

FIGURE 18-2:
Microsoft 365
Admin Center
specialist
workspaces.

From Microsoft 365 Admin Center, note that the left navigation has fewer menu items, as shown in Figure 18-3. Don't panic — you can still access the other navigation links if you click Show More. You can add or remove items that appear in the left navigation pane by clicking Edit. Any changes you make to the left navigation apply only to you.

FIGURE 18-3:
Microsoft 365
Admin Center in
Preview mode.

In the right pane, a few cards are grouped under the Essentials group. Note that when the new experience is available generally, you may see more cards than shown in Figure 18-3.

ARE YOU COVETING MY CUSTOMIZED NAVBAR?

You may have noticed in Figure 18-3 that my navigation bar (navbar) looks a little different than the default navbar in Microsoft 365 Admin Center. I've customized this area in Admin Center to display my company logo which, when clicked, takes a user to my company website. The image and color scheme are also different, although you may not see that in the black-and-white version of the image in the printed book.

To customize the navbar, you unfortunately have to go back to the Classic mode of Admin Center, which means turning off Preview mode. Then click your company name at the top right, below the navbar. Click the Edit button next to Manage Custom Themes for Your Organization, and make your customizations. When you're finished, don't forget to turn Preview mode back on!

The minimalist look and feel in Admin Center is designed to make the IT admin focus on important tasks. Smart defaults include cards that know what matters to you based on your role. The idea is not to overwhelm an admin with all the cards available when some of those cards don't apply. For example, if your role is to manage security and compliance, the Billing card may not be important to you.

If you think you're missing a card on your home page, click the + Add Card button in the top right to display all the cards you can drag to your home page.

One-Stop-Shop User Management

I was traveling out of the country recently when I got a call from a customer's IT admin. He sounded frantic because they had just fired an employee and were worried that the employee's son has the technical abilities to hack their system. The IT admin had already removed the license for the user but was confused about where to go to remove the company data from the personal device the employee owned.

Had this event happened today, and the IT admin had Preview mode turned on, I doubt he would be calling me. That's because in the new Admin Center experience, user management is greatly simplified with a one-stop-shop approach. The user interface is intuitive enough that I doubt I would have had to take a quick break from shopping to deal with a long-distance support call.

Interacting with the Users List

According to telemetry data from Microsoft, 75 percent of admin actions are repetitive. From resetting passwords to adding and removing licenses, these seemingly small but repetitive tasks add up to inefficiencies.

In the new and improved experience, IT admins can manage their users more effectively by taking cues from integrated insights served up by the system. Filtering capabilities have been improved so it's easy to find one user among hundreds. Inline actions are available, so you don't have to jump from one page to another to complete a task.

The new Active Users list, shown in Figure 18-4, displays three columns by default: Display Name, Username, and Licenses. Clicking Choose Columns opens a window that allows you to choose other columns to display, such as Sign-In Status and Usage Location.

FIGURE 18-4: Active Users list in the new admin experience.

At the top of the list, below the Active Users label, note the commands you can apply to a selected user or multiple users. Resetting a user's password, for instance, has gone from two clicks in the old experience to one click in the new experience.

TIP

In addition, when you click the three vertical dots next to the user's name, a menu of quick actions appears, as shown on Figure 18-5.

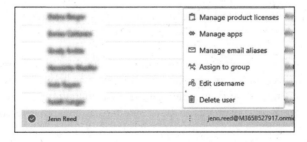

FIGURE 18-5: Quick actions you can perform on an end user.

Managing users

Remember the real-life scenario I mentioned in the introduction to this section, about the IT admin who had to deal with an employee who was fired? In the new experience he would select the user in the Active Users list to display the User Details page.

The User Details page, shown in Figure 18-6, is the one-stop-shop approach for user management.

FIGURE 18-6:
User details page.

At the top, below the username, are icons representing quick actions to reset the password, edit the sign-in status, and delete the user.

The tabs in the User Detail page are where the simplification happens. You can not only view information about the account but also manage the user's devices, licenses, apps, mail, and OneDrive. In the past, managing a user's device and the apps assigned to a user would have required a different portal and a tedious process.

Clicking the Devices tab displays all the devices the user is enrolled in — you can even see whether or not a device is compliant. From the same tab, you can either remove company data from the device or reset it to factoring settings (see Figure 18-7).

FIGURE 18-7:
Managing devices from the user details page.

Are you wondering about the difference between the Licenses and Apps tab and the User Details page? Think about it this way: To use the service, each user needs to be assigned a license. One user may have more than one type of license. For example, your marketing manager may have a license for Microsoft 365 Business and a license for the standalone higher-tier Microsoft Stream Plan 2 service. You can see which licenses are assigned to a user in the Licenses tab.

Each license comes with apps, which are shown in the Apps tab. If you need to remove an app for a user but don't necessarily want to remove the license, you can do so in the Apps tab.

The Mail and OneDrive tabs in the User Details page are carried over from the previous Admin Center experience but with additional commands. In the OneDrive tab, for example, you get a cool visual of the user's storage usage, as shown in Figure 18-8.

These and other improvements to Admin Center deliver on the promise of simplified IT management to drive efficiency. Remember, though, that as a SaaS application, Microsoft 365 will continue to evolve and be updated. The images you see in this chapter may be a little different by the time you provision your tenant. When that happens, just know that the changes were made to make your life as an IT admin even more productive.

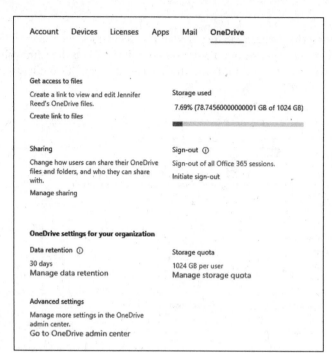

FIGURE 18-8:
The user's
storage usage is
listed on the
OneDrive tab.

Chapter **19**

Creating Reports and Alerts

I magine being the CEO of a thriving small business with a lot of goodwill from your customers and industry contacts. Now imagine that, unbeknownst to you, for three months you've been sending your customers and industry contacts emails that contain sensitive and maybe even damaging information. During these three months, you've been in meetings with some of these people and have wondered why some of them were giving you odd looks.

Then one day, you get a bounced email notification for an email you purportedly sent to a contact, the contents of which are cringeworthy. At that moment, you realize that your email has been hacked! At the next moment, you realize that your IT admin will be let go or, if he's lucky, will be spending the next few weeks — including weekends — deconstructing what happened and coming up with a plan to make sure it doesn't happen again.

Unfortunately, this scenario is based on a true story and is not rare. Although there is no guarantee that your organization will never be a hacking target, fortunately you can take preventative measures to minimize your risk. Microsoft 365 Business offers built-in reporting and alerting features to help you manage your exposure to cyberattacks.

In this chapter, you explore built-in reports and roll up your sleeves to create a custom report. You review the default alerts and configure a new one, so you can stay on top of potential breaches. You also enable audit logging, so you can start recording user and admin activities in your environment.

In the true story I shared above, the IT admin was lucky. The CEO didn't fire him. Moreover, the unfortunate event made the CEO realize that the IT admin had too much on his plate to give security the right focus. As a result, the CEO provided the budget for an additional staff member to help with the workload. We should all be as lucky as this IT admin!

Keeping Apprised with Reports

The best way to stay secure in today's threat landscape is to assume that your company will be breached. With that mindset, not only are you focused on protecting your environment, but you also have a response plan ready if your environment does get compromised. With the help of advanced technologies such as machine learning and artificial intelligence, you can stay a step ahead of bad actors who are looking for opportunities to exploit and cause trouble.

The built-in reports and alerts feature in Microsoft 365 is a great way to get started with the "assume a breach" mindset. You typically set up these reports and alerts in Security Admin Center.

The topics covered in this chapter are found in Microsoft 365 Security & Compliance Admin Center. There are plans to break out this admin center in the second half of 2019 into two separate specialist workspaces: Security Admin Center (https://security.microsoft.com) and Compliance Admin Center (https://compliance.microsoft.com). If you're reading this book after these two workspaces have been made generally available, most likely you'll find the reports and alerts in Security Admin Center.

Usage Reports in Microsoft 365 Admin Center

In Microsoft 365 Admin Center, you can access a page that consolidates the usage reports for Exchange, Microsoft Teams, Office 365, OneDrive, SharePoint, Skype for Business, and Yammer. Simply click the Reports menu in the left navigation, and then select Usage.

These usage reports give you a quick visual to help detect something awry in your environment. Figure 19-1 shows a graph of the usage across the various workloads in your tenant, enabling you to see usage at a glance and drill down on spikes if you think they're abnormal.

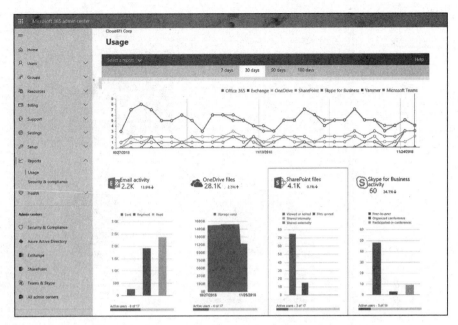

FIGURE 19-1:
Usage report
page in
Microsoft 365
Admin Center.

If you want to get fancy, you can further visualize your usage data in Power BI, a business analytics service from Microsoft that is free with basic features. To visualize your usage data in Power BI, click the Go to Power BI button below the Microsoft 365 usage analytics card on the Usage report page.

You will be guided through the process of enabling the connection to Power BI. After a few hours, the data will be available in Power BI. At that point, click the Go to Power BI button to visualize and interact with your data, as shown in Figure 19-2.

Reviewing the Reports in Security Admin Center

Several reports in Security Admin Center go beyond the usage reports you find in Microsoft 365 Admin Center. You access Security Admin Center from the Admin Centers list in the left navigation in Microsoft 365 Admin Center or directly at `https://security.microsoft.com`.

The Reports dashboard, shown in Figure 19-3, gives you an at-a-glance view of your environment's threat protection status, the movement of data in and out of your organization, and even insights and recommendations to secure your environment.

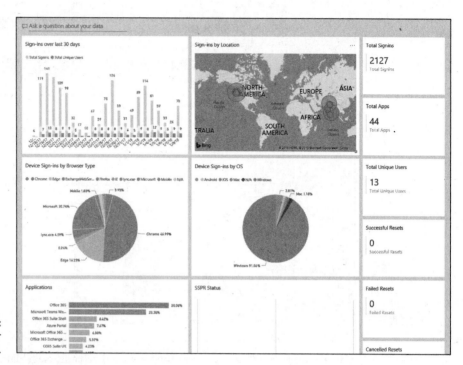

FIGURE 19-2:
Visualizing user data in Power BI.

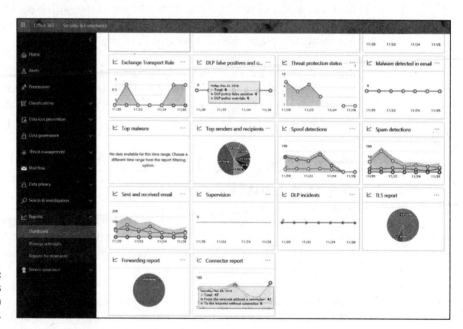

FIGURE 19-3:
The Reports dashboard in Security Center.

The user interface is due for a facelift in mid-2019 to align with the updates being rolled out in Microsoft 365 Admin Center. In the new Security Admin Center experience, insights and reports will be presented in cards with easy-to-spot actionable items to help you take the guesswork out of prioritizing the tasks to best secure your environment. Figure 19-4 is a preview shared by Microsoft at the 2018 Ignite conference on what the future Security Center will look like.

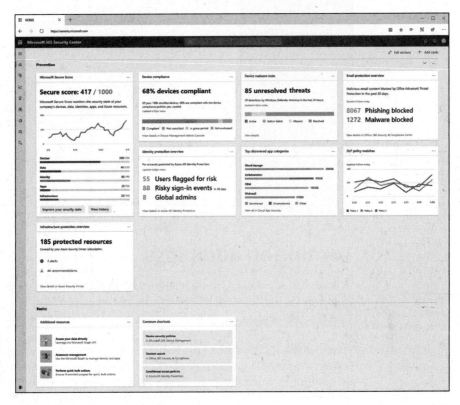

FIGURE 19-4:
A look into the future Security Center experience.

If the Reports dashboard is too much for you, you can hone in on specific dashboards for Threat Management, Mail Flow, Data Governance, Alerts, and, if relevant to your business, GDPR. Figure 19-5 shows the Threat Management dashboard, which is accessed by expanding the Threat Management group in the left navigation and then clicking the Dashboard menu item.

FIGURE 19-5:
Threat Manage-
ment dashboard.

Turning on audit logs

In the event of a breach, you'll want to look at the audit logs in your environment to do some forensic analysis. To view the audit log, you need to enable auditing in your environment.

When you first click Audit Log Search under Search & Investigation in Security Center, the Audit Log Search page prompts you to turn on auditing. Click the Turn On Auditing button (shown in Figure 19-6) to record user and admin activities in your tenant. In a few hours, you can then run an audit log and view the results in a report.

FIGURE 19-6:
Turning on
auditing.

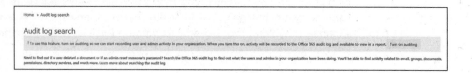

For example, suppose a breach occurs in your environment and a hacker has been sending emails on behalf of one of your users. You can use several prebuilt activity to search for mailbox activities in Exchange. One is the Sent Message Using Send As Permissions, shown in Figure 19-7.

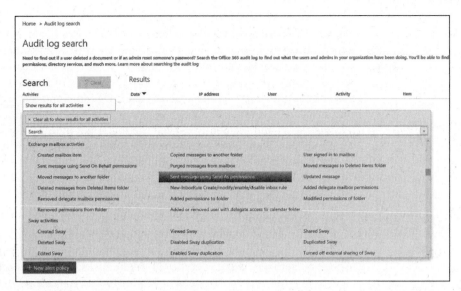

FIGURE 19-7:
Prebuilt
activity logs.

You access prebuilt activity logs by clicking the Audit Log Search Menu item in the Search & Investigation group in the left navigation.

After you select the activity log you want to search, you need to specify the start and end date for the search. You can also specify a user to narrow the search, or leave it blank to search the entire organization. As shown in Figure 19-8, when the results are displayed, you can export the data into a CSV format which you can open in Excel.

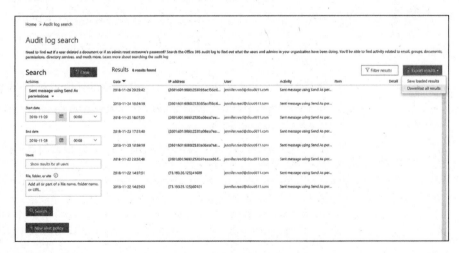

FIGURE 19-8:
Audit log search
results.

TIP

Did you know that audit logs can keep your end users honest? If you doubt that, here's an example that may convince you it's true. A customer called one day because a critical shared folder in SharePoint was mysteriously deleted. No one would admit to deleting the folder or working on any of the files in the folder. To solve the mystery, we downloaded the audit log. Sure enough, we found the culprit, a user who was working from home on a weekend. He admitted later that he was distracted and accidently deleted the folder but didn't know who to call on a weekend. By the time he got to the office the following Monday, everyone was freaking out, so he was afraid to admit the mistake.

Setting Up Alerts

When you get busy doing everyday IT admin tasks, you may forget or run out of time to monitor reports. To prevent a catastrophe, you can set up an alert so you will receive an email if something suspicious is going on in your environment.

One of the ways hacker can wreak havoc in your environment is by elevating a user's privileges to Global Administrator or Exchange Administrator. To get alerted if this happens, create an Elevation of Privilege alert by following these steps:

1. In Security Center, click Audit Log Search, which is below the Search & Investigation group in the left menu.

2. In the Audit Log Search page, click the + New Alert Policy button.

3. In the window in the right pane, enter the name of the alert.

   I entered Elevation of Privileges. I typed the same information in the Description box.

4. In the Alert Type drop-down menu, choose Elevation of Privilege.

5. In the Recipients box under Send This Alert To, enter your name, as shown in Figure 19-9.

6. Click the Save button to return to the Audit Log Search page.

Now you'll know what to do in case you need to create your own alert.

Yet another place to create an alert is in the Alerts group in the left navigation. Click Alert Policies below the Alerts group in the left navigation, and you'll see four preconfigured alerts, as shown in Figure 19-10. If you want to create a new policy, click the +New Alert Policy button.

FIGURE 19-9:
Creating an
Elevation of
Privileges alert.

FIGURE 19-10:
Preconfigured
alerts.

TIP

Now that you're familiar with Reports and Alerts in the Security Center workspace, I highly recommend doing your own exploration of the feature sets available in Security Center. You know, better than anyone else, the extent to which you should use the capabilities here, so do what you need to do to enhance your security posture.

If a breach does happen, and you feel that dealing with it is over your head, do not try to resolve it on your own. Reach out to Microsoft Support for help if you're licensing directly with Microsoft. Or contact your licensing partner for support options. You can find people with experience and expertise to bail you out of a bad situation.

Chapter **20**

Managing Collaboration Workspaces

"Keep calm. It works on my machine."

That mantra greets employees from the back of a strategically positioned monitor on the IT admin's desk at one of my small-business customers. I'm not sure how effective the sticker is in diffusing the panic or frustration employees feel when they decides that a personal visit to the IT guy is due because the ticket they submitted a minute ago is not enough. But what I do know is that the IT guy is one of the more than half a million subredditors who regularly post tales of IT admin woes at a popular subreddit for professionals in tech support.

Admit it. If you're an IT admin, you have mastered, or are on your way to mastering, the art of duplicity. You've probably used phrases like "sorry for being unclear" when you really meant "No, I wasn't unclear. You obviously didn't read my response to your support ticket, so do me a favor and read the entire email before you reply and copy your boss and my boss and their boss."

I'm not going lie to you. As an IT admin for Microsoft 365 Business, you will have your share of support tickets from users confused about what productivity tool to use when. Between SharePoint, OneDrive for Business, Office 365 Groups, Skype for Business, Microsoft Teams, Yammer, and email, you won't have a shortage of ways to create collaboration overload. A colleague once sent me an email, and then followed it up with an instant message on Skype, and then tried to catch my attention with an @mentions on Microsoft Teams. And as if that weren't enough, I got a text message too. When I asked why he went through such lengths, the response was "I wanted to make sure that I covered all the channels because it's urgent."

In this chapter, you gain clarity on the use cases for SharePoint versus OneDrive for Business versus Microsoft Teams. I then walk you through the new SharePoint Admin Center experience to prepare you for managing your SharePoint environment.

Understanding Teamwork in Microsoft 365

If you look at marketing materials for Microsoft 365, you'll repeatedly find the message that the solution is designed to unlock creativity, is integrated for simplicity, has intelligent security, and is built for teamwork. Microsoft 365 has three main scenarios for teamwork:

>> Collaborating regularly with people in your internal team: Use Microsoft Teams.

>> Connecting with people across the organization: Use Yammer.

>> Sending targeted email communications: Use Outlook.

Underpinning this triad of scenarios is SharePoint, which is the solution for content collaboration. Within SharePoint, you also have OneDrive for Business, which is a solution for storing personal files versus team files.

In this section, I cover specific use cases to determine when to use OneDrive versus SharePoint versus Microsoft Teams to help you plan your implementation and, I hope, drive adoption of the technology you've invested in.

Use cases for OneDrive for Business

Each user with the Microsoft 365 Business license gets 1 terabyte (TB) of online storage in OneDrive for Business (OneDrive for short). Typically, you save documents on OneDrive for personal use at work. Personal files are documents you don't want to share with anyone else or are not ready to share with anyone yet. For example, if I'm working on a sales report for the month and I'm still pulling in all the numbers, I might not want people to have access to that document. When the sales report is final, I might post it at a team site in SharePoint or keep the file in my OneDrive folder but give others access to the file.

Another use case for OneDrive is people management. For example, if I'm a manager who has people reporting to me, I might have a folder for each of my people reporting to me in OneDrive to store documents such as performance reviews and compensation information. OneDrive is the best place to store this information because I can control who has access to the folders. By default, files and folders in OneDrive are Private which means only the user has access to them. If the user decides to share a file, it is clearly marked as Shared under the Sharing column when the user is logged in to OneDrive, as shown in Figure 20-1.

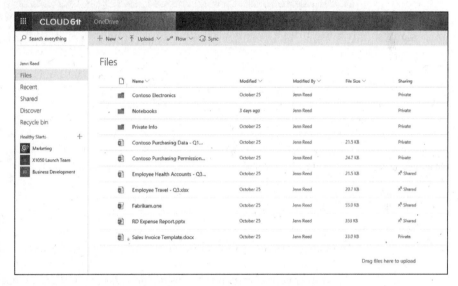

FIGURE 20-1:
Sharing status for files and folders in OneDrive for Business.

OneDrive is accessed from `https://office.com` using a Microsoft 365 Business credential. If users have an existing consumer OneDrive account, they will be prompted to choose either a Microsoft personal account or a work account. In this book, I refer to the work account, and the login credentials are the username and password associated with the Microsoft 365 Business license.

The benefits of SharePoint Online

Just like OneDrive, SharePoint Online (SharePoint for short), allows you to store documents and files online in a document library. Unlike OneDrive, however, files stored in a document library are by default shared with the people who have access to the SharePoint site. That's because SharePoint is designed for groups of people working together on projects or initiatives.

However, the site owner or site collection administrator for a SharePoint site can change the default sharing status of documents in the library to restrict access on either the file level or the folder level. For example, in Figure 20-2, I can change a group's access level to a folder in the document library from Can View to either Can Edit or Stop Sharing.

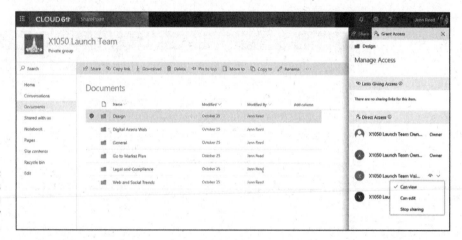

FIGURE 20-2:
Managing access to a folder in a document library in SharePoint.

To manage access to a folder in SharePoint, follow these steps:

1. **Hover your cursor over the folder you want to manage access to, and then click the circle to the left of the folder, as shown in Figure 20-3.**

2. **With the folder selected, click the Details icon (*i* in a circle) on the command bar, and then click the Manage Access link, as shown in Figure 20-4.**

3. **Click the down arrow next to the user or group whose access you want to change and then make your selection.**

   If you choose Stop Sharing, you will be prompted to confirm the removal of the access.

4. **Close the Manage Access pane by clicking X at the top right, and then close the Details pane by clicking the Details icon again.**

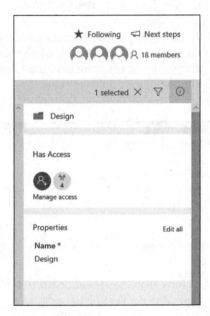

FIGURE 20-3:
Selecting a folder in SharePoint.

FIGURE 20-4:
Find the Details icon and the Manage access link.

TIP

Note that SharePoint provides more than just document storage. When a project team needs a shared task list, calendar, site page, and even integration with built-in or third-party apps, SharePoint is a better solution than OneDrive.

In Microsoft 365 Business, each organization gets 1 TB of storage in SharePoint plus 10 GB per licensed user. With, say, one hundred users, an organization would have 2 TB of storage in SharePoint. If you're administering the service for your organization, I highly recommend reviewing the SharePoint Online limits here: https://docs.microsoft.com/en-us/office365/servicedescriptions/sharepoint-online-service-description/sharepoint-online-limits.

The deal about Microsoft Teams

In previous chapters and specifically in Chapter 4, I touched on Microsoft Teams as yet another collaboration tool in Microsoft 365 Business. As a digital collaboration hub, Microsoft Teams also comes with its own document library — no surprise here.

When you create a Teams hub, you're also provisioning a SharePoint site with a document library called Documents. The default channel in a Teams hub is called General, and that channel automatically provisions a folder called General within the Documents document library. If you create a new channel called Knowledge Share, for instance, a new folder called Knowledge Share will be created within the Documents library at the same hierarchy as the General folder.

In Figure 20-5, I accessed the Knowledge Share library in Microsoft Teams by clicking the Files tab in the Knowledge Share channel. When viewing the shared library, I can click Open in SharePoint on the command bar to launch the document library in SharePoint.

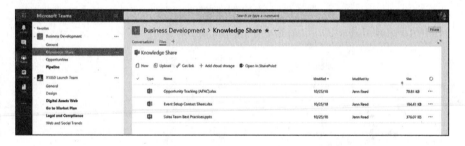

FIGURE 20-5:
Accessing the document library for a channel in Microsoft Teams.

So, what does Microsoft Teams have that SharePoint doesn't? Well, aside from the fact that Teams is the fastest growing application in the Microsoft 365 suite, it is the one-stop modern collaboration solution for today's organizations. In Teams, you can chat with colleagues, make phone calls, conduct web conferencing, interact with bots, and more.

As a bonus, you can also view all your OneDrive files in Microsoft Teams! Don't worry, even though you're using the Microsoft Teams app, the access controls set on your OneDrive documents remain intact.

To view your OneDrive files in Microsoft Teams, click the Files icon on the app bar on the left and then click the OneDrive icon from the Teams pane, as shown in Figure 20-6.

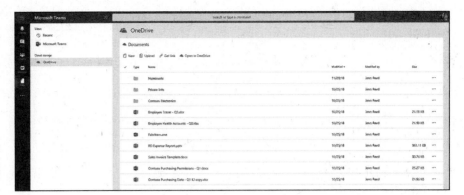

FIGURE 20-6:
Accessing
OneDrive from
Microsoft Teams.

If you want to learn how to supercharge your team collaboration with Microsoft Teams, I recommend picking up *Office 365 For Dummies*, 3rd edition, which I co-authored (shameless plug). In that book, I dedicate Chapter 15 to Microsoft Teams.

Better three-gether: OneDrive, SharePoint, and Microsoft Teams

I often get asked whether IT should direct users to use just OneDrive or SharePoint or Microsoft Teams for teamwork and collaboration. The reality is, you don't have to choose one over the other. They are better together, or in this case, three-gether!

Rather than focusing on the technology, it's best to start by asking, What kind of file am I working on? Is it a personal file that I don't want to share with others? Or is it a team file? If it's a personal file, store it in OneDrive. If it's a team file, store it in either SharePoint or Microsoft Teams so others can access the file and collaborate on it.

The OneDrive app allows you to access files wherever they are stored. To see this in action, navigate to your OneDrive app. The default view displays the files you stored in OneDrive. Look in the left navigation, and note the list of all the document libraries — in SharePoint and in Microsoft Teams — you have access to. In Figure 20-7, I clicked the Business Development icon to display the document library for the Microsoft Teams hub of which I'm a member.

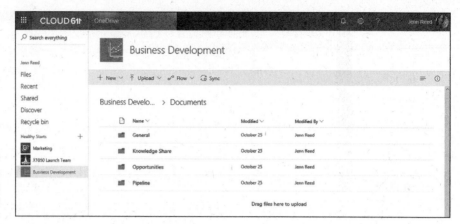

FIGURE 20-7
Use OneDrive to access files wherever they're located.

Working in SharePoint Admin Center

If you're administering your Microsoft 365 Business tenant, you'll likely run into tasks related to SharePoint administration. If you're never used SharePoint before, the knobs in classic SharePoint Admin Center may seem daunting. Don't worry, the fact that I described the current Admin Center as *classic* bodes well for you. The current user interface for Admin Center is undergoing a major overhaul to make life easier for IT admin who are not SharePoint gurus — yet.

As of November 2018, some functionalities of the new SharePoint Admin Center experience have been rolled out in Microsoft 365 tenants signed up for targeted release. More features and functionalities will be gradually released until the new experience becomes available for all tenants in late 2019. The screenshots captured in this section as based on the functionalities available in the preview version. By the time you read this, more features will probably be available. Such is the nature of a SaaS solution — things are always changing. But remember, change is good in this situation because it usually means more features.

Turning on the new experience

Depending on when you provisioned your Microsoft 365 Business tenant and whether you signed up for targeted release, you may see the classic experience when you log in to SharePoint Admin Center. You can tell if you're in the classic experience if you're greeted with the user interface in Figure 20-8 when you click SharePoint under the Admin Centers group from the Microsoft 365 Admin Center at https://admin.microsoft.com. Simply click the Try It Now button on the blue notification bar to start administering SharePoint using the new features and functionalities.

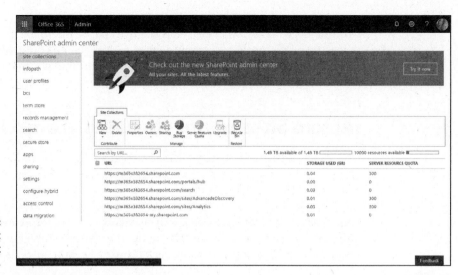

FIGURE 20-8:
The classic
SharePoint
Admin Center.

The Home Page

The Home page of SharePoint Admin Center is a great way to see, at a glance, a visual representation of your organization's adoption of SharePoint. The charts tell you activities on the files stored in SharePoint and how active the sites are. For example, Figure 20-9 does not indicate a file shared externally, but the File by Activity Type chart could help you act quickly to minimize or prevent data loss if you see a spike in externally shared files.

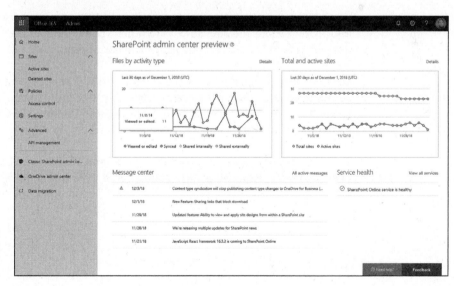

FIGURE 20-9:
SharePoint
Admin Center
Home page.

The Message Center, which is below the two charts, filters the list of all the messages from Microsoft 365 Admin Center to just the ones related to SharePoint. This feature is handy because otherwise you might find yourself wading through dozens of messages to find the ones related to SharePoint.

Active Sites under the Sites group

The Active Sites menu item, which is below the Sites group in the left navigation, displays a list of all active sites in your environment. The list is similar to the look and feel of lists in SharePoint.

And what is a list without a view? The developers at Microsoft added some built-in views you can choose for managing the list of active sites, as shown in Figure 20-10. To access the views, click the arrow next to All Sites in the top right.

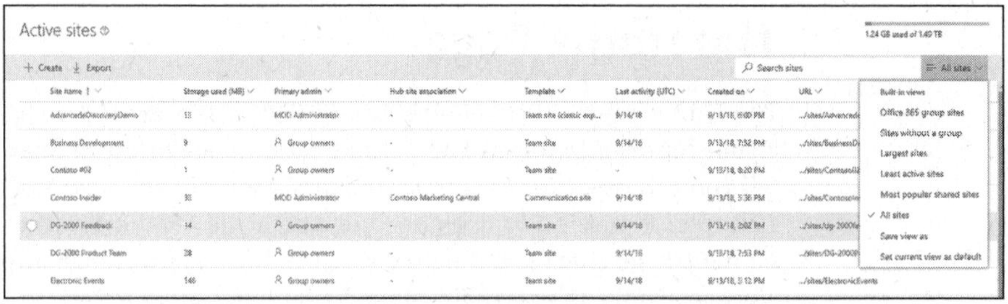

FIGURE 20-10:
Built-in views
for the list of
active sites.

If you select a site from the list, the details pane will appear, chockful of additional information about the site, such as Insights (page views and activities), properties, admins for the site, and the external sharing status.

To create a site collection, click the +Create button on the command bar. The Create a Site panel appears. The average user (without global admin privileges) sees two options: Team Site and Communications Site. IT admins, however, see a third option: Other Options, as shown in Figure 20-11.

The choices in Other Options include legacy templates such as Document Center, Enterprise Wiki, Publishing Portal, and a Team site without Office 365 groups tied to it.

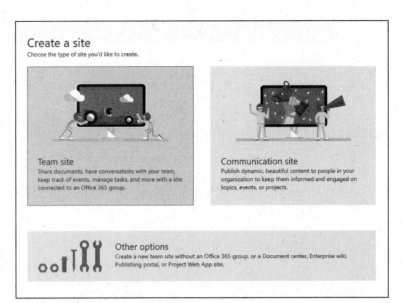

FIGURE 20-11:
Admins have
three options for
creating sites.

Access Control under the Policies group

If you head over to Access Control, below Policies in the left navigation, you'll find a number of controls you can configure to keep your environment protected. For example, under Unmanaged Devices, you can block access to SharePoint if the user is using a computer from a library that's not enrolled in MDM.

Note that additional submenus will be added under Policies later.

The Settings Menu

Controls in the Settings menu (see Figure 20-12) could help automate some admin tasks. For example, under Site Storage Limits, you can select Automatic to allow site collections to expand based on storage needs up to 25 TB without intervention. I was out skiing with my son one beautiful morning when I received a call from a frantic customer because a site had reached its maximum storage of 5 GB and the site admin wanted to increase it so she could load a huge PowerPoint presentation. If I had set that settings to Automatic, I could have gotten one more run in that day.

Note that not all the controls from the classic experience have been ported over to the new experience. Even so, the typical tasks an IT admin does on a daily basis in SharePoint Admin Center are already there. If you do need to complete a task and the control is not available, you can always go back to the classic mode by clicking the Classic SharePoint Admin Center menu in the left navigation.

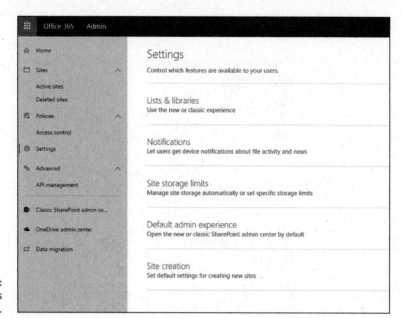

FIGURE 20-12:
The Settings
menu.

7

The Part of Tens

IN THIS CHAPTER

» **BitLocker**

» **End user communications**

» **Microsoft Flow**

» **Microsoft Forms**

» **Microsoft Planner**

» **Microsoft PowerApps**

» **Microsoft Search**

» **Microsoft Stream**

» **Knowing when issues are outside of your troubleshooting expertise**

» **Microsoft Sway**

» **Service Health**

Chapter **21**

Ten Apps and Features an Admin Should Know

Microsoft 365 Business is like the gift that keeps on giving. For $20 per user per month, your employees can have an enterprise-class email system, a robust online storage and collaboration solution, a boundary-less chat and telephony system, and the desktop version of Office applications such as Word, PowerPoint, Excel, and Outlook. All four of these key workloads have built-in security and privacy features that an IT admin can configure to his or her heart's content. Best of all, Microsoft 365 Business also comes with the

Windows 10 operating system, which simplifies the maintenance and upkeep of an organization's Windows devices.

But wait — there's more! In November 2018, I counted 27 apps available for end users with a Microsoft 365 Business license — great value for your company, but additional work for the IT admin if end users start using these apps and then ask the IT admin for support when they get stuck.

In this chapter, I provide an overview of the top ten additional features in Microsoft 365 to help you administer the services effectively and support your end users better.

TIP

The service is constantly being improved, so be sure to stay up to date by checking the Microsoft 365 roadmap at www.microsoft.com/en-us/microsoft-365/roadmap.

BitLocker

In Chapter 5, I walk you through the Setup wizard to enable device and app policies in your Microsoft 365 tenant. In the process, a set of policies were configured to protect the Windows 10 devices in your organization. One of those policies is BitLocker.

BitLocker is a disk encryption feature in Windows 10 that is included in the Microsoft 365 Business license. You will want to use this feature to protect data, especially sensitive data, saved in the computer's hard drive.

As a best practice, end users with the Microsoft 365 Business license should save their documents in either OneDrive for Business or SharePoint so they can access those documents even when they're not using their work computer. But sometimes, people will save data on their laptop's hard drive. Without encryption, the data in the hard drive could pose a risk to the organization if the laptop were lost or stolen. With encryption, you can sleep well knowing that even if someone manages to log in to a lost or stolen device, the data stored in the hard drive is protected.

Or maybe you have a broken laptop you need to mail for repair. Do you want to have unencrypted data handled by strangers? If you don't, use BitLocker.

When the BitLocker setting is switched on in the device policy for Windows 10, end users licensed for Microsoft 365 Business will see intuitive prompts to start encrypting their Windows 10 device after it's synced to Azure Active Directory. The end user can use other applications while the encryption runs in the background. The BitLocker key generated when encryption is first run is stored in the end user's profile in `https://myapps.microsoft.com`.

TIP

If, for some reason, the system does not prompt the end user to turn on BitLocker, you can start it manually. Search for *bitlocker* in the Cortana search box and then click Manage BitLocker in the search results (see Figure 21-1, left). In the , and then BitLocker Drive Encryption window that appears, click Turn on BitLocker (see Figure 21-1, right).

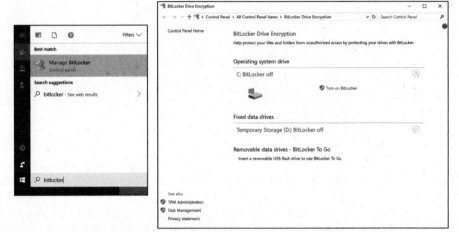

FIGURE 21-1:
Manually turning
on BitLocker.

End User Communications

Let's face it. Using a SaaS application such as Microsoft 365 Business has tons of advantages, but it can also accelerate the graying of an IT admin's hair. Why? Because Microsoft is constantly updating the service with new features and sometimes replacing features your users have become accustomed to.

I recently received a call from an irate user because something was broken in the OneNote 2016 desktop app she uses daily. After spending an hour troubleshooting, I discovered that the new version of Office ProPlus no longer includes the OneNote 2016 desktop app. Instead, users are forced to start using the modern version of the OneNote app built with the Universal Windows Platform (UWP) version.

In reviewing the notifications at Microsoft 365 Message Center, I found the announcement about the change buried in the hundreds of messages I haven't had a chance to read. Had I shared that announcement with the user, she would have been prepared for the change and I would have saved an hour of troubleshooting.

I have good news for you. Microsoft can communicate directly with your end users on changes to the Microsoft products they are licensed to use. Simply enable the End User Communications service in your tenant, and everyone in your organization will receive an email from Microsoft when new features are rolled out or old features are removed. End users can manage their own preferences for the email communication from their security and privacy settings in Office 365.

To turn on End User Communications, log in to Microsoft 365 Admin Center. Under the Settings group in the left navigation, click Services & Add-ins. Then click End User Communications, and toggle the switch to On.

Microsoft Flow

A famous quote on the Internet supposedly came from Bill Gates: "I choose a lazy person to do a hard job because a lazy person will find an easy way to do it."

If that attribution is true, apparently the people at Microsoft want us all to be lazy. I say that because Microsoft 365 Business includes Flow, which is an application that automates your workflow. You can choose from more than 200 (and growing) templates to manage your work, stay informed, and streamline processes.

For example, you can use a Flow template to automatically save email attachments to OneDrive for Business or a document library in SharePoint Online. If you have business processes requiring approval from several people, you can start with an approval template and customize it to fit your needs. You can also integrate Flow with third-party applications such as Slack, Gmail, and RSS feeds.

No programming skills are required to use Flow templates. The step-by-step instructions are easy to follow. To find these templates, click the Flow tile from the app launcher when logged in to Microsoft 365 at `https://portal.office.com`. Figure 21-2 provides a glimpse of the templates available in Flow. Go ahead and check them out before one of your end users beats you to it!

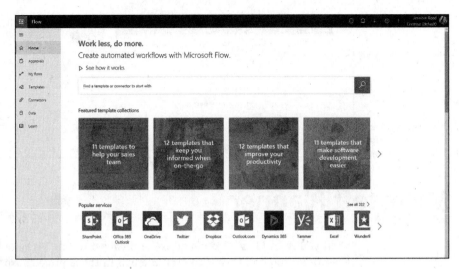

Microsoft Forms

Survey Monkey out. Forms in. Yes, it's true. You can skip paying for third-party applications to create surveys, polls, or quizzes. Your Microsoft 365 Business license includes the Forms app, which is enabled by default in your tenant.

You can create surveys, polls, and quizzes for internal use only, or you can invite people outside your organization to respond to a form on a web browser or a mobile device. Forms can have branching logic. Each licensed user can create up to 200 forms, and each form can have up to 50,000 responses. Export form responses to Excel for analysis and reporting.

You can disable Forms for an end user in Microsoft 365 Admin Center by toggling the switch Off for Forms in the user's licenses. If an end user creates a form and leaves the company, the forms created by that person will be deleted 30 days after the user is deleted from Azure Active Directory.

Aside from the Forms app at www.office.com/, you can also create a form from OneDrive for Business and Excel Online, as shown in Figure 21-3. In OneDrive for Business, click New, and then click Forms for Excel to start a new form. In Excel Online, the Forms command is on the Insert tab.

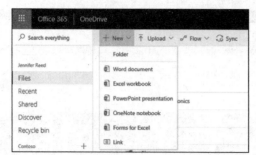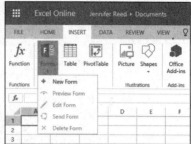

FIGURE 21-3:
Creating a form in OneDrive and Excel Online.

Microsoft Planner

When you're in IT, you're bound to be involved in one or more projects at any given time. You don't want to drop the ball in those projects, so you need some type of project or task management solution. You probably don't have the budget for a complex enterprise project management solution like Microsoft Project. You're in luck. Microsoft 365 Business includes Microsoft Planner, a visual task management solution that helps organize teams working on projects.

Planner allows you to quickly create a plan, invite others in your organization to the plan, and then start assigning tasks to the members of the plan. You can access Planner from the app launcher when logged into Microsoft 365. It has a task-board type of interface with easy drag-and-drop functionalities. A plan can be private (only members can see the content) or public (everyone in the organization can see the content). The My Tasks page aggregates all the tasks assigned to you, so you don't have to go to every single plan to manage your tasks. Planner is also synced with Outlook, so you can see the project schedule in the Outlook calendar.

You can invite people outside your organization to participate as guests in Planner. Guests have limited functionality, but their access is sufficient to perform basic task management.

Planner is enabled by default as part of the Microsoft 365 Business license. When someone creates a plan, the service automatically creates an Office 365 group and adds the members of the plan to that group.

If you must disable Planner for a certain user, you can do so by deselecting the Planner license for the user in Microsoft 365 Admin Center.

Microsoft PowerApps

I'm really going to push the envelope by saying this: with Microsoft 365 Business, you and your end users can become app creators without going to programming school!

PowerApps is a service in Office 365 that allows licensed users to create business apps that connect to data stored in various sources, such as SharePoint Online and Excel. Depending on the skill level of your end users, they can create apps in either the Power Apps Studio model or the App Designer model. The former is simplified to make building an app feel like creating a PowerPoint presentation; the latter is geared more for the geek in your organization who likes to tinker with model-driven apps.

So go ahead and explore PowerApps. After you've built your first app, don't forget to update your LinkedIn profile to include Business App Development as one of your skill sets.

TIP

One of the templates you'll find in the PowerApps portal is the Help Desk template, shown in Figure 21-4. With a few clicks, you can create a mobile app that allows end users to submit support tickets from their phone and allows you to track the progress of the support tickets — without paying an app developer a few thousand dollars.

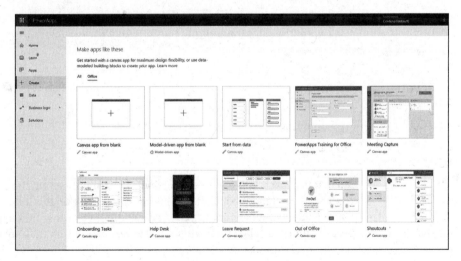

FIGURE 21-4:
PowerApps
templates.

Microsoft Search

Have you ever used Bing to search for something? Well, you're about to make the search experience for your end users better with Microsoft Search in Office 365. With this feature, searches powered by artificial intelligence (AI) technology give users search results from within or outside your organization across Windows 10, Office Apps, SharePoint, Microsoft Teams, and Bing from a desktop or mobile device.

Figure 21-5 shows my search experience when I'm logged into Bing.com with my Microsoft 365 account. Searching for the keywords *Azure AD* give me search results from my Office 365 environment (including conversations in Microsoft Teams) as well as the Internet.

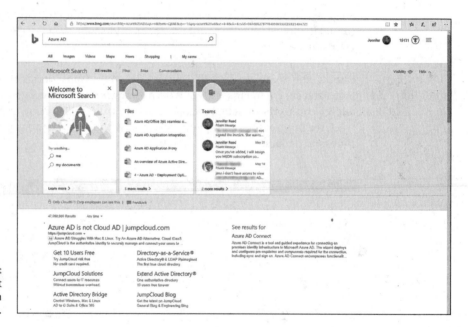

FIGURE 21-5:
The Microsoft
Search
experience.

Microsoft Search is a new service that was announced at the Microsoft Ignite conference in September 2018, so expect the service to continue to evolve. If you want to enable this feature in your organization, you must first activate Microsoft Search and then follow the Setup wizard. It took me less than five minutes to set up the service in my environment.

Ready to turn it on? Navigate to Microsoft 365 Admin Center with your global admin credentials at `https://admin.microsoft.com`. Then, under Settings in the left menu, click Services & Add-in, click Microsoft Search. Then follow these steps:

1. **Turn the toggle switch to On next to Activate Microsoft Search under Step 1.**

2. **Click Save.**

3. **Click the Get Started button under Quick Setup Wizard (below Step 2), and follow the prompts.**

   A new browser tab launches and the Microsoft Search admin portal appears.

TIP

After you've configured Microsoft Search, you're on your way to making your end users even more productive with AI-powered search results relevant to them. But what's in it for you? Well, you can reduce the number of help desk tickets coming your way by embedding answers to common questions, such as IT resources, policies, and new hire information. Happy searching!

Microsoft Stream

I touched on Microsoft Stream as your YouTube at work in Chapter 1. As in YouTube, users can create channels, upload videos, and rate and comment on videos. Unlike YouTube, however, Stream is a secure video service that uses Azure Active Directory to manage the identities of the users, so you can protect sensitive company data.

When you upload a video in Stream, you can choose to have the service automatically generate captions by using Microsoft's Automatic Speech Recognition technology. You can watch Stream videos from a browser on a Windows PC, a Mac, and mobile devices. The service automatically adjusts the quality of the video depending on your bandwidth. And because it's part of Office 365, Stream integrates well with SharePoint, Microsoft Teams, and Yammer.

Stream also allows you to broadcast live events. Suppose you have a company meeting or announcement, but some employees are in the field and can't make it to the meeting in person. With Stream, you can broadcast your meeting live and have employees tune in from their Internet-connected devices. If you are the organizer of the live event, you can monitor how engaged the participants are in real time.

You can access Stream from the app launcher in Microsoft 365 or directly at https://web.microsoftstream.com/. To manage Stream, click Settings (gear icon) beside your profile while logged into Stream with your Microsoft 365 Business global admin access. In the Admin Settings for Stream, under Live Events, you can specify who is allowed to create live events by toggling the switch On or Off (see Figure 21-6).

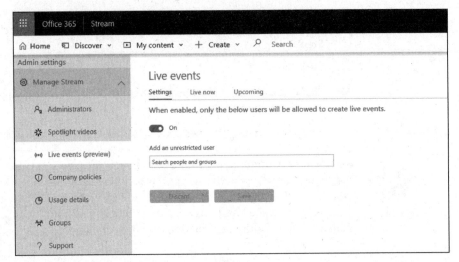

FIGURE 21-6:
Managing
Microsoft Stream.

Microsoft Sway

Do you secretly covet the web design skills of a friend or coworker? With all the work required of an IT admin, who has the time to take online courses on HTML and web development? Well, there's no need to give up that dream. Assuming you know how to use Microsoft Word, you can easily create beautiful and interactive web pages in Microsoft Sway without writing a line of HTML code!

Sway is a web-based storytelling platform in Office 365, whether that story is in the form of a financial report, a corporate presentation, or a step-by-step instruction on how to use a sous vide tool. You can add text, pictures, and videos or embed content from other sources. To get started, go to the Sway portal by clicking the Sway app from https://www.office.com/. Then you can choose from and customize a variety of templates.

Another way to publish a web page that looks great on any device is available. Suppose you have a Word document that outlines your organization's security policies and the actions your end users need to take to keep your environment secure. Your millennial employees are not interested in reading your flat, boring document.

You can quickly transform that document into a web page worthy of a web designer's thumbs up with the Transform to Web Page command in Word! Simply open the document, choose File, and then click Transform in the left menu. The Transform to Web panel appears on the right with style options. Choose the style that resonates with your users, click the Transform button, and then watch magic happens as artificial intelligence turns your boring document into an awesome web page complete with eye-catching headings and pull quotes to break up long paragraphs and make text easier to read.

Do you want to be an IT admin who can design web pages? Check that off your list with Sway.

Service Health

Like any self-respecting IT admin, I usually start my day with a prioritized list of critical items to tackle to make sure I keep our IT environment running smoothly. And like many IT admins, even before I start working on the first item, I get a phone call from an end user with an issue. So, for the next few hours, I'm troubleshooting and dealing with bugs. By the time lunch break rolls around, half the day is gone and I have not completed a single item on my list. Worse, the end user's issue is still not resolved.

Here's a no-brainer tip I wish I had adopted right away when I started administering Office 365. Before you troubleshoot any issue related to services in Office 365, check out the Service Help page to see whether Microsoft engineers are working on advisories and incidents. You can waste a lot of time trying to figure out why someone's email is not synching only to find out that there's an Exchange Online outage you can't fix.

You'll find the Service Health dashboard in Microsoft 365 Admin Center under the Health group in the left navigation. The dashboard displays incidents and advisories that Microsoft engineers are working, along with the status, the effect on end users, a description of the issue, and the steps Microsoft is taking to resolve the issue. If a service doesn't have any issues, a green mark appears next to the service name. At a glance, you'll be able to decide whether or not you should be troubleshooting an end user's issue.

IN THIS CHAPTER

» Pick up where you left off

» Share documents with confidence

» Co-author anytime, anywhere

» Catch someone's attention easily

» Figure out whodunnit

» Blur my background please

» Design like a pro by using AI

» Talk, don't type

» Go hands-free with Read Aloud

» Time travel with Windows Timeline

Chapter **22**

Ten Ways to Be Productive in Microsoft 365 Business

Your Microsoft 365 Business subscription includes access to not only the desktop application of the Office suite but also its mobile versions. Office mobile apps are rated highly across the different mobile platforms. Every day, millions of information workers around the globe, myself included, are actively using these apps to do work without being tethered to an office desk. I've found that the ability to make last-minute changes to a document when I've already shut down my computer has been a great productivity boost.

In this chapter, I share ten productivity tips available in the service. Use these tips as part of your adoption campaign to drive usage of the service and to reduce support calls to your IT team. You can confidently share these tips to your end users knowing that your organization's data is protected and managed.

TIP

I encourage you to pay attention to the notifications in Microsoft 365 Admin Center. Be on the lookout for new features so you stay on top of additional productivity tips that you can share with your end users.

Pick Up Where You Left Off

Let's say you start reading a Word document in your office and then realize you have to shut down your computer to get to a doctor's appointment. You arrive at your doctor's office and are told to wait in the reception area until someone is ready to see you. Disappointed that the magazines available are unappealing, you're relieved to remember that you have your smartphone — and the doctor's office allows the use of mobile devices.

You whip out your smartphone, run the Word mobile app, which is registered with your Office 365 account and voila! The last document you were reading back in your office is listed in the Recent documents list. You start reading the document, and close it when you're done. You are still waiting for the doctor, so you look at your Word app again and see that a list of documents has been shared with you and needs your attention. You open one to start editing, and then your name is called. No worries. You'll probably have time to finish editing the document after you get to the inner waiting room.

Share Documents with Confidence

Securely sharing documents with other members in your organization from a mobile device is similar to sharing a document from a desktop. Microsoft has invested heavily in making the mobile experiences in Office 365 as seamless as possible, so that your productivity — on a desktop or a mobile device — doesn't take a hit.

Suppose that you are on your way to work and get an email from your project manager asking you to quickly put together a presentation for your project team's kickoff meeting. While sitting on the bus on the way to work, you figure you can use the 30-minute commute to do something productive. So you run the PowerPoint app on your phone and start creating your presentation. You finish the presentation and save it to your OneDrive folder, but you then realize that one slide needs your project manager's input.

You look at the time and notice that you have five more minutes before reaching your destination. You go back to your presentation and tap the Share icon, tap the Invite People button, and enter your project manager's email address. Because the app defaults to Edit access, you go directly to the message area to type a quick message, asking your project manager for input. You tap the Send button and then tap Done. The system sends an email to your project manager with a secure link to the document so she can start editing.

Ten minutes later, off the bus and walking into your office, your project manager sees you. Perplexed, she looks at you and asks: "Didn't I just email you an hour ago? How did you manage to get that presentation in my inbox before you even arrived at work?" You cast a glance at your hero, the IT admin sitting nearby.

Co-Author Anytime, Anywhere

It happens. You finalize a document and send it to a bunch of people, and then you realize that you need to change one key bit of information in the document. So what do you do? You email everyone back, telling them to ignore your previous email and that you'll be sending an updated version of the document. The problem is, a few people had already replied with their own updated versions, so now you have to consolidate their feedback into the updated document and then send the document back to everyone. All the while, you're hoping you don't end up in an email tree nightmare where people just keep emailing their own new versions of the document back and forth.

Fortunately, you don't need to live in that nightmare. If you start using the co-authoring features of the Office applications in your Microsoft 365 Business subscription, everyone on your team can work on the same document — making edits and updates and seeing each other's comments — in real time! The co-authoring features of Office also work seamlessly in the mobile app versions.

Picture this real-life scenario. I was sitting in a meeting and a colleague was presenting a document that the team had been collaborating on. While the document was up on the screen for all the meeting participants to see, I noticed a bullet item that was outdated. I quickly grabbed my iPhone, ran Word, opened the document, and made the edit, which was reflected in real time on the screen. People went "Whoa, what was that? Who made that change?" I didn't have to confess because a notification popped up on the screen, saying that I was editing the document.

Catch Someone's Attention Easily

In social media such a Facebook or Twitter, @mentions are a great way to tag people and let them know you want their attention. You simply type @ followed by the name of the person you want to tag. As you're typing the name, a list of suggestions is presented, so you don't have to type the entire name.

Well, guess what? @mentions are now part of your Office suite! In Outlook, for example, you can @mention a co-worker in the body of an email or in a meeting invitation, and the system will automatically add the mentioned user in the To line of the email or meeting invitation.

As in Facebook, when you @mention someone, the full name is added automatically to the message. If you want to make the message sound more like the way you would normally relate to your co-worker, you can delete a portion of the mention, so it displays only the first name, for example. Don't worry, the email address in the To line will stay intact.

If you find that a lot of people are trying to get your attention with @mentions, you can filter your mailbox to display only the emails where you were @mentioned. To do this, click the arrow next to All in the message list, and then click Mentioned Mail. This feature works in both the Windows and Mac versions of Outlook.

Figure Out Whodunnit

If you've read the previous sections in this chapter, you'll know that in Office 365, you can co-author documents in real time with multiple people. This feature is great because you're all dealing with a single source of truth. But what happens if you one day open a document and realize someone has deleted an entire paragraph you painstakingly wrote the day before?

Well, you could email everyone and ask the culprit to fess up. Or you can go the stealth route and simply view the version history of the document to see a log of the different versions that have been saved along with the name of the person who saved it and a time stamp of when the version was saved. You can even open the previous version of the document and restore it.

To display the version history in Microsoft Word, click the filename in the top bar and then click Version History, as show in Figure 22-1. The Version History pane appears on the right of the screen, providing quick access to the versions of the document and the name and icon of the version author.

FIGURE 22-1:
Accessing
the version
history from
Microsoft Word.

In the web version, click the History icon at the top right to display the Version History pane.

This feature not only improves productivity but also promotes harmony when used correctly!

Blur My Background Please

Imagine being on a live interview broadcast worldwide discussing the ramifications of the impeachment of a South Korean president when your toddler crashes your interview by walking into your home office and starts dancing. Now imagine the situation getting even worse when your infant child in a walker waddles into the room, followed by your panicked spouse trying to drag both kids out of the room. Well, this did happen, and it made for a hilarious viral video back in March of 2017 when Professor Robert Kelly was interviewed by BBC.

The new Blur My Background capability in Microsoft Teams avoids this scenario. If you schedule a meeting with Teams, click the More Options (. . .) button, and then click Blur My Background, everything behind you will be subtly blurred. I tried this with a coworker a few days ago and it worked well. His face was crisp and clear, but the background was blurred, concealing the basket of laundry on the sofa behind him. When he moved, the background stayed blurred while his head and face remained clear.

Imagine how much more productive you're going to be now that you know you can skip the commute, have video-conferencing meetings from your home office, and look professional without worrying about your kids or dog coming in during your meeting and becoming distractions. I bet Professor Kelly would love this feature. But then again, if his hilarious interview hadn't happened, he wouldn't have inspired the folks at Microsoft to add this feature.

Design Like a Pro by Using AI

Let's face it. Not all of us have been gifted the talent to create presentations that pop and capture people's attention. Unless you're one of those creative ones, creating a TED-worthy presentation is out of reach.

There's good news for all us design-challenged individuals! With the help of artificial intelligence (AI), creating PowerPoint presentations that have the touch of a highly paid marketing guru is now achievable.

In the desktop or web version of PowerPoint, start a new presentation. Just plug in the details you want to convey in your slide and don't worry about the look and feel. When you're finished, go to the Design tab on the ribbon, and click the Design Ideas button. The AI technology in Office 365 automatically generates some design ideas for you to choose from. Figure 22-2 illustrates how AI generated icons to represent the sentiment I was trying to convey in the sample slide.

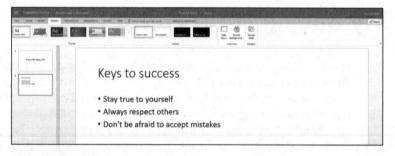

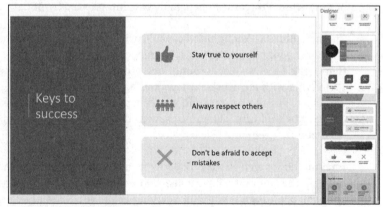

FIGURE 22-2:
The Design Ideas feature in PowerPoint.

Talk, Don't Type

As a cloud service, Office Apps in Office 365 gets smarter over time. Machine learning and artificial intelligence enable Office applications such as Word, Excel, PowerPoint, and Outlook to adapt to how you work, saving you time and even improving your writing skills.

One of these intelligence services is the Dictate feature, which allows you to dictate text instead of typing. In fact, starting with this section, the content in this chapter was dictated using the Dictate feature. This was handy because I had been writing for four hours and my wrists were sore.

In Microsoft Word, the Dictate button is on the Home tab on the ribbon. If you're using Outlook, start a new email, go to the Message tab and then click the Dictate button. When the Dictate icon turns red, you can start talking. As you talk, text appears in your document. Just make sure your microphone is enabled and you're talking clearly and conversationally.

You can insert punctuation by saying the name of the punctuation. For example, at the end of the sentence, say "period" or "question mark" or "exclamation mark." If you want to start a new paragraph, say, "new paragraph."

What are you waiting for? Give it a try!

Go Hands-Free with Read Aloud

Productivity in Office 365 is designed to meet the needs of people all over the world with different abilities. Dictate (described in the preceding section), Tell Me, which gives quick access to commands without cycling through the different tabs on the ribbon, and Accessibility, which works seamlessly with screen readers, are just a few of the features in Office 365 that drive productivity and promote inclusion in the workplace.

Yet another nifty feature you'll find in Office applications is the Read Aloud feature in Word. Although touted as one of the capabilities in the Learning Tools in Office especially useful for people with dyslexia, I find the Read Aloud feature helpful in driving productivity. It's great for proofreading because it highlights the text as each word is read.

I have an hour-long commute to work and I sometimes use the Read Aloud feature to get me ready for the day. One time, this feature saved me from looking unprepared. I had forgotten that I was supposed to read a 15-page document before walking into my first meeting of the day. So I opened the Word document and had the Read Aloud feature read it to me while I was driving.

A bonus for people whose first language is not English, the Read Aloud feature is also a great tool for learning how words are pronounced.

I encourage you to test this feature and incorporate it into your workflow. The Read Aloud button is in the Review tab in Microsoft Word.

Happy reading aloud!

Time Travel with Windows Timeline

Have you ever found yourself wasting 30 minutes looking for a document that you worked on a few days ago but can't remember where it was saved? Or going through your browsing history to find a search you did for a renovation project?

If you've had that unpleasant experience, you'll be happy to know that you don't need to waste time in that fashion again. The Timeline feature in Windows 10 helps you reclaim that lost productivity by enabling you to see all your activities during up to 30 days in one screen.

Figure 22-3 shows a screenshot of my Windows Timeline. The slider bar on the right allows me to go to different points in time and see my activity. I can also use the Search box to do a keyword search of my activities.

To activate the Windows Timeline feature, click the Task View button next to the Cortana search bar, or press the Windows and tab keys.

So go ahead and pick up where you left off with Windows Timeline. You may not be able to go back in time, but at least you can always go back in the Timeline!

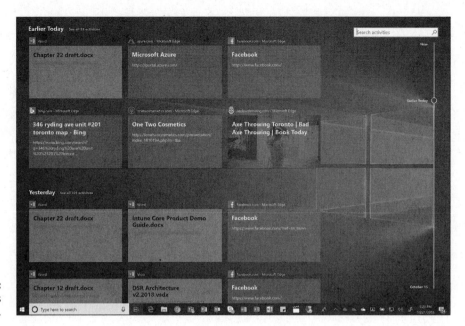

- » Recruit and activate champs

- » Communicate the change

- » Develop and execute a training plan

- » Start with "easy win" scenarios

- » Provide self-service resources

- » Highlight the wins

- » Check the usage report

- » Be ready to provide support

- » Bring in the pros

Chapter **23**

Ten Tips to Drive Adoption

For most of the IT admins I know in the SMB sector, getting the budget for a Microsoft 365 Business deployment is not easy. In my career, I've been in numerous meetings and conducted dozens of onsite and remote demos to support the IT team's efforts to convince business leaders that investing in Microsoft 365 Business is the right decision. If we're lucky, we get approval in three months. Sometimes, it takes more than a year. And these budgets usually have strings attached.

It's understandable for a leader approving a significant budget for a SaaS solution to want to see the return on the investment (ROI). Guess who's on the hook for demonstrating that ROI? Your IT team.

One of the ways you can convince your leaders about the ROI is to show your success in getting end users to adopt the technology. Unfortunately, though, technology adoption is tricky. If you think you can just roll out the changes and expect users to start using the technology and singing your praises, think again. Change is usually met with resistance. Studies have shown that only 34 percent of the user population typically will adopt a new technology, as illustrated in the theory of Diffusion Innovations in Chapter 4.

In this chapter, I share some of the best practices, tips, and tricks for driving adoption based on my own experience and what I've learned from my cohorts in the industry. Feel free to customize and tweak these suggestions to fit your organization. Do take credit if any of the suggestions here bring you success.

Get Leaders to Sponsor the Effort

Executive sponsorship in technology implementations are usually a foolproof way to get users to adopt a new technology, even if begrudgingly. Let's be honest, an IT admin does not have as much clout as the president, CEO or owner.

After you identify the executive sponsors for your technology implementation, make sure you agree on what's expected of them. Ideally, you want executive sponsors to assume a shared responsibility for the success of the implementation. They can provide air cover when you run into political challenges in your organization or when end users push back on the changes you're rolling out.

For your part, make sure to give your executive sponsors training on the functionalities of the technology based on relevant scenarios. For example, if they tend to use email a lot versus co-authoring documents, train them on the new features in Outlook instead of teaching them how to save and share files in SharePoint. When they see the value of the technology, they'll be able to share their experiences with the rest of the organization.

Recruit and Activate Champs

Scientists have not figured out a cloning machine yet, but you can create clones of yourself to scale up your training efforts. How? By recruiting and activating a network of champions for your cause. Usually, these people are early adopters and super users of the current technology in your organization. Give them access to the full suite of the Microsoft 365 Business services and conduct a focused training for them. Apply the "train the trainer" model so that they understand that they will be tasked with training other people in the organization. It might help if you give them an incentive to be in the Champs network (such as a new laptop) in exchange for going through the experience of a Windows 10 AutoPilot deployment.

Ideally, you'll want a champ from each department who understands the workflow for the users in a department. You might find that people in the Marketing department, for example, are excited about Microsoft Stream, but the folks in the Finance department, not so much.

Communicate the Change

It has been said that 90 percent of a project manager's job is communication. This statistic is true and applicable when you're implementing Microsoft 365 Business in your organization. Whether you have an assigned project manager or are tasked with the role of the project manager, it's best to have a solid communication plan.

Be mindful of the cadence for the communication. If you send an email every day for three months reminding end users of an upcoming change, you may end up with annoyed people who will create a rule to automatically delete your emails or route them to a folder to read later. If you space the communication too far apart, they might miss a communication and be unprepared when you finally make the switch. You need to find the right balance based on what you know about your end users.

TIP

For small businesses, I make an initial announcement about the Microsoft 365 implementation around the time that licenses are procured. Then about three weeks before the email is cut over to the new system, the drip communication starts, and the frequency gradually increases as the cutover date approaches.

In Chapter 7, I outline the communication emails we intended to send to end users to prepare them for migration. Even though we ended up not sending emails, we used their content to verbally prepare our users for the change at the specified time. Feel free to use the titles for the emails from the project plan. In fact, if you'd like to have the content of the emails, send your request to info@cloud611.com with the subject "Ten Tips to Drive Adoption" so I'll know your request is a result of reading this book.

Develop and Execute a Training Plan

The saying, "fail to plan, plan to fail," couldn't be truer when it comes to implementing a new technology. Key to the overall implementation plan is the training plan for end users. The training plan doesn't have to be complex. Even an outline of who's going to be trained on what and when is sufficient, especially if you have a small organization. Remember the champs network and the executive sponsors? Those groups need to be included in the training plan.

You may find that you need to adjust your training plan as you get a feel for how well your initial groups of trainees are responding. As such, create your training plan in a format that can be easily updated or collaborated on. You can expose your trainees to the new technology by using SharePoint lists or document libraries as the repository for your training plan. They will start to get trained on the functionalities without even realizing it!

Start with "Easy Win" Scenarios

I was once asked to deliver a four-hour training on Office 365 for a small business with 25 users. I was unsuccessful in trying to get information from the business owner on the training needs and the technical skill sets of the employees and was told to just train the users "the dummies way." What that signaled to me was that I couldn't have a fixed topic for the training. I ended up preparing different scenarios to fit a variety of personas. Based on the flow of the conversation, I pulled a certain scenario and focused the training around it.

So, what is a scenario? In my example, a scenario went something like this:

> Jane, Rob, and Paul work in the marketing department and are constantly emailing each other documents they're collaborating on. It's hard to keep track of the latest version of the document and figure out who's made what comment. Jane, who is in charge of culling all the feedback, is getting frustrated because just as she thinks she's made the final version of the document, someone sends belated feedback. Or someone pulls into the conversation another person who then provides feedback on issues, not knowing they have already been dealt with in previous conversations.

I presented that scenario to the workshop attendees and asked if that happens in their organization. The response was overwhelmingly yes. Based on that, I spent 30 minutes showing them the co-authoring features in Word, OneDrive for

Business, and SharePoint. They then used their own laptops to practice what I showed them. By the end of 30 minutes, everyone had a good grasp of the concept and figured out which people were better at it than others. The ones who were more skilled became the go-to person for the ones who needed more hand-holding.

The lesson here is that if you want users to adopt the technology, make it a quick win for them and tailor the training to a scenario that is real for them. It wouldn't have worked if I simply started the training with Outlook and how to send encrypted emails. Although we did cover that topic, by the time we got to it, the participants were already exposed to the integration of Word, OneDrive, SharePoint, and Outlook as well as access controls, so it was easier to pile on the concepts of security and encryption.

Provide Self-Service Resources

If you have a small or one-person IT team, you can reduce the burden of supporting many users during the implementation of Microsoft 365 Business by creating a self-service portal in SharePoint or Microsoft Stream or both. You can post 30-second how-to videos to give end users a refresher on the training. You can ask the champs to post content at your portal, or open your self-service repository to anyone's contribution. By doing it this way, your end users will be practicing what they've learned as they load content in SharePoint or Stream. If you want to get fancy, you can gamify the process by giving incentives to users who have the most-liked video.

TIP

The Internet has a ton of videos on different scenarios for Microsoft 365 that you can include in your resources. However, I find that raw videos created by a co-worker showing the organization's environment resonate more with users than high-production-value marketing videos from Microsoft on YouTube and other channels.

If your users are not into videos, another option is to start a OneNote notebook from a SharePoint site. In the notebook, create different sections focused on a technology. In each section, include step-by-step instructions showing how to complete a task using the technology. For example, you could have a section on Outlook where you have a page for email, a page for the calendar, and a page for tasks. As users read your content, they'll be learning about not only Outlook but also OneNote and SharePoint, albeit unknowingly.

Highlight the Wins

Implementing a new technology such as Microsoft 365 Business is not an easy task. When you have success stories, take the time to celebrate and share the win with your end users. When users understand the value of their contribution to the success of the implementation, it helps motivate others who may not be participating much.

An example of a win is showcasing how much the company saved by reducing travel costs since people started having videoconference meetings using Microsoft Teams. A win might also be a testimonial from someone about the increase in productivity from co-authoring documents in real time versus emailing documents back and forth.

SharePoint Online has a nifty feature called News, an out-of-the-box service that allows you to create content that then gets shared across the different SharePoint experiences and apps. You can highlight your wins by using SharePoint News to further drive adoption of the technology. To find out more about SharePoint News, download the PDF file at `https://aka.ms/SharePointNewsPDF`.

Check the Usage Report

As a global admin to your Microsoft 365 tenant, you have access to usage reports that provide insight into how your user base is adopting the technology. The reports include activity and usage metrics for Exchange, Microsoft Teams, Office 365, OneDrive, SharePoint, Skype for Business, and Yammer. You can export the reports into Excel for further analysis. If you're so inclined, you can even analyze the data in Power BI, yet another tool from Microsoft for visualizing data.

One way to act on the available data to drive adoption is to look at OneDrive for Business usage. The report includes information on the user, the last activity date, the number of files, the number of active files, and the storage used. If you notice that a user has zero (0) files and very low storage used, that might be a good indication that the user isn't adopting OneDrive for Business. Based on that information, you could target training for users who have low usage of OneDrive for Business.

Be Ready to Provide Support

When deploying a new technology, nothing fails as spectacularly as a deployment with no support model in place. Following a deployment, I have seen people get fired from their jobs because of bad user experience and no clear path for escalation.

Depending on how you acquire your licenses, you may have different options for support. If you bought your Microsoft 365 Business licenses directly from Microsoft through their website at https://office365.com, your support is provided by Microsoft. Unless you're paying big money for Premiere support, only the global admin can submit support tickets to Microsoft Support. That means you, as the IT admin, will be on point for providing support for your end users. However, you can submit a ticket on behalf of your end users, and Microsoft Support may end up working directly with them to resolve an issue.

I have a SharePoint site where I curated the most common issues in Office 365 with links to troubleshooting steps from Microsoft. I am happy to share that with you; simply send a note to info@cloud611.com and specify "Access request to Knowledge Portal" in the subject line. You will also find free e-books on Microsoft technologies at the site, but be forewarned — those books are more advanced than the Dummies series.

If you purchased your licenses from a Microsoft Partner, either through the Cloud Solutions Provider (CSP) or Enterprise Agreement (EA) model, the partner is on the hook for providing support. Depending on your agreement with the partner, you can either send your end users directly to the partner's support team or act as the intermediary between your end users and the partner's support team. Be aware that partners may charge an extra fee for support on top of license fees. At https://cloud611.com, you can purchase Microsoft 365 licenses that include 24/7/365 end user support for a minimal fee on top of the license cost.

Bring in the Pros

If you have followed all or most of the tips provided in this chapter and still aren't having success in driving adoption for Microsoft 365 Business, it may be time to bring in the pros. The Microsoft Partner Network is replete with highly qualified training and adoption partners who can help you unblock adoption challenges. Although you have to shell out good money to engage these partners, the investment may be worth it in the long run.

You can search for Microsoft training partners at www.microsoft.com/en-us/solution-providers/home. Just a heads up — when I entered that URL in the Chrome browser, I got an error message, but the URL works perfectly in the Microsoft Edge browser.

One of the partners you'll find from the Microsoft Partner Network is Softchoice Corporation. They have a robust end user adoption professional service that includes defining use cases to understand the end users' needs all the way to the creating an implementation plan to drive desired business outcomes. You can learn more about this service at www.softchoice.com/solution-studio/services/professional-services/professional-services-to-enable-end-users.

Yet another training partner I have direct experience with is www.brainstorminc.com/. They were contracted by Microsoft to provide training for the Customer Immersion Experience program for which I am a certified facilitator.

If you feel your organization has unique training needs, I may be able to connect you to the right partner. Please send an email to info@cloud611.com with the subject line "Need help with training." I will respond ASAP.

Index

A

Accessibility feature, 275

Access Requirements blade, 163

Active Directory (Azure)
- Intune and, 160–161
- Microsoft Authenticator app, using, 121, 124–125
- multifactor-authentication, 151
- overview, 31–32
- password reset, 116–117

active sites, SharePoint, 252–253

Active Users list, 229

Activity icon, 100

Add Configuration Policy blade, 209–210

Admin Center, Microsoft 365
- Exchange, 23
- expanded view, 23
- experiencing, 224–226
- group, creating, 174–176
- home page, 21–23
- interacting with Users list, 229
- IT management in, 224–228
- logging in to, 22
- navigation bar, 228
- one-stop-shop user management, 228–232
- overview, 21, 223–224
- personalizing, 226–287
- Preview mode, 227
- Release Preference window, 224
- Security & Compliance Center, 24
- Setup Guidance card, 42–43
- Setup wizard, 23, 55–58
- SharePoint, 24
- specialist workspaces, 226, 227
- Teams and Skype for Business, 23
- updates, 22
- usage reports, 234–235
- user management, 230–232

Admin Center, SharePoint
- access control, 253
- active sites, 252–253
- classic experience, 250–251
- home page, 250–251
- message center, 252
- overview, 24, 250
- settings menu, 253–254

admin centers, 32

adoption of Microsoft 365 (ten tips)
- checking usage reports, 284
- communicating changes, 281
- developing and executing training plans, 282
- getting leaders to sponsor the effort, 280
- highlighting the wins, 284
- Microsoft Partner Network, 285–286
- overview, 279–280
- providing self-service resources, 283
- providing support, 285
- recruiting and activating champions, 280–281
- starting with easy win scenarios, 282–283

Advanced Threat Protection (ATP)
- overview, 70–71
- Safe Attachments, 71–74
- Safe Links, 73–75

AIP (Azure Information Protection)
- activating, 137–138
- applying labels to documents, 144–145
- client, downloading, 143
- client, installing, 142–143
- configuring, 136–141
- data protection in, 136–137
- defined, 136
- evolution of, 136–137
- global policy, 140–141
- labels, 76–77, 138–140
- layered approach to security, 15
- policies, 140–141
- revoking information access, 145–146

alerts
- overview, 233–234
- setting up, 240–241

M

machine learning, 53

Macs, 52

mail. *See* email

mail-enabled security groups, 174

Mail Migration Advisor, 42–45

malicious links, 74–75

malware, 14, 70

MAM (mobile application management)
- adding Excel app to Company portal app, 201–202
- application policy for iOS, 198–200
- application policy for Windows 10, 197–198
- app protection policies, 194–196
- choosing, 167
- default app policies, 196–200
- downloading Excel app from Company portal app, 202–203
- groundwork for, laying, 194–196
- versus mobile device management, 164–166, 195–196
- overview, 159, 193–194
- scenarios for, 196

Mashable, 206

Master Wizard level, 52

MDM (mobile device management), 34
- administering enrolled devices, 187–188
- configure stage, 171
- device compliance policies, assigning, 184–185
- device compliance policies, setting up, 182–184
- device configuration profile, creating, 185–187
- device enrollment, 34, 178
- device lifecycle and, 171
- end users, 188–191
- enroll stage, 171
- groups, setting up, 174–176
- manage and protect stage, 171
- versus mobile application management, 164–166, 195–196
- overview, 159, 169–170
- portal, 177–178
- preparing for, 172–176
- removing devices from, 34
- retire stage, 171
- users, setting up, 172–174
- validating users, 173–174
- Windows 10 device management policy, 164–165

meetings, recording, 107

@mentions, 95

Message Center, 252

MFA (multifactor-authentication). *See also* security
- admin tasks for setting up, 127–132
- Azure, 125–126
- for Azure Active Directory Administrators, 125–126
- best practices, 125–126
- bulk update option, 129
- choosing, 125
- defined, 124
- deploying, 126–132
- disabled, 133
- enabled, 132
- enabling multiple users at same time, 129
- enabling users for, 128–129
- end-user experience, 130–131
- enforced, 133
- managing, 132–133
- mobile apps, 126
- notification from mobile apps, 125–126
- for Office 365, 125
- overview, 123–124
- page, 132–133
- phone call, 125
- remembering, 129
- statuses, 132–133
- verification code, 126
- verification code from mobile apps, 125–126
- versions of, 124–125

Microsoft 365
- Admin Center, 20–24
- adoption of, 279–286
- plans, 18–21
- roadmap for, 258
- self-service resources, 283
- tenants, 31
- training plans, 279–286
- usage reports, 284

Microsoft 365 Business
- Bookings app, 24–26
- decision tree, 20
- implementation road map, 32–33
- implementing, 29–38
- licenses, 285

About the Author

Jennifer Reed is a technology solutions professional who founded Cloud611 (www.cloud611.com), a Seattle-area-based IT services firm focused on helping small and medium-sized businesses and nonprofit organizations achieve their goals using cloud technologies. The firm is a Microsoft Silver Competency Partner in Small and Mid-market Cloud Solutions. This recognition of competency is awarded to Microsoft partners who are selling and deploying Microsoft Office 365 cloud solutions to SMB customers. It also requires customer references based on successful implementation and customer satisfaction.

Currently, Jenn manages a high-performing team of solutions architects helping organizations in North America in their journey to the cloud. Jenn's focus is enabling IT departments to adapt to evolving technological innovations and adopt the best approach to digital transformation — whether it's all in the cloud or a hybrid solution.

Jenn holds a bachelor's degree in Economics and has for many years provided consulting services to a wide range of clients including a Fortune 500 company. She is a frequent speaker at business forums about Office 365 productivity and provides training facilitating user adoption of Office 365. Her certifications include Microsoft Certified Professional in Office 365 Administration, Customer Immersion Experience Facilitation, Project Management Professional, and Scrum Master.

Jenn lives with her husband Rick, a writer, a retired Hawaii state senator, and a former All-Coast defensive back who played at Washington State University. Jenn and Rick live in the lush farming valley of Snohomish, where Rick grew up and through which flow not one but two rivers, 45 miles northeast of Seattle. When not working on a cloud technology-related book, Jenn enjoys tending her organic garden, skiing, running, and hanging out with the Reed's son, Siddha, who has inherited his mom's interest in cloud technologies and his dad's writing skills.

Dedication

My work on this book would not have been possible without the love and support of my husband and best friend, Rick, our wonderful son, Siddha, and our large, exuberant housemate, Rama the Great Pyrenees/German Shepherd. I dedicate this book to you three for understanding my late nights and pressured weekends. Thank you, Rick, for ensuring that I stay healthy physically and spiritually. Thank you, Siddha, for putting up with my quirks and for translating Gen Z-speak to a Gen Xer like I. Big thanks to Rama for keeping me company during my late nights of writing and helping me stay awake with his big dog snoring. You guys make me laugh and inspire me. I love you.

Author's Acknowledgments

I owe my deepest gratitude to my customers for giving me the opportunity to help with their cloud journey because those experiences have provided me with valuable insights into real-life applications of Microsoft 365 and other cloud technologies. I will continue to use the knowledge I've acquired to benefit the underserved business sector: SMBs and nonprofit organizations.

I am indebted to my employer, co-workers, and friends for the opportunities to learn and enrich my life, and grateful that I can share those positive, relevant experiences in this book. I want to call out special friends Stephanie and Angie Smolen for providing much needed help with doggie outings.

It's been an honor and a pleasure to have the support and guidance of Katie Mohr, Susan Pink, and the rest of the Dummies team, including Siddha Reed in his role as technical editor of the book. They are truly a dream team without whom this project would have been impossible.

Publisher's Acknowledgments

Associate Publisher: Katie Mohr

Project Editor: Susan Pink

Copy Editor: Susan Pink

Technical Editor: Siddha Reed

Editorial Assistant: Matt Lowe

Sr. Editorial Assistant: Cherie Case

Production Editor: Mohammed Zafar Ali

Cover Image: © JGI/Jamie Grill/Getty Images

Leverage the power

Dummies is the global leader in the reference category and one of the most trusted and highly regarded brands in the world. No longer just focused on books, customers now have access to the dummies content they need in the format they want. Together we'll craft a solution that engages your customers, stands out from the competition, and helps you meet your goals.

Advertising & Sponsorships

Connect with an engaged audience on a powerful multimedia site, and position your message alongside expert how-to content. Dummies.com is a one-stop shop for free, online information and know-how curated by a team of experts.

- Targeted ads
- Video
- Email Marketing
- Microsites
- Sweepstakes sponsorship

20 MILLION PAGE VIEWS **EVERY SINGLE MONTH**

15 MILLION UNIQUE VISITORS PER MONTH

43% OF ALL VISITORS ACCESS THE SITE **VIA THEIR MOBILE DEVICES**

700,000 NEWSLETTER SUBSCRIPTIONS **TO THE INBOXES OF** *300,000* UNIQUE INDIVIDUALS EVERY WEEK

# of dummies

Custom Publishing

Reach a global audience in any language by creating a solution that will differentiate you from competitors, amplify your message, and encourage customers to make a buying decision.

- Apps
- Books
- eBooks
- Video
- Audio
- Webinars

Brand Licensing & Content

Leverage the strength of the world's most popular reference brand to reach new audiences and channels of distribution.

For more information, visit **dummies.com/biz**

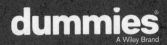

PERSONAL ENRICHMENT

Staying Sharp

9781119187790
USA $26.00
CAN $31.99
UK £19.99

Facebook

9781119179030
USA $21.99
CAN $25.99
UK £16.99

Guitar

9781119293354
USA $24.99
CAN $29.99
UK £17.99

Investing

9781119293347
USA $22.99
CAN $27.99
UK £16.99

Beekeeping

9781119310068
USA $22.99
CAN $27.99
UK £16.99

Digital Photography

9781119235606
USA $24.99
CAN $29.99
UK £17.99

Meditation

9781119251163
USA $24.99
CAN $29.99
UK £17.99

Pregnancy

9781119235491
USA $26.99
CAN $31.99
UK £19.99

Samsung Galaxy S7

9781119279952
USA $24.99
CAN $29.99
UK £17.99

iPhone

9781119283133
USA $24.99
CAN $29.99
UK £17.99

Crocheting

9781119287117
USA $24.99
CAN $29.99
UK £16.99

Nutrition

9781119130246
USA $22.99
CAN $27.99
UK £16.99

PROFESSIONAL DEVELOPMENT

Windows 10

9781119311041
USA $24.99
CAN $29.99
UK £17.99

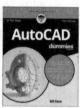
AutoCAD

9781119255796
USA $39.99
CAN $47.99
UK £27.99

Excel 2016

9781119293439
USA $26.99
CAN $31.99
UK £19.99

QuickBooks 2017

9781119281467
USA $26.99
CAN $31.99
UK £19.99

macOS Sierra

9781119280651
USA $29.99
CAN $35.99
UK £21.99

LinkedIn

9781119251132
USA $24.99
CAN $29.99
UK £17.99

Windows 10

9781119310563
USA $34.00
CAN $41.99
UK £24.99

SharePoint 2016

9781119181705
USA $29.99
CAN $35.99
UK £21.99

Fundamental Analysis

9781119263593
USA $26.99
CAN $31.99
UK £19.99

Networking

9781119257769
USA $29.99
CAN $35.99
UK £21.99

Office 2016

9781119293477
USA $26.99
CAN $31.99
UK £19.99

Office 365

9781119265313
USA $24.99
CAN $29.99
UK £17.99

Salesforce.com

9781119239314
USA $29.99
CAN $35.99
UK £21.99

Coding

9781119293323
USA $29.99
CAN $35.99
UK £21.99

dummies.com

dummies
A Wiley Brand

Learning Made Easy

ACADEMIC

9781119293576
USA $19.99
CAN $23.99
UK £15.99

9781119293637
USA $19.99
CAN $23.99
UK £15.99

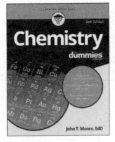

9781119293491
USA $19.99
CAN $23.99
UK £15.99

9781119293460
USA $19.99
CAN $23.99
UK £15.99

Physics I

9781119293590
USA $19.99
CAN $23.99
UK £15.99

9781119215844
USA $26.99
CAN $31.99
UK £19.99

9781119293378
USA $22.99
CAN $27.99
UK £16.99

9781119293521
USA $19.99
CAN $23.99
UK £15.99

9781119239178
USA $18.99
CAN $22.99
UK £14.99

9781119263883
USA $26.99
CAN $31.99
UK £19.99

Available Everywhere Books Are Sold

Small books for big imaginations